M000035082

Broken By War

"A Powerful Story Of Death, Trauma and Recovery"

By Anthony Lock

COPYRIGHT

Some names, characters, incidents and locations mentioned within the book, Broken By War, have been purposely changed to protect those mentioned. No affiliation is implied or intended to imply any organisations or recognisable bodies mentioned within. All persons identified within Broken By War by their nicknames or known names have given permission.
COPYRIGHT Broken By War 2019©

Warning Statement

Broken By War whether by paperback, hardback or eBook is licensed for your personal enjoyment only. The paperback, hardback or eBook may not be re-sold or given away to other people. If you would like to share this book with another person, please purchase an additional copy for each recipient. If you're reading this book and did not purchase it, or it was not purchased for your use only, then please return to your nearest retailer and purchase your own copy. Thank you for respecting the hard work of this author.

I would like to thank my partner Rhiannon and daughter Katie for sticking by me when times were hard. You cared for me, when I needed caring. You calmed me, when I needed calming. You loved me, when others wouldn't. Your commitment, passion, willpower and positivity is the reason I am who I am today.

For almost ten years I struggled for the support I desperately needed. I began to write down my horrors that stalked my every thought.

Thanks to the generosity of two people, I am able to share my story with you.

Darren & Bobo
Thank you

During eleven years' service to Queen and Country,
colleagues would become friends and brothers.
We trained together, we lived together and we fought
Side by side together, but for some,
they Paid the ultimate Sacrifice.
Gentlemen – Rest in Peace

To all the Men, Women and Animals
Who paid the ultimate sacrifice for
Queen and Country – Rest in Peace

Jen – You were my inspiration,
When times were hard, you stood tall,
you gave me the courage
And resilience to fight on.
Rest in Peace x

Gone but Not Forgotten

PROLOGUE

I didn't grow up intent on becoming a Soldier. In fact, I had wanted to be a Police Officer. Life was very different back in the late 1980's, with no social media to help persuade you career wise, I only knew what I could see around me. My education was poor and a fresh start away from my home City was always key for me as I wanted to make something of my life. Something I could look back upon in years to come and tell stories to the grandchildren of my adventures.

Growing up, I didn't play soldiers with my friends, I grew up knocking people's doors and running away. I didn't want toys that I could sit down and play with and use my imagination on. I did have everything I had asked for, even though times were hard for my Mother. I wasn't a bad kid or a trouble maker. I did the same things growing up as most of the other children did. My estate was a tough estate, but if you stayed low and stayed out of sight then there was plenty to do.

On the estate I grew up on, there was a large Victorian House, which had a huge area of land to discover; there was a lake, woodlands and a big adventure park no further than a five-minute walk away from my home. I would often go over and visit the grounds of the Victorian House with my brothers and friends. Walking around the lake far away from the troubles on the estate was where I first begin to think about my future and the escape away from the City I grew up hating.

My City was like any other City but being so young and naive I just wanted to move as far away from it as I could. If It was possible to have emigrated to the moon as a child, I would have. I wasn't the most confident of children, the loss of my brother at such a young age knocked my confidence massively as I wasn't much older than him.

I had attended the junior school on my estate and my late brother attended the infants. Both schools were separated by a metal fence. After my brother passed away, the children in the infant school would taunt to me through the fence over my brother's death.

Growing up back in the late eighties and early ninety's and forced outside to play come rain or shine, was a different world to what it is today. Technology and Social media has destroyed the whole dynamics of a modern childhood, although looking back at my own childhood – if I had the internet back then, I guess my education may have swung more in my favour. Nethertheless, I am who I am today and I wouldn't change it for the world.

Moving away from the City when I took my chance had its benefits, but I still missed the place more than I wanted to. I always dreamt of moving to a bigger City like London or Manchester, somewhere that offered more hope of a better future for me and my girls.

I met my first love whilst serving close to the City I was born and bred in, she was the sole reason I finally got over my hatred for it and returned home. It didn't take us long to realise we were meant to be together and within a year we had bought our first home and had our only child together - where we have remained for fourteen years.

Broken by War wasn't an easy book to write, in fact it had taken almost ten years of suffering at the hands of regular nightmares and bad memories to be strong enough to put them all into words. I was diagnosed with Post-Traumatic Stress Disorder in mid-2010 and I have struggled to overcome the illness ever since. I have had my ups on route to recovery but I had twice as many downs. I suffered a brain injury in 2009 and my memory was worst affected, every fine detail in my brain up until the moment I was severely injured, stayed, everything after, lost. As I struggle to retain new information – the old memories continued to eat away at me.

I often think about how easy life would be if I was dead. I would finally be free of all the pain and memories that have already killed me inside. I would no longer have to see other Veterans struggle like I have, let down by a failed and flawed system that is resulting in a steep incline of suicides. The truth is, I just want to move on, be normal again and live a happy life – but I can't.

Back in 2010 I sat in a room full of medical experts, they would discuss in detail the extent and severities of my injuries. They would make the decision to cut my promising Military career short. Facing reality hurt, it killed me inside. I only ever knew one job – I had joined up almost from school. Having to start fresh in the real world mortified me.

I would remain too injured and unable to start my resettlement package prior to leaving the Armed Forces, so I missed out – the Government, Military and many of the bigger charity's chose to turn their noses up at me, leaving me to struggle alone, desperate for help. My cries would go unnoticed. My anger towards the world grew. Everything I tried to do, got knocked down, I felt as if I was being silenced. I chose to join the Army, the Army didn't choose to join me, but they do have a duty of care and an obligation to prepare me for life outside of the wire, especially after being seriously wounded on the frontline – they failed me, like they failed many.

R.I.P to all those who have been failed by the system and have decided to end their torment.

If you don't speak up,

you don't get noticed.

If you don't get noticed,

you don't get help.

If you don't get help,

you're left to rot.

If you're left to rot,

You die.

Anthony Lock©

CHAPTER ONE
EARLY DAYS

As I turned my back on the school gates for the very last time, GCSE results in hand, I knew It was time to grow up. I never fully understood the process of schooling or the need to knuckle down and get the grades which would eventually come back to haunt me twenty something years later when I would need them most.

The truth is, I had a poor childhood, growing up in a rough area of Newport, where we fought to survive on the estate from the day we learned to walk. My brother, James, born two years after my birth, was run over and killed by a car at the age of five. He walked out in front of a parked bus - pulled over because it was early for a change. The car was being driven slowly and cautiously, but sadly the driver of the car that day turned out to be my Step Dad's father. He was driving under the recommended speed limit of 30mph for the road. The impact was too much for my baby brother, even at the low speed the car was being driven, he still died of serious head injuries just a few hours later. My Brother had been over at his friend's house playing, so we thought. His friend lived just three doors down when they decided to sneak out of the house to go over to the newly built supermarket, literally just a two-minute walk from the street that we had lived in. They went across together to see his favourite action heroes, The Teenage Mutant Ninja Turtles. His death prepared me for what I would eventually go on to do and witness later in life.

Mum and Dad split up when I was just six years old and memories of them argue in the kitchen still haunts me to this day. I never expected them to split up and get divorced, I thought in my early years growing up that we were a happy family. Looking back now, I realise that my Mum broke the relationship up because she moved her next partner into our home almost instantly. I had four brothers and two sisters, three older and three younger, so we always had loads of things do with each other and we never got bored. Although we hated each other most times, we never got bored of each other either.

My estate was a square of council houses that fenced off the primary school. This is the very school where kids would stand at the gates and shout vile nasty things to me as I arrived. The horrible little bastards would taunt me over the loss of my little brother! From such a young age, I always said to myself that I would move away from the shit hole I called home as soon as I could.

Shortly after my brother died, we moved away to another estate in Newport, hoping for a fresh start. We didn't want to see the spot where my brother had died every time we left the street. Those memories are memories no-one should ever have to live with. The new estate was no better than the previous one, there was less fighting, so it was safer growing up, but with less things to do. I had to start in a new school though, which totally petrified me. My older siblings were already in high school. The high school sat on the previous estate we had lived on, so it made sense for them to stay in the same school. The bus route to the high school was on the opposite end of the estate to where my brother had died so we wouldn't be forced to see the spot. I had no other choice but to attend a new primary school. My younger brother and sister were too young for school, so I had to go it alone.

I was always a shy, timid lad growing up. I had pointy out ears that often got me name called by bullies. Flapper and Dumbo just two of the names often yelled at me. The good old saying of "Sticks and stones will break my bones, but names will never hurt me" always got me through the name calling and it helped thicken my skin. It didn't really bother me that much after I met my first friend at my new school because he had a severely disabled brother, so I knew my problems weren't as bad as his. I ended up having my ears pinned back after I started attending high school because the name calling started to get out of hand.

When my brother passed, I became quiet and struggled with my education for a while. I was put into a special class with my own teacher to help me catch back up to all the other kids in my year. I couldn't concentrate much at all, I would often break down and cry. I missed my little brother so much. For such a long time after his death I believed it was my fault for not walking home with him that day. I struggled to sleep after he passed away. I often suffered with sleep apnoea after his death, my eyes would often open as soon as I fell off to sleep. I couldn't move, it felt as though someone was sat on top of my body, strangling me. I would have to try and stay calm whenever it happened to me and I would try to fight it by forcing myself back to sleep which was the only way I could get out of it. It was horrible, I was too scared to fall asleep. I never told my Mum, with whom we lived with after Dad had left.

On the day of my brother's death, I had stayed behind after school to play in a football match. The game was a spur of the moment for me as I wasn't in the team. The team was short of players so I volunteered to play. I would normally walk home with my brother after school which was a short walk across a field but that day I stayed behind. I saw my brother and told him to head on home and that was the last time I ever saw him.

I hadn't left High School with a positive future in mind. I left unsure of what I wanted to do as a career. Deep down I always wanted to be a policeman, but I was below the age to enroll when I finally left school.

My High School, at the time of attending, was probably one the worst schools in the UK - let alone Wales. It was a mixed-race school of all faiths. The school had a major discipline problem. There was also a Catholic school on the opposite side of the estate and the kids would go over at dinner time to fight one another. One fight got that bad and out of control that teachers from both schools attempted to break it up and a teacher ended up in hospital hit by a flying missile, thrown from the very kids they were trying to educate.

Most of my time in school I spent with three mates, hiding in the library playing pranks. The librarian was a very friendly and caring lady called Mrs. Schindler and on entering the library you had to sign in for access. So, me and the boys would write on her signing in form - which we had renamed between us "Schindler's List" after the film - with false names like Mike Hunt, I.P. Freely and Brian Haemorrhage, the latter name would come back to haunt me and the boys later in life. We also started to stalk the caretaker thinking his name was Logan we would constantly scream his name every time we came close to him and, fair play, he chased us every time. The name calling, and the chases continued on for years afterwards. We later found out his name wasn't even Logan.

The school had cameras newly erected and we wanted to test them out to see if they were being monitored and were, in fact, real. We would pretend to start fighting in front of the cameras; and yes they were monitored because we ended up with detention over a pretend fight.

My mate was called in front of the head teacher one afternoon, so me and the other boys decided to cover our faces and pull our underwear down and show our bare bottoms to the cameras. My mate came out laughing his head off, he went in for a ticking off over something he didn't do and ended up being told to leave the room instead because of our actions on the screen in the head teachers office, thankfully we were never caught.

I wasn't really that bad in school, most of the other students smoked weed, bullied other kids and were just plain nasty towards one another. That's why me and my small group of friends would hide away playing pranks. I hated my school and my life, I just went to school to see the boys. I wasn't forced to go to school by my Mother either. I didn't fully understand how much an education would benefit me later in life.

As I stood in nervous anticipation, considering whether to open the envelope with my GCSE results inside, I knew this was make or break for me. The pinnacle of my life so far was right in front of me in the envelope I was holding. I honestly thought, deep down, I was going to get good grades because I tried my best in school.

I tore the envelope open and read the results and gulped as reality instantly hit home. I had two GCSE's, a C in English and a C in Drama. I failed everything else. I was devastated. All my friends had achieved good grades. I put my results down to the death of my brother because of the effect it had on me.

Most of my friends, from both estates I grew up on, were starting to get involved with drugs and trouble making. This could so easily have been my route, but I chose differently. I wanted a life, a career. But most of all, a way out of the shit hole I called home.

I never thought about college, probably something the school I studied at should have promoted more. But they never did, so leaving school with no real educational qualifications to write on my CV, I had to rethink my entire life structure. Was it worth living, I thought to myself?

Luckily for me though, life was about to change dramatically. I was in town shopping with a friend who lived in England and often came to visit his lovely Grandmother - who lived opposite me - whenever his mum could find the time to visit. We saw a soldier walking around our town. He was a big man, scary looking and very intimidating. He tried approaching us, but we just ran off in fear. We didn't know what he wanted to do to us, we were just 15 and 16 years of age at the time. As we stopped running and took a breath we suddenly heard a voice behind us that said in a friendly manner,

"Alright lads, I only want to know if you're interested in joining the army and seeing the world?"

I was sold, instantly, seeing the world was enough for me, this was my ticket out of here.

I headed nervously to the Army careers office, with the soldier who had followed us when we ran off. He wasn't as intimidating as he looked, in fact he was really friendly, polite and knew exactly how to sell the Army.

As I sat down at the desk of the recruiting Sergeant, not knowing what I was about to hear or be asked to do, there was a cheeky glimmer of hope finally appearing in my life, one I hadn't had or ever felt before.

I was sold again; this time by everything the recruiting Sergeant had just told me. He promised me my driving license, plenty of adventure training, to see the world and a chance to gain an education that I failed so dismally at. All I could think about in my head was sign me up Now! But unfortunately for me I was underweight! The recruiting Sergeant put a plan into place for me on how to gain the weight I needed. I went home and raided the fridge, freezer and even the dog's bowl, but still the weight was escaping me.

Almost three months later, and still at the same weight, the recruiting Sergeant looked me in the eyes, I gasped as I had it in my head he was about to tell me that I wasn't going to be able to join and to go home. But he didn't, he just looked me square in the eyes and said

"Ant, get a job in McDonald's mate, give it a try."

I laughed out loud, I didn't quite understand at the time what he was saying. I thought he meant try McDonald's rather than the Army. But it soon dawned on me as I walked home what the recruiting Sergeant meant,

"Ant, get a job in McDonald's" ... This could be the way I gained my weight!

Back in the late 90s, technology wasn't like it is today, the internet only really offered the bare minimum and Google wasn't the Google it is today. Although the porn was pretty good. So, if you wanted to find a job it either involved going to the job centre or visiting the actual place you wanted to work for and fill out an application form by hand.

Luck was on my side. A new McDonald's had just been built, not far from my house, so I went down and applied straight away. I got the job and started full time. My first ever job. When I started, my manager showed me around the store and explained the type of jobs I was expected to do. I only had one job in mind and that was making burgers and chicken nuggets, so I could fill my face with them when nobody was looking.

My manager had tried to train me up on the till at the front of the store, but I found it difficult to cope with some of the rude, abrupt customers. I had one customer call me a cunt for no reason at all! Madness how some people think it's okay to be abusive towards people who are just trying to make a living. I was only sixteen and still had a babyface at the time, so it wasn't hard to tell I was young.

Because I had been deliberately struggling on the front till, my manager finally put me in the kitchen area to work, the place I had been pestering him to work in since I started the job. I was in heaven, food heaven. Ok, it's unhealthy food, it's the late 90s but it's food and its food that would hopefully make me gain the weight I required to leave Newport and start my life.

After three months of eating burger after burger, I had gained my weight. I was ready to travel to Pirbright, a training centre that puts a candidate through a number of tests to determine their strengths and limits. You are also required to have a full medical including the dreaded "cough and drop". A medical examination of your groin area where you place your ball sack into the palm of the doctor's hand and he works his magic. I'm guessing the doctor was looking for lumps, well I hope so as I was a scrawny little lad with hardly any confidence and it wasn't easy whipping your manhood out for another man to caress.

At the end of a very long and draining two days, I had an interview, I was told I had passed and I could now start my training at the next available date if it was still what I wanted to do. I was over the moon. For the first time ever, I had a meaning in life, I knew what I wanted, and I knew the new found dream was so close.

I headed back to the Army careers office and signed my Military contract, I had to swear an Oath of Allegiance to the Queen, then I received my Military number. The number was cool, I loved it!. Easy to remember as well. That was it for the Army careers office, no more visits for me. It would be the last time in a long time I would see the place again. I returned home to prepare myself for the day I was to start my training. This would start in just three weeks' time - after Christmas. January 2000. Not only the start of a new millennium but a new start to my life.

When the day arrived, I said my goodbyes to my friends and family then climbed on-board the Birmingham bound train. I was heading to Lichfield, my phase one training base for the next three months. It took some courage for me to leave, especially having to leave my life behind back in

Newport. I was so small and skinny as a kid, with hardly any confidence, so leaving was a massive step for me. But I did it and I left. I knew deep down that better things would come my way, finally.

I arrived at Lichfield and was escorted over to my new accommodation, in a dormitory bedding around 10-12 guys and we would eventually become a section when we started the tactical phase later on during our training. The lads were great, really friendly with no real stand out characters at the time because we were all as nervous as each other. All of the lads in my room had come from Wales and most of them were joining the same Regiment as me! I knew that as long as I passed all of my training, I wasn't going to be joining my new Regiment alone.

As the first few days of training kicked in I thought I had joined a Far East clothing factory, because all we seemed to be learning was how to iron and fold our clothes, or how to polish our boots. But fair play, nobody moaned, everyone got on with it and everyone helped each other out.

Our instructor was a nice guy, an incredibly loud voice on him too, loud enough to make a little bit of wee come out if he screamed your way. There were three other sections with the same number of lads as mine, who were joining other Regiments, so this was the planning and reason behind what group of lads were roomed together from day one of training.

Bringing all four sections together we were now known as Minden Platoon and had four Corporals, a Platoon Sergeant and a Platoon Commander in charge of our training.

As training progressed, I had started to think about home. I guess I was missing everyone and becoming home sick. I pondered whether to quit once or twice but the thought of going back home to nothing made me want to carry on. There was no way I wanted a crap life.

Three months later I had finished the first half of my training; a step closer to becoming a fully trained professional soldier and reaching my goal of escaping home. Next step for me was to pass the next three months which would now be in a base up in Catterick, Yorkshire. A more intense and physical half to my training that included live firing and learning new weapon systems was ahead of us.

CHAPTER TWO
PHASE TWO

On arrival at my new Training Base I had recognised loads of familiar faces from my time at Lichfield and it helped to settle my nerves. My new Platoon Sergeant was a giant of a man, arms bigger than my body. He was a scary looking monster of a man who towered over everyone else, but strangely he was a gentleman who had served with the Regiment I was preparing to join. With all my friends and myself settled in to our new accommodation for the next three months we could start concentrating on the next phase of training and try to enjoy the experience. This part of my training saw us learn all the tactics and weapon systems, the fitness regime became much tougher than the first phase of training back in Lichfield, so Catterick was a much harder experience for us all. We still had the occasional locker inspection, but that was about as much bullshit as we had compared to Lichfield.

One of my fondest memories during my time at Catterick was the bayonet training. This was one of the most intense days of training we did. It was designed to either make you or break you.

The day started off at around 05:30 am. The instructors woke us up screaming orders at us; we were required to crawl from A to B; the instructors ran us ragged in full Military kit that included helmet and weapons. After being run stupid we were taken to some field with a dirty looking swamp in the middle of it. There were mannequins made from straw and plotted around in different locations, ready for us to fix our bayonets and KILL.

I was first in line ready to attack the mannequin when the instructor started screaming in my face - he was trying to get me angry and in the right frame of mind to attack and kill the enemy - he was screaming at me with his nose literally touching mine

"Your mother's a fucking dirty slut who fucked every man in your village!!!"

I couldn't help thinking to myself,

"I don't live in a village, I live in a City."

I had to quickly learn to ignore what was being said to me because it was a horrible experience. I was too scared to answer back in case I got run ragged again and even more than I had been forced to run already. The abuse from the instructors was aimed at getting our aggression out and to prepare us to fight the enemy in combat, by hand if necessary. All in all, the experience was extremely emotional but amazing at the same time, and afterwards it was all we could talk about, we loved it. I still look back to that day with fond memories and I can still taste the pig shit that filled the swamp the instructors made us crawl through.

I have many fond memories from my time in Catterick. Another one was our Platoon Sergeant. We were on exercise, it was a freezing cold Yorkshire night and one of the other platoons were being attacked while they were sleeping in their area of the woods by the enemy (bugging out we called it, the instructors would fire their weapons and make it sound like we were being attacked). This was done to get us to think on our feet. We would end up going on a fast march to get to a safe location. Nobody enjoyed being bugged out, you could guarantee that every exercise we went on, we'd be bugged out more than once, at some point. That night whilst the other platoon was being bugged out I got my kit on and Stood To (*stand to* means being prepared for a likely attack) only for my Platoon Sergeant to tell me and the other lads in my section to get our heads back down and go to sleep.

"We aren't running anywhere boys," he said.

He had taken our platoon to another wood without telling his boss because, like me, he couldn't be bothered to get bugged out! What a legend. He literally stuck his two fingers up at the training program and did his own thing. Mind you, nobody would say anything to him as he was a towering monster.

So, the time had come. I passed all my required training tests and left the training base behind. I was now a soldier in one of the finest Regiments in the British Army with a history of battle honours to be proud of.

Two weeks after passing out of Catterick, I boarded a plane to Germany to join my new Regiment, based in Paderborn. I was super excited about leaving the country. I had never really travelled abroad before, apart from going to Disneyland Paris on a coach trip one Christmas. I had never flown before either, so the excitement was unreal. As the plane took off and we got up high into the air, a German guy sitting next to me turned his head towards me and said,

"We're about to crash and die."

I literally pooped myself. I couldn't understand why this man just said that to me, but I'm guessing he was just scared of flying or mentally insane. Well guess what? I am now also scared of flying too, so thank you, Danke.

As the coach arrived outside my new barracks, the reality was beginning to sink in that I couldn't turn back. I was now committed and under a contract that forced me to work for four years before I could attempt to leave. As I stepped off the coach, I was greeted by an officer who signed me and five others into the barracks for the first time. He walked us over to our new Company accommodation. All five of us were kept in the same Company together. We were now attached to 'A' Company. We were split up amongst three different platoons. I was placed into Three Platoon with Payney, a mate I had become good friends with through training. All the lads I had just met within Three Platoon seemed fantastic and instantly took me under their wing. One lad was extremely funny. He called me into his room and at first I was nervous as I didn't really know anybody. As I entered his room with another lad I'd just met, he performed some sort of weird homemade Kung Fu fighting action. To gain the right to do this, we would need to complete his very own, made up, Kung Fu course called the Nin-can-do Karate Cadre which I did because I wanted to be part of the Platoon I had just joined. It's hard to explain in words without the vision to go with it but it was funny, this was the type of morale I had longed for all my life.

I had heard that some of the other lads who joined the Regiment with me were having a tougher time in their platoons, they were in a platoon that had some bigger characters than them; characters who liked to fuck the newer lads about by making them become their slaves and force them to run to the shop for them, clean certain things, carry out extra duties and so forth. I was lucky, I fitted straight into my platoon without any problems. I had a cracking platoon.

It was now 2001 and the first year of my Army career had passed. I had been briefed by my Platoon Commander that the Regiment was going on Tour in early November. I was about to deploy on my first Operational Tour to Kosovo. Kosovo was located in the South-Eastern side of Europe, we had around seven months to prepare for our deployment.

One evening after a long day of training we went out on the piss as per usual with my platoon. Most of our nights would entail finishing work and heading straight for a sunbed, then we would go for food afterwards. We would then, dependent on time, head to the famous German wank booths located in various shops around the City. A wank booth is exactly as it sounds on the tin. A booth that you go inside and watch porn and masturbate. Seems weird, but it was normal in Germany. We wouldn't go for a wank though - we were British - we were brought up better than that. Instead, we would stand outside clapping and cheering the local men leaving the booth.

Afterwards we would head to the aftershave shop and spray ourselves free from the sweaty sunbed stench before heading to Roy's bar for a few beers and then onto Savoy's for some serious drinking.

Roy's was a Welsh bar based in the centre of Paderborn town. The bar had a great atmosphere and it would always be our first stop. After finishing at Roy's, we headed to the local nightclub, Savoy's. It was one of those nightclubs where the bouncers would ask to see your knuckles to see if you had any bruises on them. If you did then you wouldn't be allowed into the club, apparently everyone with a bruise on their knuckles was a troublemaker. I understood the nightclub's theory regarding the knuckles because Paderborn had a few rival Regiments that often fought each other outside the nightclub or at the taxi ranks at the end of the night. It's what we did. We had an English Regiment based close to ours, so being Welsh you can guess what would happen if you ever crossed paths - especially drunk.

Late one evening - after a long night of drinking - I was extremely drunk. I couldn't walk apparently, but the lads I was out drinking with looked after me and put me in a taxi, telling the driver where to take me. During the drive back, I woke up being sick all over myself, gallons of the stuff pouring out of my nose and mouth. I looked at the driver as I was being sick, and I saw him masturbating. Yep, that's right, masturbating whilst he was driving. I immediately told the taxi driver he was good at multi-tasking because my sense of humour had kicked in, hiding my fear of what was happening before I calmly opened the taxi door and exited out of the moving vehicle. Then the taxi screeched to a halt. Next thing I knew the taxi driver was attacking me in the middle of the street, kicking and punching me in my face, breaking my nose. I managed to walk the short distance back to camp, covered in blood and now almost sober after the close encounter. The Guard Commander took one look at me and called an ambulance and the police.

As I left the hospital the SIB (Special Investigation Branch) had arrived to interview me about the attack. I wasn't bothered about making a complaint, but I felt pressured and gave in. I wrote my statement and told them that the taxi driver was committing a sexual act in front of me, then attacked me when I escaped. This was now being treated as a serious case. The SIB had gone out of their way to find this disgusting taxi driver.

The next day, while on parade, I had become a laughing stock. The butt of all jokes. Being in a Regiment with around four hundred men you can guess how much stick I had to endure from them. It was all light hearted, squaddie banter at its best. I also found it funny, even though he attacked me afterwards breaking my nose. I used to say to myself at least it was me he was wanking over and not doing it in front of a child. Maybe he had a beautiful lady in the car before me and was still horny and saw me sleeping and thought... let's crack one off!

Later in the day I was in front of my Platoon Commander over the incident and instead of sticking by my side, he said to me that he thought I made the story up because I didn't want to pay for my taxi ride. What an absolute tool he was for even suggesting that, but it was very typical of the way officers thought. The taxi driver was never found but it couldn't have been too hard to track this man down? There is only one taxi firm in Paderborn.

Two weeks later and still the Regiment's laughing stock, a mate had gone out one night and met a young lady and went back to hers for a nightcap. She stripped him off and tied him to the bed ready to make sweet passionate love together. But that wasn't going to happen. Out of nowhere, a man came into the room and had sweet passionate sex with him instead. He was now the laughing stock of the Regiment and I could breathe easily walking around camp once again, my new-found fame had fizzled away. We didn't know the full exact story about that night, but what we did know, he probably had a few stitches afterwards!

Germany was a beautiful country and I was living the dream. Every weekend that we had off from working, I would try and visit different areas. Düsseldorf and Dortmund were my two favourite locations for a bit of shopping or a night on the town. Being in the heart of Europe, we had Belgium, Holland and France at arm's length, so I was really loving life. Amsterdam was a favourite spot for many of the lads. I'm guessing they liked Amsterdam for the window shopping and not the drugs.

I headed to Amsterdam on the weekend of the football World Cup Final held in Japan. Germany were playing Brazil. Me and the lads boarded the train at Paderborn and headed to Amsterdam. We had to swap trains somewhere in Germany and the match had just ended 0-2 to Brazil. Myself and two others were wearing bright yellow Brazil jackets and people were starting to give us funny looks. As we boarded the second train, around a hundred drunken German fans were being ushered onto a platform opposite. Me and a lad from 'A' Company had stuck our heads out of the train window and shouted across at the German fans,

"2-0 to the Brazilians, 2-0 to the Brazilians!!!"

All hell broke loose; the fans started charging towards our platform and thankfully for us the train had just starting to pull out of the station as the fans headed for our train. I won't lie, I literally shit myself. A stupid thing to do, but it was funny at the time.

In Amsterdam we headed straight to the red-light district because we had heard so much about it. The place was littered with whores in windows motioning to us with their fingers to come inside for a good time. I wasn't the confident type to step inside either, or part with my cash. After a few drinks we headed back through the district where two big ladies called us inside and we agreed. There was a load of us and we all piled up the stairs into their shagging room. They were trying to haggle prices with us for sex and I assumed we were just there for a laugh. Anyway, one of the ladies laid down on the bed, she spread her legs and pointed to me and said,

"Sniff..."

I was eating a banana at the time and almost deep throated it in shock. I bent down to sniff her like she asked and, as I did, I noticed that she had scars all over her nether-region. She was once a man. I panicked and told the lads and we told her to fuck off. They both became abusive. They wanted money from us for wasting their time. I barged through one and headed at speed for the stairs, closely followed by the boys. We made it out of the building and headed down the street, running for our lives. We stopped to take a breath and realised one of the lads was not with us, but actually still inside. We headed back to the building and the door was locked. Before we had chance to boot the door through, he opened the window from above and hung out shouting down to us,

"I'll be down in a few minutes boys," in his Cardiff accent.

I was eighteen at the time, so I didn't really understand the issues people had with their sexuality and the moment in the building for me was a really scary experience when I saw the scars. Back in the late 90s early 00s, people who changed their gender were treated like freaks and the same attitude taken for same sex relationships, but thankfully, people are starting to realise that the laws have changed on human rights and more information and promotion have become readily available. Nobody should be treated any differently to anyone else, no matter how they looked.

CHAPTER THREE
BRIGHT LIGHTS AND WINNERS MEDALS

Growing up, my father and my friends were all massive football supporters, they supported both Liverpool and Cardiff, so I grew up to support them both also. My partner would say to me that she thought she was second to them in our relationship and I always jokingly replied back to her that,

"Actually you're third, because my daughter is second."

Following both clubs made me happy in life. I had nothing in my childhood to be happy about, so it soon became my obsession and gave me something to focus on whenever I was feeling low. My dad would take both me and my older brother to watch Cardiff City at the old Ninian Park stadium and the buzz of the bright lights, lighting up the pitch and the packed-out stadium would leave me dreaming of becoming a footballer. I played in goal as a child. I loved diving around and getting dirty. My mother used to hate me coming home covered in mud, but it made me happy. Pretty much every game I played in goal for my local team, I would be asked to go for trials, but my confidence and my shyness prevented me from going.

Growing up on the new estate there wasn't much to do other than cause trouble and I wasn't a trouble maker. The boys living on my street were very much the same as me. We had a good-sized area of land behind our homes that we had used for playing football on. Some days when we turned up to play football it would be littered in dog faeces from the miserable old man living close. We would ignore his constant moans about us playing there because we were doing no harm just playing and staying out of trouble. We built our own goalposts and we bought our own nets. The goalposts often got pinched by kids from other parts of the estate, but we went searching for them and always found them. It would piss us off though, all our hard work building them to keep us out of trouble and they got pinched no matter where we had hidden them; including in one of the boys' back gardens. Yet, my estate had plenty of goalposts on it that were there to be used. For us though there weren't any goalposts that were close enough for me and my friends to use, that's why we built our own.

It was May 2001 and Liverpool had made it to the European Cup Final against Deportivo Alaves, a team from Spain and the game was to be played in Dortmund. With Dortmund being just an hour down the road, I was desperate to get to the stadium just to be part of the atmosphere. There was a Corporal in my Company who never seemed quite all there in the head, but the one thing he wasn't lacking was a heart of gold. He offered to drive me to Dortmund which I couldn't resist, the temptation was unbelievable, but we had a problem, we were working. The Army didn't allow you to do your own thing during the working hours even if you had nothing else to do. I had to consider doing a runner for a few hours - or AWOL in military terms (absent without leave) - and hope nobody noticed I was gone, because going to a cup final, especially a European Final, was nothing more than a dream to someone like me, I so wanted to be part of the experience.

I decided to do a runner with the Corporal. We stopped at his house first and his wife made us sandwiches to take along with us. We had made it to the Westfalenstadion stadium in Dortmund, where the Final would be played, just in time to watch the Liverpool team bus arrive outside the ground. The atmosphere was unbelievable; red smoke and flags littered the sky, the fans were singing "you'll never walk alone" which pinged loudly around the outside of the stadium. I had taken in the most amazing atmosphere I had ever witnessed, I was buzzing. We didn't have tickets for the game as it was a spur of the moment decision, so we just travelled down for the pre-match atmosphere. We decided to head back to the car when the Corporal I was with - who wasn't even a Liverpool fan but actually a Manchester united fan - had started to sing out loudly at the top of his voice,

"United!!! United!!!!"

and suddenly a group of scousers passing by overheard him shouting and rushed at us. They had surrounded us, locking us inside a semi-circle, their faces were full of anger and hatred. I literally almost died on the spot, I couldn't believe what he had just done and what was about to happen. I believed they were ready to beat us to death, so I had to act quickly and use my head to get us out of the situation. So, I did, I said to the gang of scousers surrounding us

"Guys, I'm sorry, my mate is retarded and doesn't understand what he is saying, I'm also his carer".

The look on their faces suddenly changed from hatred to the "oops, we're sorry to bother you look" and they left us be.
As we made our way back to his car, a gentleman with a scouse accent stopped us. He said he had two spare tickets for the game as his two sons couldn't make it to the game and we could buy them off him for the price he had to pay for them. We agreed to buy the tickets for around fifty Marcs each, which for a game like that was dirt cheap. My mate was going to buy the ticket for me which took me aback as he wasn't a Liverpool fan, yet he wanted me to live my dream. We got into the stadium and watched the game together, it was the best day of my life, at the time, and to top it all off Liverpool won the match. We returned to camp with no voice left. What a legend the Corporal was.

The next day I was called to my Company Commander's office, known as the OC. I was expecting to get a ticking off from him for yesterday's disappearing act, but that wasn't to be. In fact he had heard how big a Liverpool fan I was and asked me if I fancied representing the Regiment at the Millennium Stadium. I would be carrying the Charity shield onto the pitch at the end of the game and the teams playing the match were Liverpool and Manchester United. Ooh my god, I had to ask him if this was a wind up! I had goose pimples, I was buzzing with excitement, what was happening to me?

At the Millennium Stadium my changing room was located right next to the Liverpool team's. I was on cloud nine and over the moon. I got to see my heroes and talk to them. Adrenaline started rushing through my veins as it was nearly time to walk out onto the field. There were over 70,000 people in the stadium at the time and live on TV, so I was really nervous. The game had ended, I was stood waiting in the back area near the players' changing rooms, whilst holding the heavy winners shield, ready to march onto the podium being erected on the centre of the pitch. I had three of my Military friends with me who would be carrying the medals out. Nobody was carrying that shield out other than me.

It was time, I was now stood just inside the tunnel behind the England Manager and eventually we marched onto the field with him, but first came the announcement!

"Ladies and gentlemen, the soldiers about to march the Charity shield onto the pitch are about to deploy on operations to Kosovo."

Then the announcer said our names and the entire stadium stood up and gave us a standing ovation, it was unbelievable. The noise was deafening, they were clapping, whistling and cheering for us.

I was given the nod and I started to march the shield onto the pitch. I got to choose the route as I was leading and as my favourite team just beat Manchester United 2-1, I wanted to walk the trophy past the losers and rub it in. I marched towards the losing team who were sat down on the pitch looking disappointed with themselves for losing the game to their arch rival. I gave a quick wink in their direction as I passed heading for the podium. My life at that moment was complete. Just two years earlier I had left school with no education and now I had just lived every fans dream.

Now the fun was over it was time to start our pre-deployment training, ready for Operations in Kosovo the following November. My Regiment would deploy by train to Poland on a four-week training package. We boarded the train with no food or water after being told we were going to be fed en-route. I don't think we realised how long the train journey was going to take, bearing in mind Poland is next door to Germany and should be a straightforward trip, but no! The journey took over twelve hours, with over three hundred starving men squeezed into the carriages of the train.

The journey took so long due to the weight loaded onto the train. Not only was there three hundred men on board, but the train was also carrying the Regiment's armoured personnel vehicles (known as a Warrior), plus we had our Recce Platoon vehicles - the Scimitars - also loaded on. I think we had around thirty-six Warriors each weighing around twenty tonnes and a large number of scimitars. These tracked armoured vehicles looked like tanks, they were designed to carry troops into battle, capable of pushing right up into the thick of the action. The Warrior also had its own weapon system, a machine gun and a 30mm cannon. A kick arse piece of kit that I was dribbling and foaming at the mouth to be trained to use, but for now, I would be in the rear of the Warrior as a dismount soldier.

I hated being in the back of the Warrior, as I suffered with motion and travel sickness. I had suffered severely as a child with travel sickness and once, whilst returning from holiday, I was so severely sick it shot out of my mouth and went all over the back of my mother sitting in the front seat. She had just forked out big money on a new perm as well, but hey, she knew what I was like and should have let me sit in the front.

As we arrived in Poland, starving hungry like the poor kids we passed while travelling on the train, we pretty much jumped straight into our usual battle prep as soon as we stepped off the train, ready for the training package to begin that evening.

The exercise itself was a good laugh, hard work, but very enjoyable. We were using this awesome state-of-the-art piece of kit that we attached to our helmets, weapons and kit and it fired invisible laser beams that told you if you had been shot. It was like playing laser tag like I did as a kid back in my local ten pin bowling centre.

Every four to six days we had a maintenance day, where the exercise would come to a halt for twenty-four hours in order to carry out some much-needed maintenance on the vehicles and fix any damage that been caused during the exercise. But more so, to give us a rest from all the physical activities and to catch up on our lack of sleep from the exhausting exercise.

Being deployed on long exercises like these, nine out of ten times - depending on the country we were in and their rules and regulations - if we needed a poo we would have to dig a hole, do the deed, then fill that hole back in. I found it embarrassing to be honest. Reality is what it is though, if I was at war would I be close to a toilet?

Anyway, one maintenance day I needed a poo and luckily there was a large wooded area to the rear of our location. So,

I decided to grab a shovel that was located on the side of the Warrior and go for a poo in the woods. I found this quiet spot deep inside the woods and far away from the lads. I dug my hole, had my poo, wiped my back-side, then filled the hole back in. Later that night we had our orders ready for the mission starting the following morning. The brief was usually given to everyone in the platoon by our Platoon Commander or Platoon Sergeant on the upcoming mission.

We had the brief and when it finished the Platoon Commander turned around and said,

"Oh, gosh, wait there gents. I nearly forgot to mention. Earlier today, somewhere in the wood behind our location, someone took a dump. Well, whichever person it was, you wasn't alone. You were in fact being watched by another Unit who are using the wooded area for reconnaissance. Be warned lads, there are eyes everywhere."

I nearly choked on my own vomit after hearing that. I knew it was me he was talking about. I did ask if he had any names as to who it was, but he said no names had been given. Lucky me I guess, wasn't that long ago I woke up inside a taxi and the driver was bashing one out while watching me sleep and now I nearly became the butt of all jokes once again.

During the exercise I started to break out in a horrible rash all over the area of my face and neck I had applied my cam cream to. Cam cream is a cream we apply to help blend our faces into the surrounding areas, green, black and brown in colour. I hated it because it was greasy and messy. The rash was itchy and sore, the doctor said I had an allergic reaction to the cam cream and I was not to wear it again during the exercise. This was now a problem, everyone else was running about concealed in the surroundings and I was doing the same, but with a white, rash covered face. I was taken out of my section and I worked with my Platoon Sergeant instead for the remaining days of the exercise. I won't say I wasn't embarrassed, because I was, but the one good thing that came of it, I was no longer running about tirelessly.

During the same exercise it had been raining for days, the ground was sodden and almost everyone's feet were soaked right through and freezing cold. Some of the lads had trench foot from the wet conditions and one particular lad in my platoon could no longer walk from the pain. I was with him when the medics were looking at his feet. One medic asked if anyone wanted to do him a favour and I jumped at the chance, thinking I might be taken off the exercise with him. It never happened though. The medic told me to open my jacket, leaving it zipped up slightly at the bottom and then I had the shock of my life. The medic placed the lads cold, wet and smelly feet inside of the jacket that I was still wearing and told me I had to hug them until they warmed up. From that day on I never ever volunteered for anything again.

CHAPTER FOUR
THE FIRST TOUR

The day had arrived, in early November and close to Christmas, I was going on my first Operational Tour to Kosovo, where I would remain until May 2002 in a peacekeeping role.

We arrived in Kosovo after a traumatic six-hour flight on the back of a noisy and cramped Hercules aircraft. These aircraft aren't the usual aircraft people would fly on in the normal world, these things are horrid. Passengers have to sit on hard strapping, a type of material that felt like an egg slicer cutting through your arse cheeks. Due to the loud engines, we were forced into wearing ear plugs which then prevented us from having conversations with mates. We, literally, ended up sitting quietly with the overpowering noise coming from the engines, whilst thinking about all the danger we could expect on the Tour.

After landing safely, we were bussed from the airport to our new base. We were now on operations. From now on, every time I had to leave the base and go outside the wire - as it was known in the Military - my weapon would need to be loaded with a full magazine attached to it. During this bus ride, though, there weren't any weapons to be seen. I was sitting at the back of the bus thinking to myself,

"What if we were to be ambushed right now?".

How much fun would that be for us knowing we were completely fucking defenseless. Needless to say, we arrived at our new base alive and well. Our new base was known as Station Two. The building was a very large block of flats and apparently some of the residents had been massacred in the building during the war. The cellar area itself looked and felt like it was haunted and closely resembled a dungeon in my eyes. It was somewhere I tried to dodge, if I had the chance. However, our armoury was located in the cellar, so I couldn't dodge it as much as I wanted because every time I had to sign my weapon out for a patrol I was required to go down there.

During the first couple of weeks, we had a number of new boys arrive, fresh from training, who joined my platoon. I looked at my platoon as the best platoon in the Regiment. Everyone got along so well and there was never anyone falling out with each other. One of the new lads was extremely young, just seventeen - not much younger than me. I thought being nineteen was young. He was a nice lad, but very quiet. We became friends from the moment we met each other which was probably down to us being so close in age.

I was glad we had some new boys arrive in the platoon because my platoon was slightly under strength in man-power and most of our time was spent guarding empty buildings. So the more men we had, the easier it would be. The buildings had a profound meaning to the Pristine residents though.

One building in particular was the Serbian Church. My platoon had been tasked with protecting it. The church itself was a derelict building, it had no windows or doors and was completely gutted out. On top of the church was a golden cross, which I guess was the sole reason we were guarding it. Inside the empty, cold church there was an eighteen-foot military tent erected which was heated by a generator located outside. We could almost guarantee that the generator would run out of fuel as soon as we got inside our sleeping bags to get our heads down.

The winter months in Pristina were freezing. If I remember correctly, the lowest recorded temperature hit around minus twenty-five. So the heater was desperately required. We would stand at the front of the church during our stag (in the Military a guard duty is called a stag or sentry), we had a small wooden box to sit inside at night or if the weather turned bad during the day.

My platoon was required to supply the man-power for the guard down at the church on rotation, which would consist of just three people and we would usually spend around three or four days at a time down at the church. The way the guard was split between the three of us worked well enough by splitting the duty down to one person on guard at a time, which wasn't ideal but due to the lack in man-power. We decided that two hours on guard at a time was more than enough, per person, due the weather conditions. It would leave us with around four hours of rest which would be more than appropriate for the few days of guard.

Two hours of guard duty on your own would drag by extremely slowly. Everyone hated the guard at night, including me. It was bitterly cold during the winter months and boring. There was nothing to really look at during the night as it was too dark, but in the day we had all the college girls passing by, so it wasn't too bad.

We would eat from container meals filled with slop, designed and cooked by the glorious military chefs. The meal was known as range stew. Range stew was a famous meal within the Armed Forces which we would have if we were live firing on the range. Hence the name "range stew". It probably took the lazy chefs all of five minutes to prep and cook. It usually consisted of a range of everyday foods like baked beans, some sort of mince - that was probably horse meat knowing the Military - Broccoli, potatoes, vegetables and whatever else that was found hiding behind the sirloin steaks belonging to the officers as the chef cleared the fridges. The ingredients would then be mixed together, cooked, placed into foil trays and brought down to us with a loaf of the finest stale brown bread the lovely chefs could find.

There was a portable toilet located just inside the entrance to the church which you would almost certainly need after your meal. Every time someone used the toilet, the door would slam shut sending a gunshot sound echoing around the empty church. No matter how many times I heard that toilet door slam shut, I thought the sound was a gunshot and it would instantly send a shiver down my spine and, at first, running for the entrance, rifle in hand.

The second location my platoon had to protect was the Post Office. This was a building near the centre of the town and not too far from the Serbian Church. The man-power at the Post Office was around six men, due to the Post Office opening for business on certain days to allow the locals to attempt to apply for a passport. The Post Office was a good little duty as well, it was warm and had a working shower. Each of the three platoons within my Company had different locations to guard so we barely crossed paths during the first three months or so.

Winter was in full swing, snow was falling freely; the temperature was dipping well below minus twenty degrees come nightfall. I was in the Serbian Church and just starting my three or four days of guard duty. I wasn't looking forward to it as I'd already done a few rotations at the church since I started my Tour of Kosovo. Each day that had passed felt so long. Standing at the front of the church, showing a presence to the Serbian locals for peace of mind, was a boring job. Occasionally, there would be locals passing, i.e. the college girls, but that was about as much action as could be expected at the church. I hated the place. Two hours on and four hours off, over three or four days at a time. Just an hour into a stag, my legs would be aching, the weight of my kit and ammunition weighing me down. My shoulders would be aching from the webbing straps digging into my shoulders.

Everywhere I looked at night, I could see nothing but complete darkness. As a nineteen-year-old man, in a foreign country, on guard on my own at night, it was an extremely frightening experience. I remember I used to sit inside the freezing cold guard box and hold the door handle so tightly my left hand would be covered in blisters. One of my roommates noticed the blisters on my hand and assumed I had been masturbating vigorously and he kept going on and on about it like it was a massive deal or something. In the end I just started to agree with him and play along to shut him up,

"Yes, I've been wanking..

I know wanking wasn't the cause of the blisters because I'm actually right handed.

Back in the guard box with nothing to do bar just sit there freezing and wishing my life away, I would constantly be rethinking and re-evaluating my life. The one good thing about that particular guard duty was it turned out to be a brilliant stress reliever. No matter how stressed I was in life, after two hours of doing absolutely nothing but shiver and stare into darkness, I just wanted to crawl into my bed and sleep. Being part of a small, three-man team, without any authority in charge of us - that's exactly what we did.

On one occasion, whilst I was asleep and out cold in my sleeping bag all comfy and warm, dreaming away, I was woken up by a late comedian whom I had loved as a kid. Yes, the man himself - who I had idolised - from the TV and best known for video camera mishaps, was in my tent in the Serbian Church and was waking me up. He had travelled out to Kosovo to visit the troops. It was a total surprise to us. I woke up to my childhood hero leaning over me, stroking my face with his small disfigured hand, while grinning away. It was like a scene from that funny film where the butler would say to the girls,

"...Touch my strong hand..."

Looking back now, I still laugh at it, he was at his best that day, a very funny man indeed.

As my four days came to an end, I packed my kit away and carried out the handover of the church to the lads replacing us. Also here, to replace me, was my mate the new lad. My friend didn't look right, he looked so unhappy and lost. I asked him if he was okay, but he just looked at me and nodded in my direction. He had just finished his guard duty at the Post Office. I turned to him as I was about to leave the church and said,

"If you get time, when you are free next, come and see me and have a chat if you fancy one, ok.".

He said nothing, and I just left it there.

That was it, guard done, for a few days at least. Feeling depressed and a bit sorry for myself due to the cold weather and the long guard duty, it was now time to head back to Station Two for a few days of patrolling around the beautiful City of Pristina and some much-needed chill out time.

I loved my chill out time in Kosovo, we didn't get much time to chill out while on operations, so when we did get the chance we jumped at it. I had a computer game console that I had brought over with me to play on during my down-time - or, if Liverpool were playing on TV I would watch them. Although the commentary would be in Serbian, I'd be more cut out on the actual game being played than the language.

As I was chilling out, I had a parcel arrive from home and inside was a box of celebration chocolates sent out to me by my mother. Little treats like this went a long way while away on operations, it would boost morale so much and always gave me a much-needed pick-me-up. It felt the same when receiving a letter.

As I sat on my bunk bed, I shared with the dirty fucker who slept above me. I opened my chocolates and closed my eyes. As I did, I felt a cold breeze that sent a shiver down my spine. The feeling was weird, I thought one of the ghosts from the cellar had come to share my chocolates with me, it was a horrible feeling and one I'd never forget.

I had just fallen off to sleep when suddenly all hell had broken loose around the building, people were running around panicking, I could hear people shouting,

"QRF, kit on - outside - now!!!"

I literally hadn't a clue what was happening, but I'll tell you one thing, I wasn't opening my door to ask just in case some fucker picked me - in the blind panic - to go and do whatever they're being tasked to do. (QRF means Quick Reaction Force). It may sound selfish but after four days of sentry in that cold church, my legs were still numb, like jelly and aching. My non-wanking hand still covered in blisters from squeezing the guard box door handle so tightly at night. I just wanted to chill out and eat my chocolates.

Around ten minutes later my door opened. One of the boys from my platoon walked in, looking clueless as usual and unaware as to what had happened out there on the ground. He told me that everyone had to go straight downstairs to the cookhouse for a brief. At this point I was still tired, but I did as I was told and I made my way downstairs.

I arrived at the cookhouse and sat down on the same table as the rest of the lads from my platoon. I was still clutching my box of celebration chocolates, as I was going to eat them and didn't want to leave them in my room. The cookhouse was now full, every man and his dog were sat in that cookhouse and nobody knew why. A few minutes later in walked the OC (Company Commander). Everyone stood up as a sign of respect - something we do in the Military. Then he let the cat out of the bag. The mother of all news.

"Gents, a short while ago, down at the Serbian

Church, we sadly lost a member of the Company. We do not know at this point what has happened, but we do know that, sadly, we have a deceased soldier, a member of 'A' Company."

Gasps of shock and disbelief rippled around the cookhouse. We all, from my platoon, sat stumped in silence. Whoever the lad was that had just passed away, was a soldier from my platoon. A friend; a brother forever.

As everyone was coming to terms with the news of the loss of one of the lads, some twat of an officer screamed angrily at me,

"You boy!! How on earth can you just sit there with a box of fucking celebrations in your hands?"

It wasn't my fault someone had died, plus I hadn't known why I was being called downstairs in the first place. Next thing I knew one of the Sergeants in the Company had told me that the officer was kicking off over the box of celebrations that I had brought downstairs with me in the rush. I told him I had been opening my mail when I was told to get down to the cookhouse and I just forgot I had them in my hand. He looked at me and then reached forward and took them off me.

"Give them here," he said.

I wanted to tell him to fuck off because they were given to me as a gift. As I handed them over, thinking I'd lost my treats, he opened the box and took a chocolate out and began to eat it. Then he passed the box back to me and told me not to worry, tempers were high, understandable, someone had just passed away and the officer just assumed, as usual, that I was being disrespectful. I couldn't have known the reason we were being called downstairs.

As we were still waiting inside the cookhouse, the Company Sergeant Major walked in with the Colour Man. Our Colour Man oversaw the admin and the kit side of life and the weapons, ammunition - even the little tuck shop. The Sergeant Major explained that a few guys were needed to go to the Serbian Church to help clean up the area. He also required a few guys to go down and take over the guard duty, so the lads who were down at the church at the time of the death could come back and sort themselves out. The truth on the events down at the church still hadn't come to light, or who had died. The man power-down at the Serbian Church was now to be doubled. From this moment on, nobody would ever standalone guarding the church.

As the hours passed and the patrols started making their way back inside of Station Two, the story of what happened was beginning to slowly start emerging. My heart sunk, my eyes started to fill up, I was shaking. I was told that the person who died was my young friend, whom I had spoken to that day. I didn't click at the time and although I did ask him what was wrong with him, I wish I had spoken to someone and made them aware that he wasn't looking right. I was told that he died from a single gunshot wound to the head. His suicide had not yet been mentioned because there would be an investigation. Although everyone thought it was suicide, everything else would need to be ruled out. My friend was a young boy when he died, at the age of seventeen.

Why had the British Government allowed the age limit for an Operational Tour to be so young? Why were we even over there in the first place? Nothing was happening and the actual war ended well over a year before our deployment. This was tough news for me, I had my downs in life before I joined and nothing but ups since, but this was heartbreaking. I felt lost, we had no support from outside sources. Our Platoon Sergeant at the time was a real legend during the death, he gave us all courage and strength to continue on with our heads held high and constantly asked the lads in the platoon how they were feeling. He also told us that if we needed a chat his door was always open. As for any outside professional support? We had nothing, literally nothing.

Horrid memories still to this day remind me of how PTSD was allowed to progress unnoticed throughout my career. Professional support should have been made available to help us through the dark difficult times in our young lives. We couldn't talk to anybody in the Military about how we felt. We knew it would damage our reputations and affect our career progression. Back in my early career if we wanted to go and see the doctor if we felt unwell, we would be made an example of. We were ordered to dress in our full No2 Parade dress, complete with bulled boots, then we would have to parade in front of the entire company holding a bag packed with overnight clothing. We would be humiliated just for feeling unwell and this was one of the reasons anyone dared to seek help. Instead we would crack on with the days tasks until we finished work, where we would head straight for the pub and drink all night long to hide our suffering.

CHAPTER FIVE
THE FUNERAL

As the days passed after the death of my friend, stories about how he died started circulating around the base. The two lads who were at the church at the time of his death had said they were both in the tent talking at the time, whilst my friend was on guard duty. As usual, they heard what sounded like a gunshot, but ruled it out as the portable toilet door slamming shut. They ignored the ever-familiar sound and carried on doing what they were doing. It wasn't until it was time to change over the guard that they uncovered the horrific tragedy. One of the lads had gone to the guard box to replace my friend on duty and when he opened the door to the guard box and he saw my friend slouched, lifeless and motionless on the freezing cold floor. His blood had started to freeze over from the extremely cold temperature. The alarm was then raised back to base and that was when I started hearing all the noise and fuss outside my room in the corridors of my accommodation.

No sooner had my friend's body been recovered back to the main base, which was home to all the top-ranking officers and the remainder of my Regiment, we had the task of stripping the guard box down and burning the wood. The guard box was no good to us, nobody wanted to go back inside it, not now. As the guard box was broken down, under the floorboards, his blood had leaked through onto the outside floor. It was frozen solid. The sight of his blood made me feel like vomiting. Again, everything that had frozen to the ground would require to be removed and burnt. It was a horrible sight. Luckily, I wasn't tasked with doing that job, but for the lads who were, they had to scrape away at the ice to get it all up.

With the guard box now broken down and destroyed and the clean-up complete, it unfortunately meant we were still required and expected to continue doing our jobs. Guard duty at the church would need to resume. We were given no time to mourn; we were soldiers and soldiers don't mourn, they simply lift their heads high and continue on. The attitude back then stunk. He had friends and most of them, including me, were just as young as he was. They needed a hug and some advice on how to deal with a death - especially one like this - not extra guard duty. Losing my brother at such a young age meant I learned the hard way how to deal with death. Death was totally new to some of these lads.

My platoon were back on guard at the Serbian Church. The Royal Engineers had arrived to build a new guard box for us; this time it would be located away from where the last guard box was positioned. The portable toilet was still inside the church, the tent had been taken down and removed from the premises, but the generator remained. We were now guarding the church in pairs, but no longer sleeping at the church after our duty finished. We were now based back at Station Two for the foreseeable future and would patrol down to the church in time for our guard duty to begin. When our guard duty was finished, we would patrol the short distance back. The stag list was a pain to write as well, nobody wanted to do the eight o'clock shift, that was around the time my friend pulled his trigger and passed away. It was known as the "dead time" to us. I wasn't the type to believe in ghosts, but after his death I now felt extremely uncomfortable being around the spot where he had died. I think most people would get the same uncomfortable feeling being down at the church knowing what had happened there. Apparently there had also been a massacre inside the church before the British and NATO forces put a stop to the Serbian War. The brain works in mysterious ways though.

Later that day after my guard duty had finished and I was back at the accommodation, our Platoon Commander called us all together for a brief. Our Platoon Sergeant wanted to have a discussion regarding the death, to ensure that, we, as a platoon were all coping with the tragic event. We had a lot of younger soldiers in our platoon, including myself, and not everyone had experienced the pain of a death in their life like I had from a young age. My Platoon Sergeant at the time was probably one of the best Sergeants I ever had leading me. He always put the lads and their problems first.

After the discussion, the Platoon Sergeant asked for volunteers to return to the UK and attend his funeral, where we would be part of the coffin bearer party. His family had agreed to a Military Funeral and there were no better people to carry his coffin than the lads in his platoon who were close to him. The Regiment would be pulling out all the stops to give him a good send off, with a Military Funeral, minus the gun salute at the end. Obvious that one to be honest. The last thing his poor family wanted to hear was the sound of gunshots.

Within the week, five private soldiers, including myself and a Corporal from the platoon, flew back to Germany where we would start practicing as the coffin bearers almost immediately. We would need to learn how to fold the flag in a particular way together, while either side of his coffin. The flag would be pinned over my friend's coffin on the day of his funeral and require folding just before we lowered him into his final resting spot. I was nervous about doing it, but I wanted to do it, he was my mate and although I hadn't known him all that long, we still got on really well with each other right from the very day we met.

We spent a few nights in Paderborn, Germany, training hard so we could do his parents proud at the funeral. We went out for a few beers during the evenings to let off some steam and try to keep focused and stay normal inside, because it was easy to forget who you were after being away for so long at a time.

The day of the funeral was almost upon us and we had travelled back to the beautiful part of the UK every Welsh person knew as God's Country. We were based and accommodated at the 2nd Battalion Barracks in Cardiff until the funeral was over. We were allocated a pit to use in one of the vehicle workshops in the Barracks which we were staying at and used the pit for practicing lowering the coffin into the ground. This was tricky at first. The more we trained together at it, the better we got.

We visited the funeral home where my friend's body was resting until the day of his funeral. We had travelled there in order that we could see the coffin for ourselves and get a feel for the size and shape of it, to ensure we were absolutely ready for the funeral. We would also need to dress the coffin with the British flag that we had frantically practiced folding. As we entered the building we were led into a waiting room while the staff of the funeral home prepared the room we would be viewing my friend's coffin. The funeral home was really peaceful and quiet and had a strange smell in the air, one that I had never smelt before. We were sat patiently waiting for the go ahead to view the coffin, when one of the boys just come out and said

"Dead quiet in here today, isn't it?"

We all started to snigger quietly to ourselves, whilst trying desperately not to break out into laughter. We were then taken into his room and there was his coffin. I started to shake, the reality of his death had just dawned on me. Once again I was in a room with my friend, but this time the situation was different. He was gone and there was nothing I could do about it. I had already been feeling guilty after his death because I hadn't said anything to anyone the day he died. Seeing his coffin and knowing he was inside made me want to just run away from the world and hide.

We placed the British Flag over the coffin and tied it down using pins; then we placed his beret and his Regimental belt on top of the flag and pinned them down tightly too. Job done and off we headed back to Cardiff. Tomorrow was the big day and soon to be over.

As dawn broke, we were up very early. We had to travel to Swansea for the funeral so we decided to start the morning off with a full English breakfast before we travelled up by car. As we sat in a local café in Cardiff, just up the road from the Barracks, our breakfasts had been ordered. We sat talking to one another and there was a newspaper on the table. I don't normally read papers, but I decided to have a read while I waited for my breakfast to be cooked. I was only interested in the sport section to see how my team were getting on. Most of the football talk is usually on the centre pages of the newspaper, so I opened the paper straight to the centre page and to my shock and disbelief, right there on the centre pages staring right back at me was a massive picture of me and another lad from my platoon. We were standing proud outside the Serbian Church on guard in our pairs - in the snow - with a big storyline trailing the picture underneath. Strangely, nothing was mentioned about the death of my friend that had happened there. I couldn't remember any reporters coming out to do that story either, possibly due to all the grief and emotion I had been silently going through over the days after the death of my friend. Apparently, the reporter came out with a photographer and the picture which appeared in the paper - that I had in front of me - had proved it.

After seeing myself in the paper at breakfast and our bellies now full of unhealthy, but pleasurable food, we travelled down to Swansea to the church and then the cemetery for a quick look about and a rehearsal before the funeral started. We then headed over to the church and waited outside patiently for the hearse to arrive. As we waited outside, more and more people arrived to attend the funeral. There were so many people in attendance that the church was full and those who couldn't fit inside started lining the streets instead. I was beginning to feel anxious and nervous, as were the other lads.

Right on time, the hearse arrived outside the church. We marched to the hearse where the driver had opened the rear door and pulled the coffin out using rollers. We raised the coffin up together and then placed it onto our shoulders. We proudly and passionately headed slowly into the church, taking a slow step together. As we entered the church there were gasps and screams from my friend's family and friends. Their moans echoed around the church; people were crying in every direction we could see. I tried my very best not to burst out into tears with all the sadness around me, but I had no tears left to cry. We marched down the aisle and we placed the coffin down. We then turned around and marched to the back of the church to watch the service. The service was beautiful. The vicar told the mourners to open their hymn books and everyone, no matter how upset, started to sing. All I could hear to my right was my Corporal's singing... It was dreadful, I was trying not to snigger to myself and be respectful - but his voice was something else. If the famous music mogul had been at the church that day then he would have pressed his big red buzzer, instantly.

After the service ended we marched back to the front of the church and we carried the coffin back out. His parents and family looked shell shocked and lost as we marched past holding their son on our shoulders. I guess the death of a young seventeen-year-old boy, deployed on his first Operational Tour, came as a massive shock to everyone from his area. The way they had all come together for the service was heartfelt and lovely to see.

We headed over to the cemetery to complete the last part of the funeral service, which was the flag folding and then the lowering of his coffin into the earth to be laid to rest. We carried the coffin over to his final resting spot and lowered the coffin onto two plinths and then carefully, one at a time, removed his head-dress and belt that had been pinned onto the British flag covering his coffin. We then folded the British Flag one corner at a time into a large triangle and we then quickly prepared ourselves for the final part of the service, the lowering.

As we lowered him down into the ground, I looked at the coffin one last time and almost burst out crying. Again, I had no tears left to cry. I knew he wasn't himself that day, I fucking knew it. Until this day I still wish I had done something about it. Deep in my heart I also know that I could not have predicted what he had planned to do to himself - if he even had planned it at all. It must take some serious circumstances to force someone to commit suicide.

That was it for us. Time to relax; the funeral was over. We did our jobs professionally and I know my friend would have been super proud of us that day.

I was handed the flag which had covered the coffin that had been folded into a triangle and asked by an officer attending the funeral to give the flag to his parents, as a gesture. I went to find the family, but they had left almost immediately. I guess seeing their baby boy disappear in front of their eyes had taken its toll on them. I ended up taking the flag home as everyone I tried handing the flag too refused to take it off me.

The flag was massive, it was the size of a single bed sheet. I used the flag to cover the rear seats of my first car. Which had boy racer stripes up and over it. Whenever I had people sat in the back of my car and sitting on the flag they always asked me where I got it from, as it looked expensive and good quality, I would be straight forward about it and tell them,

"The flag's off my mate's coffin and somehow I ended up with it after his funeral. Nobody wanted to take it off my hands, so here it is and you're sat on it".

That would be it, I'd end up being forced to pull over and my passengers would get out, feeling sick. They would rather walk the rest of the journey than sit on the flag covering my back seats. I had the flag in my bedroom at first, but the missus had threatened to leave me if I didn't get rid of it, so it ended up in the car - which she wasn't best pleased about. I had to remove it from there as well after a few weeks of ignoring her moans.

Our flight back out to Kosovo was a few days later, so we were allowed to stay home with our families until the flight departed. When we landed back in Kosovo we heard the news that our Company had moved back to our Regiment's main base and swapped places with 'C' Company. We were now staying in two-man rooms inside of a porta cabin. The rooms were awesome and much better than the crap we had stayed in at Station Two. I was sharing a room with a lad we called, Side-Show-Bob, he was a funny guy who didn't give a shit about feeling down. I had bought a video camera before flying back out to Kosovo and brought it over with me. I had taken it over to the tank park as we had now switched back to a Warrior role that 'C' Company had previously been doing. At the tank park, with the camera rolling, Side-Show-Bob walked to the toilet. The toilet was a single portable one and blue in colour. As he stepped inside the lads in my platoon ran over to the portable toilet and tipped it over! They then lifted the portable toilet back up and Side-Show-Bob literally fell out covered head to toe in shit.

It was mid-January and life in Kosovo was getting better after the hard month that had just passed. It was a horrible Christmas for the platoon with my friend's death coming just days before. I was offered the chance - if I passed my drivers' theory test - to fly back to the UK and undertake a two-week driving course, where I would go on and gain my driving license. Exactly what the recruiting Sergeant had promised me the day I walked into the recruiting office for the very first time. I had finished the driving course early due to having been put in for my driving test sooner than I expected, so I had a few extra days at home and bought my very first car. A green Vauxhall Corsa that I fell in love with as soon as I saw it on the forecourt.

CHAPTER SIX
THREE MORE FUNERALS

After departing Kosovo, I went on to gain Promotion to Lance Corporal, after passing the junior non-commissioned officers' course in March 2003. I was then promoted in June, whilst out on Exercise Medicine Man in Batus. Batus is short for British Army Training Unit Suffield and based in Alberta, Canada.

After gaining promotion in the British Military and usually from the rank of Corporal, to further your career, you are required and expected to go away on a posting from your Regiment. Usually it would be a training establishment you would be sent to and spend anything up to two years away. Your Regiment would send you away to help mature you as a leader and help you gain experience in a number of fields. I was lucky for my posting though; a spot had become available on my Regimental Recruitment Team based in Cardiff - literally fifteen minutes away from my home. I was ecstatic and could not turn the chance down, buzzing was not the word. I remember my Company Commander asking me if I wanted this posting whilst I was sat in the back of his Warrior in Canada. I was his driver for the duration of the six-week exercise, so I guess that helped.

Being based in Cardiff had all the perks you would want in a job. I was single at the time, so working in the City of Cardiff and the local town centres recruiting, had its perks. We had a decent start and finish time and hardly ever worked a weekend let alone work at all. While I was away on my posting though, I had missed out on the first two Iraq Tours my Regiment would serve. I was disappointed not to go on Tour, which was mainly down to missing my friends back in the Regiment, but I was also relieved, to be honest. News of the Iraq Tour had broken after I left my Regiment and started my posting in Cardiff.

The only really negative part of the posting was the possibility that me, and the team, may be called upon to carry out any funeral duties if anything was to go wrong while my Regiment had embarked on its first Tour of Iraq. Iraq would be different to Kosovo. Nobody within the Regiment would be allowed home from Iraq to attend any funerals, like we did in Kosovo. The Recruitment Team, including myself, would be responsible for handling the funeral party commitments if required.

Unfortunately, within weeks of my Regiment being in Iraq, we lost another brother, friend, colleague. He was a lovely guy; a guy who touched everyone's heart and a soldier everyone would want to work with on the frontline. He died in a freak accident whilst out on the ground patrolling in a Military Snatch Land Rover.

As the news broke, morale fell silent in the office as we were not expecting it. Our boss at the time explained to me and the rest of the boys that we would now be representing the Regiment and the family of our deceased friend as the funeral party. We would be required to start training and preparing for the funeral almost immediately.

We had roughly two weeks to prepare for the funeral and we spent every spare minute we had practicing in the same pit, with the same coffin we had used and practiced with when my friend committed suicide in Kosovo. The emotion and the stakes for me were even higher for this funeral. Although it is no mean feat to carry a coffin or a job anyone wanted to do, in the circumstances, it was a privilege and an honour to be part of it.

On the day of my second Military Funeral, we headed West to a small village in Neath where the funeral service would be held. We got changed at the vicar's home and then made our way to the church to wait for the arrival of the hearse. We didn't get the chance to visit the funeral home beforehand and get a feel for the size of the coffin, nor were we able to dress the coffin with the British flag. That would be done by someone else. At the church, like my last funeral, there were hundreds of people gathered outside. I had wondered why nobody had made their way inside the church yet. Military representatives and dignitaries were also in attendance and some high-ranking officer came over to us for a chat. He had told us that the church was already full to capacity inside and all these people standing outside were here of their own accord to pay their respects to a local fallen hero.

A message was passed to us to get ourselves ready and prepare for the arrival of the hearse, which arrived shortly after. I was centre man and on the left-hand side of the coffin and grateful not to be on the front this time. You may ask why but imagine carrying a coffin being at the front. Everyone's eyes are on you first and it can be emotionally draining, as the family and friends weep louder as the coffin passes by.

We carried our fallen comrade into the church. Hundreds of mourning eyes set upon us. The service went well. It was hard and very emotional inside and outside the church. As the funeral ended, our fallen hero's favourite song played out as we carried his coffin out of the church. The Police - Every Breath You Take; a song I had loved until hearing it play that day. We raised the coffin up onto our shoulders and slowly marched in step towards the church doors. At the foot of the door there were two steps on leading out. We had already negotiated the steps on the way in, so getting out should be fine. As the first two men leading at the foot of the coffin stepped down out of the church, some of the personal possessions - that were supposed to have been pinned down to the top of the coffin - slipped off, falling to the ground.

Gasps, moans and cries screeched out from the crowd outside. I had tears running down my face. I felt let down. Whoever dressed the coffin clearly couldn't be bothered to pin the items down correctly.

We raised our heads high, held off the emotion and carried the coffin back to the hearse placing it back on the rollers that slid the coffin in and out. We then slowly marched behind the hearse, all the way to the cemetery. As the funeral was finishing there was a military gun salute which sent the noise of gunshots echoing through the air. The noise buckled me, I instantly thought of my poor mate who died so terribly in the guard box in Kosovo. The funeral was finally over, and we were asked by the family to attend the Wake, where we had the privilege to meet his family, friends and everyone else that was there to pay their respects.

Death is an unfortunate occurrence in the Military, due to the danger and the nature of the job. I always said to myself when it's my turn to go, it's my turn to go. Something I had picked up from my partner. I guess it helped take the fear of death out of me, because nobody really knew when their time was up unless you had a serious illness.

A few months later, while enjoying the recruiting job, we were given a Warrior to use for recruitment purposes. Being the only qualified Warrior driver on the team - other than Mikey, who was a Warrior driving maintenance instructor - I was given the task of driving the armoured Warrior into the Cities and town centres across South Wales. The buzz I had driving the Warrior around Wales was incredible. The looks we had from people who were not expecting an armoured vehicle to pass them by, was crazy. People just stopped doing whatever they were doing to watch us pass by.

My boss called me and two others into his office and told us we were to travel up to Nottingham and represent the Regiment at a funeral of a fallen hero who had died many years ago. This gentleman had fought in the great Battle of Rourke's Drift in the Anglo-Zulu War back in January 1879, where around one hundred and fifty British Soldiers - mostly from my Regiment - defended a small garrison against over three thousand Zulu Warriors in the Natal Province in South Africa.

I was honoured and humbled to have been told I was going up to Nottingham, because it was history. My Regiment has strong links to this battle and it is our biggest achievement and honour to date. Every year on the 22nd of January, my Regiment would hold a Rourke's Drift Day; a day of history and remembrance, followed by a meal and then some kind of sports activity.

The funeral had come and gone and although I had not known this gentleman, it was still humbling to attend and to see the huge crowd of people who also attended. That was it for a few more months, everything was running smoothly back in Cardiff.

I had met my long-term partner whilst on the posting to Cardiff. It was love at first sight for me. My partner was on crutches after falling over and rupturing her cruciate ligament, when I met her, but that never turned me off her. After a few months of living together she fell pregnant, but unfortunately it wasn't meant to be for us this time and she suffered a miscarriage. We just had a new boss take over at the time and he was the biggest prick anyone could imagine. I had to tell my boss about the miscarriage because, not only was I gutted and destroyed over it, but so was my partner and I was about to head up to Wrexham for two days of recruiting. He gave me one sodding day off to mourn the loss and comfort my distressed partner.

He called me into his office on my return to work the very next morning and his sick, disturbed mind saw him accuse me of causing my partner's miscarriage. His reason? In order that I could have some time off. Obviously, I went absolutely mad and gave him a fucking mouthful which resulted in me being the one in trouble. Even though a captain from my Regiment had overheard the entire conversation and came into the office to calm the situation down. I was then sent back to my Regiment which was then based back in the UK, in Tidworth, Wiltshire, but still currently away on its second Tour - in quick succession - of Iraq.

I returned to my Regiment's new location a few days later, extremely angry and disappointed at the Regiment for allowing my treatment at the hands of the arsehole who was a trusted Sergeant Major and supposedly "...a leader of men...". I had been forced to leave my distraught partner at home. With the Regiment still away on operations in Iraq, our camp was quiet and empty of soldiers, bar the biffs and those deemed useless. I was attached to Rear Party when I arrived; carrying out camp guard duties. Rear Party was made up of basically those not worthy or trusted to serve on the frontline, not all of them were useless though. Some injured and some, like me, returning from postings, while others had viable excuses.

I had another falling out with the Rear Party Commander in charge - a Major at the time - over the incident back in Cardiff. He was obviously good friends with the wanker who had accused me of causing my partner's miscarriage. I had tried to make a complaint about the accusation made against me, but I was treated like a criminal instead. I was given the choice to withdraw the complaint or continue to be pressured. I did eventually withdraw my complaint because I found that I had no support on my side and low and behold I was treated normally again as if nothing had happened. But it had. Snotty twats.

Whist on Rear Party, I met a couple of new lads who hadn't long joined the Regiment and one particular lad, I instantly became good friends with. We'd sneak off together, head up the Warrior sheds to smoke cigarettes and chill out all day while hiding in the back of a Warrior - out of sight and out of mind. We pretty much just sat there talking, smoking and having a laugh together. But unfortunately, later, life would change for one of us.

My Regiment returned from Iraq for the second time in two years and after their leave, normal camp routine kicked in. I was attached to Javelin Platoon in Support Company. All the lads in my new platoon were really nice, friendly guys - including our Platoon Commander and Platoon Sergeant, who quickly sent me away on a Warrior driver maintenance instructor's course which lasted around six weeks. However, I went on to fail my final assessment, due to my instructor missing a key point whilst teaching me beforehand. I ended up having to re-attend the last two weeks of the next course and re-sitting the assessment again. This time I passed and was now a fully qualified Warrior driver and maintenance instructor. Passing this particular course would qualify me on the promotion board, up to the rank of Sergeant.

When I returned to my platoon after the course ended for the second time, my mate, the lad I had been sneaking off smoking and skiving with during Rear Party, had also been attached to my platoon. Unfortunately for him though he decided to take himself absent without leave (AWOL) sometime later and in July of 2006 he ended up getting into serious trouble. Subsequently, one high positioned officer within the Regiment, abused his position and demanded to see him in his office and made it very clear that he was to be made hot and sweaty first. The poor lad ended up passing away from the beasting, aged just twenty-two. Rumours spread around the camp like wild-fire about my friend's actions the night before. He had soaked the officer in question's wife with a fire extinguisher as she walked past his accommodation block. Everybody was shocked by his sudden death, it came from nowhere and totally out of the blue. He did not deserve to die the way he did and for the reason he did. In my eyes, what he did with that fire extinguisher, that evening, could have been legendary if he chose to soak the officer instead. However, either way, he should never have done it in the first place. The lady was just making her way past innocently and should not have been involved.

The morning after the night before, I recall seeing him lying on the concrete floor from the window of my accommodation block, I wasn't to know he was on that floor clinging on for his life. His body was shutting down, until his heart finally stopped beating en-route to hospital. R.I.P my friend. What a great lad he was and what a horrific way to go - all because of what exactly!? Anyway, shocked and horrified, we had the TV crews, with their cameras and the press queuing outside of our Regiment's camp gates trying to get stories from anyone leaving our base. Our Sergeant Major at the time, a wonderful leader and role model, had asked me if I wanted to be part of the bearer party and carry his coffin for the family - if they agreed to the Military Funeral as offered. Coffin number three.

I said yes to the bearer party. He was a good friend of mine and even though I hadn't really known him all that long, I wanted to do it. The funeral was a doubt from the start because of the nature of his untimely death. I couldn't blame his parents for not wanting a Military Funeral for their son, he was let down by the very people there to protect him. A life gone, and needlessly, a life wasted. This added even more stress onto my small shoulders although I had to continue - carrying on as per usual with, again no support being offered. All this within a relatively short career.

We had trained vigorously for his funeral; the coffin drills were becoming almost routinely normal to me. But unfortunately for all of our preparing for the day, no matter how long and hard we trained, the family stuck their fingers up at the Army and told them to stuff their Military funeral where the sun doesn't shine. Fair game to them, I'd have done the same. The Military had started to lose its pride long ago, thanks to the ever-changing human rights and freedom of speech that continue to turn the United Kingdom into a spectacle of embarrassment around the world. All the men, women and animals who died in both world wars had fought to give these people that very freedom of right, but all it has done, sadly, is spiral out of control into a Country where we now have to watch our every word, action and step.

CHAPTER SEVEN
I WOULDN'T WANT TO THINK

With the Military funeral cancelled, I was now back training with my platoon. We had been informed that there was going to be another Tour of Iraq coming up in just over a years' time. This would be my Regiments' third Operational Tour of Iraq in just four years, with each one lasting over six months. Op Telic 10 would be the name of the upcoming Tour and the preparation would slowly start gaining pace for the Regiment's deployment. It would begin with another trip to Batus in Canada, we had a requirement to train out there to gain the usual tick in the box to prove we were ready to deploy. Canada, for us, was a luxury, I loved the place. The exercise was the toughest I had faced in any training I had undertaken and would last so long. We were guaranteed that the weather would move through the full four seasons - in one day. At some point in the exercise, the best bit, the night sky.

It's said, the training area we used is the size of Wales and is ideal for every type of Military vehicle, including tanks. After the exercise finished, we worked tirelessly preparing the Warriors for handover. Straight from the gates of the camp - as we entered - there would be no leeway given; no time to shower or to phone home for the first time in 6 weeks. It would be an all-out cross-country race to the back gates when the exercise finished. Just inside the camp gates was the washdown and with only four bays and over a hundred vehicles that required to be blitzed clean, we had to get back, as close to the front of that queue as we could or spend the next twenty-four hours queuing.

During the years, I would teach numerous Warrior driver courses back in the UK. I didn't mind teaching them; I enjoyed my own free time, I was left alone to run the courses and the reward of seeing the lads qualify at the end of the course and then go on to become stronger drivers, was more than enough. With Iraq fast approaching I was still teaching the driving courses as my Regiment wanted as many men as possible, qualified in the role. To be fair, I understood why and preferred to teach over running around all day anyway, I hated fitness.

Some of the lads were hard to teach. Each course I ran entailed a few weeks in the classroom learning all the Warrior knowledge and characteristics, then we moved into the maintenance phase, before finally starting the driving phase. The driving phase I had to teach were; cross country, driving on main roads and night driving. Each course would end with a mountain of paperwork and course reports that often took my free time and nights away from me, but the way my head was screwed from the deaths of my friends over the years, I only ever finished work and hid in my room, locking myself away from the world outside.

The final course was taught before I re-joined my platoon, to start my own pre-deployment training would be dramatic. The lads on my course were good lads and one in particular stood out the most because he was a big character, a friendly giant that loved his banter. During the driving phase of the course he struggled to fit into the driver's hatch. He was a giant of a man and inside the driver's compartment there wasn't much room at all - so for him it was always going to be a squeeze.

During the driving phase, which would end with a driving test by an independent, outside examiner, we were on the busy dual carriageway of the A303 when a gentleman driving a Land Rover came side to side with the Warrior I was commanding. He started honking his horn at us and I watched him throwing his arms about like he was being attacked by a hyperactive wasp. I started to get annoyed with him because I hadn't seen any issues whilst moving along the dual carriageway. I was looking at him shouting pointlessly,

"Piss off, you prick."

The number of arsehole drivers who drive dangerously close to the back end of the Warrior was unbelievable, just one bump and the fuckers would know all about it.

I decided I had no choice but to pull the vehicle over in a safe position and confront the guy still following behind vigorously flashing his main beam lights. This would be the first time driving a Warrior on the main road for the big man sat in the Warrior's driving seat. Pulling over on a busy dual carriageway was no mean feat for anyone, let alone a new, incompetent driver but to be fair he pulled over superbly with my guidance and I jumped down to confront the man behind.

As I approached the man's vehicle, a little bit nervous and prepared to headbutt the arsehole, the passenger window was down on the Land Rover. I put my elbows over where the window should be and leaned into the car. The driver just looked at me and said,

"Oh, do be careful young man, you just took my window out as I was overtaking you some time back," in a very posh accent.

I looked at the window and looked down at the passenger seat which was covered in broken bits of glass, then I looked at him again. I was confused as to how the Warrior had smashed his Land Rovers window because it didn't add up.

What had happened was one of the Warrior wheel nuts had somehow became loose, causing it to repel up off the wheel, high enough and at the right angle to hit the overtaking vehicle's window. It was a good job the gentleman had just dropped his wife off to work shortly before or God knows what injuries she may have had.

The guy turned out to be an Admiral in The Royal British

Navy and was extremely calm over the incident. When I asked him why he had to beep, flash and wave his hands at me in the manner he did, he just said that he was trying to get my attention.

The next day we headed back up the A303, along the dual carriageway, down and around Stonehenge and then back up the way we came. This time I had a different driver in the seat - and the rest of the lads were sitting in the back. I shared the driving out equally and managed to allow the lads to drive the same routes as each other.

As we drove up a steep stretch of the A303 and reached the top, I felt a knock and then heard a bang which came from the track area. As a Warrior Commander I would be stood up in the turret giving myself a safe and clear 360-degree view at all times. I turned around when I felt the knock and heard the bang to see one of the tracks rear idlers hurtling at speed down the hill. Somehow the rear idle had broken away from the Warrior, leaving the vehicle undriveable - but that wasn't my main concern. My concern was the idler wheel hurtling down the dual carriageway at speed. The damage the idler would cause if it collided with a car would be the similar to the impact caused by hitting a horse. The idler wheel had disappeared down the hill out of my line of sight by the time I had managed to get the Warrior safely pulled over and out of danger.

Once the Warrior had stopped, the hazard lights were switched on and the beacon light on top blinking away furiously. I had to go and look down the hill. I had to see what damage the idler may have caused. I approached the top of the hill with my driver, caterpillars were crawling around in my stomach. I hadn't seen any cars come up the hill and pass us since the idler wheel broke off. Luckily for me, far in the distance, the idler wheel had come to a halt on the hard shoulder causing no damage to anybody.

I sent the driver down the hill to collect the wheel and

used the other lads on my course to start breaking the track apart. The track would now be required to be split down into small segments and placed inside the back of the Warrior, ready for its recovery. Back at the Warrior sheds - after the Warrior was recovered safely and inspected for damage - I had a cigarette and a chat with the lads about what might have been before we started the long strenuous job of reconnecting the rear idler and the track ready for the lads' final day of road driving in the morning and before they sat their driving tests later that day.

The final day arrived, the last phase of driving left to do. I allowed the boys to drive the same route they would be examined on during their driving test. The last driver I had left to drive the route was the big guy himself. He was a little excited to drive the Warrior every time he sat in the driver's seat. On many occasions I had to warn him to calm his driving down and listen to my every command over the headset. During the night driving phase, every time we stopped the vehicle, regardless of the reason, he would open his driver's hatch for some fresh air. This was a No-No, he had to learn to deal with the claustrophobic feeling inside his driver's hatch. I had actually told him that,

"If you don't keep the hatch closed whilst on operations...I wouldn't want to think what may happen to you."

Mark my words, down the line I would regret ever saying it.

We set off in the Warrior towards another big Military base just a short drive away. There was a roundabout ahead of us, the lad would usually drive around the roundabout like you would in a car, taking care and driving it slowly, but this time for some unknown reason, he decided to drive straight up and over the fucking thing. I screamed at him to pull over. I was furious with him. I Jumped out of the turret when we stopped and went hell for leather on him over it. His test was coming up later in the day.

He laughed the entire thing off, not seeing the problem, I wasn't sure whether to still put him in for this driving test after that stupidity. I had to go and get some advice from my training wing boss who said to just stick him in for the test anyway. Once again, course after course, the lads passed their tests and would go on to become great drivers within their platoons.

With my last driving course complete, now the hard work would begin as I start my pre-deployment training back with my platoon. That wasn't to be though. Well not with my platoon anyway. As I re-joined my platoon, my boss had called all the lads together to give a brief on the upcoming deployment. He told us that we would be attached to Bravo Company and would now be heading out to Iraq over a month earlier than the rest of the Regiment. Bravo Company was currently understrength in the manning department, so it made sense to attach us. My platoon, a specialized platoon, would be split down between each of Bravo Company's three platoons so they had an equal amount of Javelin trained operators in it. For me though, I was going across to four platoon because they required a qualified Warrior Sergeant.

The Warrior Sergeant's role would be my first, major, responsible role whilst serving on operations and I looked forward to the challenge. My job was to ensure that all four Warriors under my control were constantly in good shape and ready to be deployed into battle when required. I had to ensure the drivers had all the correct tools required for their Warriors, so they could keep them maintained and running well and then there was the paperwork side of it and the oils, lubes and everything else that came with the role.

Many private soldiers never fully understand the added

responsibilities you get when you're promoted up the ranks. You were once just a soldier like them, a chess piece, someone to take the blame when a higher rank fucks up. As soon as you get promoted you become their leader and are expected to step aside from them, including no longer being allowed to eat on the same table as them. Then came the added pressure of the many other jobs, tasks and responsibilities involved.

I would be attached to Four Platoon for the duration of the Iraq Tour. I did not know many of the lads - if any at all - within Four Platoon as most of the them were new boys who hadn't long joined the Regiment and having been away on a posting, most of the lads I had known back in the day had left the army or decided to move to other Regiments by the time I was sent back by that wanker in charge in Cardiff.

To be fair though, the platoon had a great Sergeant leading it, a man that would happily lead anyone into battle and always have our backs. I didn't see eye to eye with my Platoon Commander straight from meeting him. It felt to me that his head would be firmly up the arse of the other Corporals in the platoon.

'B' Company was still very much short of manpower, even after my platoon had joined them. We had a number of Scottish soldiers join us for the upcoming Tour. They were a fantastic bunch of lads, so happy and positive, which instantly changed the morale within the Company. The Scottish lads would stay together in the same platoon for the duration of the Tour, with the remaining half of my platoon forming a third platoon together. Each Company had three platoons in it anyway, but with the retention being low meant 'B' Company had enough men to form two platoons.

We deployed out for our training as a Company of three platoons and a recovery and fitter section from the REME - Royal Electrical Mechanical Engineers - onto one of the many training areas surrounding Salisbury Plain. When that came to an end, we then headed down to Castle Martin training ranges in West Wales to prepare for the upcoming Tour.

We trained alongside the other Regiment who were deploying with us, they were also an infantry unit. We would be working closely with them in Iraq during our upcoming Tour and we would also be living closely together in Basra Palace. They would deploy out onto the ground using the armoured bulldog, which was a tracked vehicle. They were similar to the Warriors, but lacking turrets and firepower. They looked similar to the 432's the Army once used as field ambulances back in the olden days as they were built on the same chassis as them.

The Regiment that we would be working alongside had a good chain of command, good leaders and good men, everything you wanted your own Company to be, I guess. We would deploy to numerous live firing ranges and trained extremely hard. The training was designed to match, as far as possible, current war zones and the current operational theatres. So every angle had to be covered ready to deploy. First aid, language training, riot training, you name it, we trained hard at it. With both units now ready to deploy we would be released home for our pre-Tour leave.

CHAPTER EIGHT
HE'S BEHIND YOU

With our Pre-Tour leave coming to an end, I had to say my goodbyes to my partner and my two-year old daughter. It would be my first Tour away from them and the longest time I would be away from them. I had deployed away on long exercises already and also deployed on countless trips over to Canada, but nothing as big as this, or as long. The girls were my life and my soul, my only reason to wake up every morning. Nothing prepares you to say goodbye when you are about to leave them behind for such a long time. It's the hardest thing you'll ever be forced to do whilst serving in the Military.

Six to eight months is the expected length of time an Operational Tour lasts and with just ten days off, to recuperate in between, it kills you. Children never really understand why you have to leave them, they just assume you are leaving them for good, moving out, running away or whatever else runs through a child's mind. I relied heavily upon my partner to keep my child focused for the duration of the time I spent away. There was a twenty-minute phone call per week, for free, whilst on operations and dependent on where you were based out there, then you may be able to write a letter home as often as you could. The only real morale on Tour was either the phone call home or a parcel from a loved one. A parcel was our way of getting hold of simple luxuries from back home. Things that we needed and were unable to buy while on Tour. The simplest of everyday products would be the hardest products to buy on Tour, so a parcel was our life-line.

All of my kit had been packed onto the coaches waiting on the Regimental Square, I was about to leave with 'B' Company, heading for Iraq. As I stepped onto the coach my Company Commander stopped me in my stride and told me I was incorrectly dressed. I was confused, I thought I had the same uniform on as everyone else, but he soon pointed at my Lance Corporal tape on my clothing and said again to me that I was incorrectly dressed. I had just been promoted to Corporal. I was so happy and proud as it was totally unexpected and out of the blue.

The promotion was not done in the normal way, usually you'd be promoted in front of the entire Regiment, but I was happy not to because nobody enjoyed marching out in front of over four hundred men and women. You feel pressured with all eyes on you, waiting for you to fuck up and make a mistake in front of the Commanding Officer.

As I sat down at the back of the coach, the lads congratulated me on my promotion. I placed my new rank slide on, thanks to a mate who had a spare one with him. I was now a Corporal in the British Army. They say it's one of the hardest ranks to achieve, the easiest to loose but the most rewarding.

In today's Army though it seems that you can get promoted way too early in your career. Mainly through licking arse or brown nosing as we knew it in the Military. Back in the day stripes were earned the hard way. Soldiers were expected to serve a certain number of years in each rank also, usually around four years and progress steadily making you a better soldier. Nowadays, sadly, you can make it to Sergeant in five or six years. Guess it's due to keeping the soldiers happy and the man power up or the lads are finding their rank slides at breakfast time in their cereal boxes, like you used to find toys back in the good old days.

We flew from RAF Brize Norton, a Military Airport, often when travelling overseas. A small terminal, lacking in seats. We would often find ourselves sitting on a hard-concrete floor, or in the children's play zone until our flight departed. Like most airports, we would often find our flights out delayed for long periods of time and sometimes for days

My Regiment lost its name when the Government

decided to cut the funds for the Armed Forces. We swapped to a new name, which made no sense at all and meant the Regiment over time would start to lose its identity. Before the swap, the Regiment had the initials RRW - those initials went a long way towards creating a new meaning linked to being fucked around like naughty little school children, most mornings, by our higher ranks. We would call it RUSH-READY-WAIT. We would always leave for an exercise or a day on the live firing ranges a few hours earlier than made sense. No matter where, or what, that task was. It was the Army's way of fucking the boys around for no reason. For instance; if we had a range day coming up which we often did being an Infantry Regiment, the range itself wouldn't allow us to start live firing until 09:00am at the earliest due to the rules and regulations governed by the rulers of the land. Our Regiment was based in Tidworth and the closest range was, literally, a five-minute walk away and yet we would still be ordered to collect our personal weapons from the armoury around four hours before the first live round would even be fired. Then we would be ordered to congregate on the square, formed up like convicts in a Mexican Prison, ready for the transport to arrive three hours late hence the name RUSH-READY-WAIT! Rush to the Armory, be Ready on the square and then Wait about four hours, in the rain and cold, for the transport.

So, we boarded the plane and took to the skies. For some, they will never return. We headed to Kuwait, where we would have a short stay as a battlegroup to carry out any last-minute training. In case any drills we had been taught already had changed on the ground. The week would also help prepare us for the extreme heat about to hit us, as summer was fast approaching and we used the week for acclimatization training, which would only help to save lives.

As we landed in Kuwait we had a brief over the tannoy from a high-ranking officer, telling us not to switch our mobile phones on - that we were warned not to bring with us, or contact back home from them either. Using the phones over in certain middle-eastern Countries came with huge risks because your message or phone call home would be intercepted, and personal details used to send hate messages and phone calls to our families. Nobody would listen to the advice though - including me. We all turned our mobiles on and sent text messages home to our wives and families to let them know that we had landed safe, like you do.

A few days into our Kuwaiti acclimatization training a few of the lads, including me, finally got the chance to phone home and speak with our loved ones. Some of our partners though, mine included, had received sick phone calls after we ignored the advice on the aircraft and used our phones to send messages. The phone calls our families received were all very similar.

"Your husband's just died," the caller would say.

Obviously some of the wives freaked out from the call, thinking it was true, because their husbands had left on a Tour. I had mentioned the hacking and the hate calls in my message to my wife on landing and told her to ignore all phone calls because if anything would happen to me then she should expect a knock at the door.

Midway through the acclimatization training, I had a huge blister on my right heel from the Military boots I had been issued with shortly before flying out. I had to see a doctor for advice as the blisters weren't healing and I had vital training to conduct. The doctor put me on the sick for two days after taking a look at them and then wrote me a letter to hand to my boss stating I should be supplied with better boots as the ones I have are shit. The letter worked and within days of arriving at Basra Palace my boots had arrived which only a few of us had.

While I was left back in camp with two other lads from

within the Company - all suffering the same problem - I decided to head for a shower to cool down from the blistering heat. As I was having a shave, from nowhere, a Kuwaiti man appeared right behind me, looking at me and checking me out as I was bending over the sink with just a towel protecting my cute little backside. I instantly thought I was about to get knocked out and raped, or worse still, murdered and with my own razor. I literally shit my towel and that was quite possibly the reason why I didn't get raped. I turned around to face him and stood as tall as I could trying to make myself look big. I wasn't a big guy though, I was in fact a skinny little fucker who was still only eight and a half stone. I would struggle to get wet in a highly powered shower because I was that skinny forcing me to run around the shower trying to get hit by the water. The Kuwaiti man backed off and I told him to get the fuck out of the shower block "now" before I punched him on the nose. In his best English he replied "ifbvhfvbeuvb" or whatever the fuck it was he was muttering. I could not understand him, he wasn't speaking in the native language because we had been given Arabic language lessons during our pre-deployment training and the words didn't sound Arabic.

Come the end of the acclimatisation package, we headed to the C.O.B (Contingency Operating Base) in Iraq, via an hour or so flight. The base was huge, shared with many other Armies from around the world, including the American, Swedish and Danish Forces. My Company would be staying in the C.O.B for a very short period of days, which was enough time for me to sign-over the four Warriors that would be my responsibility on the Tour and get them prepared and ready to roll out of the camp gates heading for Basra Palace.

The weather was starting to get extremely warm and humid. I hadn't felt heat like it before. The Warrior is made up of metal as well which meant being inside it felt like a barbecue. Due to the threat worsening over the last few weeks, we were forced to wear our full body armour including helmets. I was a little skeptical as to how our bodies would even cope in the heat. The Warrior had just been fitted with a fridge that was placed by the Commanders knees, but like all the other equipment supplied in the Military, it was shit and instantly broke down because it couldn't cope with the demanding heat.

With the weather being so warm we had to drink triple the amount of water we would usually drink back home in the UK. I hated drinking tea and coffee. The water that we had to drink - thanks to a broken unfixable fridge - while out on patrol would be hot enough to make a brew. As I was preparing my Warrior with my crew, several Apache helicopters took off and flew directly over our heads, lifting the dust up and tossing it all over us like a nasty sandstorm in the desert. A few minutes later several tanks started whizzing past us heading for the gates. There were a few British Tanks heading out also, the Challenger 2 tank. Something seriously big had just happened. Later that day word spread that a Swedish patrol had been ambushed by the Al Qaeda murdering terrorists. I didn't know what to think to be honest. On one hand I now realised where I was and how real the threat was - but on the other hand, seeing the quick reactions of the friendly forces and the way the nations quickly pulled together gave me a sense of relief and hope that if I ever became stranded on the ground, captured or even injured out there on the streets of Basra, then people will come for me and could potentially die saving me.

The Warrior's pads were struggling with the blistering heat, the pads that fitted to the track wore down extremely quickly. In the United Kingdom we would change the pads every six or so months. We hadn't even had time for lunch in this fly infested, shit hole and we found ourselves changing them. We knew the changing of the track pads as track bashing and it was one of the most hated jobs in the Armed Forces. As the light fell on the tank park we would stay behind in the darkness, still sweating from heat that was now rising from the ground in order that we could reach the deadline for the move to Basra Palace.

The ground was littered with camel spiders and other creepy crawlies trying to stick to our dark shadows where the ground would be the coolest for them to scuttle around. We could hear and feel the sand underneath our feet moving about so It was obvious to me that it was the spiders crawling below me, because Saddam Hussein, the ex-leader of Iraq had been hung the year before our deployment to Iraq, so it wasn't him digging himself to freedom below my feet.

CHAPTER NINE
THE JOURNEY

The time had come to deploy as a Company down to Basra Palace, one of Saddam Hussein's former Palaces and stronghold. The British Army had taken over Basra Palace and moved into it using the Palace as a F.O.B (Forward Operating Base) as the base was ideally located inside the centre of Basra City. The journey itself would take around two hours to complete due to our Warriors needing to negotiate some very narrow and dangerous streets and the threat was growing towards NATO Forces. En-route, we encountered the occasional suicidal camel running out in front of the Warrior, luckily for us the camel wouldn't be wearing a vest as it tried to commit suicide.

As we made our way towards Basra Palace, everywhere we looked was an unpleasant picture of rubbish littering the streets, leaving a horrendous smell in the air that could never be forgotten. Some of the buildings had been damaged, or destroyed, by airstrikes. Most though had been hit by their own weapons, rocket propelled grenades or mortars which the enemy regularly fired at each other from across Basra. With the unpleasantness forced upon the local people, they would continue getting on with life and going about their day trying to earn whatever little cash they could to put food on their tables and feed their families in order to survive. The local people seemed happy enough and normal, totally different to what I had imagined, although some would look at me and you could see the evil in their eyes. You knew by the stares, that the city wasn't as friendly as the drive-in was making out.

We made our way through the streets, taking visual notes whilst en-route to Basra Palace, every possible enemy firing position we noted, potential hazards and anything that really didn't look right or out of place. We arrived safely at Basra Palace without any problems. I was expecting some contact with the enemy at any time, because our intelligence had pre-warned us. The enemy have nothing better to do other than watch us. They watch every move we make, they know our strengths. They also know when a new battle group is in town. They have people known as "dickers", who sit and wait patiently wherever we may be. As soon as the Military Forces leave camp or drive down a certain street, the enemy would pull out their mobile phones or walkie-talkies and pass the information onto the next guy, until they all knew we were heading their way.

To be honest, in an ideal world the dicker, is as bad as the enemy - however, we also knew through the media and intelligence that the enemy preferred to control innocent Iraqi families using violence, torture and rape. Al Qaeda were known to either kidnap members of local families or simply terrorize them in a ransom to force them and their families to fight against us.

But the journey was good, everything seemed okay and the people friendly enough, which gave me some reassurance. On arrival inside Basra Palace, we parked our Warriors onto the sandy area of ground outside our new, hardened accommodation. The accommodation we were moving into used to house Saddam's cleaners, we were led to believe, back in his dominant years in charge as the Iraqi dictator.

The lads were glad to be out of the back of the Warriors having been squeezed into the back for the journey, with no cold air either, everyone had a buzz about their step because we were finally here and starting the Tour. As a Warrior Sergeant I had to ensure my Warriors were shut down and locked correctly, all the correct kit and equipment would be required to be taken off and moved into the accommodation.

I would stay behind with the drivers and gunners to ensure this was done correctly which also included any minor repairs or replacement of parts like track pads, road wheels and even the oil filters.

As all the un-trained Warrior personnel quickly made their way into the accommodation like they would always do, (and this is throughout every Armoured Regiment) most lacking the intellectual capacity to understand what working as a team meant. That would mean we had to crack on with the work ourselves, which would take longer with less hands, but as soon as the guys were finished and the Warriors were closed down and secured the lads themselves could then go and do the same as the others and head for the safety of the accommodation. As my crew and I started walking from my Warrior to the accommodation - which wasn't far away, roughly twenty meters or so - a loud, piercing alarm sounded. It was a sound I hadn't heard before, during my training I had been warned that I would know what it was if it ever sounded, it was also drummed into each man and women to never ignore it.

Panic set in, the mortar detection alarm system had sounded. We hit the floor fast and hard. I was literally scared for my life, this was my first bit of hostility from the enemy and real action from within the country. All around us, in every direction, you could hear the sound of explosions where the mortars bombs had been landing.

The mortar detection system was known as the C-RAM and is a land version of the Phalanx CIWS radar-controlled rapid-fire gun used by the Navy for the protection of its vessels from incoming missiles. Anything fired in its direction would be picked up and located almost instantly. The system would lock-on to any incoming missile or mortar hurtling towards it and send a volley of explosive rounds towards it. Hopefully destroying the missile well before it even gets a chance to land.

It wouldn't always be successful though!

As I lay face first in the dirty Iraqi sand that covered the tank park, I heard shouting directed my way. The voices were ordering me to get up and run towards them where they stood, just inside the hardened cover. I hesitated because I wasn't taught to just get up and run during an attack, but to hit the floor and lay down flat until it finishes, and the alarm stops ringing out. We had to lie on our stomachs, with our faces in the ground and pray we wouldn't get hit - although some did. Nevertheless, I did get up and I ran the short distance into cover, probably faster than Usain Bolt could run the hundred meters. As I was running, I could only think about not seeing my girls ever again.

As I breathed a sigh of relief and buzzing from my first mortar attack, I had a tap on the back,

"Welcome to the Palace,"

said one of the officers who had been shouting at me to run towards the hardened cover.

I wasn't feeling welcome that's for sure. I had just swallowed half the sand and probably caught some kind of MRSA infection by snorting it through my nose while trying to breath face down in it. I was still alive that was the main thing. Now the attack was over I could head to my own accommodation and find the bed space that would become my home for the next few months and my only get away and privacy.

My room was upstairs in the main building, next to the Company Commanders and Sergeant Majors' room. It was no hotel either, even though we were inside the Basra Palace grounds. We had just a small, cramped room with eight beds crammed inside it, six as bunk beds and two on their own. I was lucky, my bed was in the corner of the room hidden behind two tall lockers. I had to share a bunk bed though and so I took the bottom bed and laid my sleeping bag down onto the mattress to claim it as mine and then I hung a bed sheet around the frame of the bed, giving me some extra privacy. I looked around the room after claiming my bed and noticed that the windows had been replaced with breeze blocks! This wasn't a good sign, but it was a safer one, at least it should stop the missiles coming through it!

I decided to familiarise myself with my new home as I had a spare few minutes. The toilets were outside of the accommodation and portable ones too! The showers were also outside in a cabin made from thin steel.

Basra Palace was quickly becoming known for how dangerous it had become over the past few weeks or so, the threat had increased just in time for our arrival and the biggest threat to us within the grounds of Basra Palace was the mortar threat - thanks to the enemy's precision - yet the toilets and the showers were still located outside? Every time we needed to go, we had to leave the accommodation and head outside. We were required to wear our helmets and body armour, which was annoying at first. Trying to work out how to fit inside a portable toilet with your gear on and secondly, how do you take a shower with all your gear on? I had to ask that question during the welcome brief. No matter how stupid I sounded, I was asking. The fact is we were now in an extremely dangerous and hostile environment that came with a massively accurate mortar threat. When I asked the question, there was the obvious eyebrow movement from one or two higher ranks, but the rest agreed - or thought it was funny. I wasn't trying to be funny, just trying to stay alive, I want to see my girls again.

From now on, anyone who had previously suffered with any form of constipation would become cured of their condition. If the heat inside the thin, plastic portable toilet didn't make you shit any quicker, the threat of the mortar alarm sounding usually did the trick! And may I say, many a time I was caught mid flow when the alarm sounded and it was horrendous! Unfortunately, a guy attached to the Regiment we shared Basra Palace with, was tragically killed by a direct hit from a mortar on the portable toilet he was using during an attack.

I had trouble finding the canteen in my accommodation and wondered how we were going to eat. I asked about to see if anybody knew where we had to go and I was pointed in the direction of the palace itself, around two hundred meters away!

"What the fuck...," was my first reaction.

Surely, we weren't expected to walk over there three times a day, dodging missiles? But we were, and we did. We had a walkway built using hesco bastion sand filled containers that could easily stop a bullet and hopefully a missile. Not all the walkway was protected though, we still had a few short distances to sprint between. The things we had to endure just for a fly infested spam sandwich made by the Army's finest chefs.

In the centre of the Palace grounds was a large lake which was often hit by the incoming mortars. Everything else was based around the outside of the lake. The main headquarters was on one side of the lake. This is where we could go to sort out any administration issues, or cash a cheque. Also based inside the Main Headquarters - or HQ as we knew it - was the medical wing, intelligence room and the Commanding Officer and his merry men.

Then we had the REME, who were attached to us. We relied on the mechanics to keep our Warriors on the road and they were our spine - if one can call it that. These guys were the ones who would keep our armoured vehicles ticking over if there were any serious issues. Just over from the REME's location was our hardened accommodation, with the tank park just in front. Further on from the tank park, the Special Forces were located and some of our guys, from Javelin platoon, were based there with them.

Next to that was another hardened accommodation block belonging to one of the other Regiments Company. Following along to the end of my accommodation block, was the start of the rat-run that took us straight to the cookhouse. Just past the cookhouse - and over a small bridge - was another block belonging to the remainder of the Regiment sharing Basra Palace with us. There was also a live firing range located at the Palace.

The camp was surrounded by blast walls, designed to stop a bomb blast and they were located all along one side of the camp-grounds. Located on the other side was a river. We shared the camp with a small team of American Special Forces and some Nepalese soldiers. The Nepalese soldiers were only stationed at Basra Palace to man the gates and guard the Base which was a great relief for us because nobody enjoyed guard, let alone doing it at a targeted location like Basra Palace.

CHAPTER TEN
THE PATROL

The first few days in Basra with 'B' Company would revolve around orientation of the City with the few remaining members of the unit we had just replaced. We would travel outside of Basra Palace as a platoon, in the four Warriors we each held as a show of strength travelling through the known areas that terrorists often used.

I would try and take in as much detail as I could, whether it was a tall, odd-looking building or a dodgy looking backstreet. Anything that I could recognise and aid me if things went Pete Tong whilst on patrols. We patrolled both day and night to get a feel of the areas - including when the lights go out, the streets fall silent and the enemy became active.

A few weeks into routine and we were being heavily mortared at random times of the day. The feeling of the mortars smashing down into the tank park, or the accommodation blocks, was unreal and I for one wasn't prepared for it. One particular day, I was doing some paperwork for my vehicles when my Platoon Commander warned me that I and another Commander in my platoon, "Bati", would be going out on patrol with a platoon from the other Regiment. The other Regiment used the Bulldog vehicle and had asked for a couple of Warriors to patrol with them for some added protection. It would only be a routine patrol around the city during the evening but being picked by a boss who had other Commanders in the platoon pissed me off because I had things to do. They could have gone instead of me, as I was busy with my paperwork for the same Warriors that he expected to be looked after by me.

My boss and I were still not seeing eye to eye. He was the type of boss who liked you more if you sucked up to him - like many did within the platoon. I hadn't once during my career ever sucked up to a higher rank. Every man was equal to me, we needed to be equal. You wouldn't want to be a prick in charge of the lads and then expect them to save your life if ever you found yourself in need.

Off I went, on patrol with my Warrior and Bati with his. We went out early evening and spent several hours on patrol in the heat of the night; sweating profusely in the metal cookers we called a Warrior. We took cold-ish water on patrol with us but guaranteed within a few hours that water would be extremely warm and uncomfortable to drink. Nethertheless we patrolled all night, but it turned out to be a quiet patrol and nothing happened - like we anticipated. As we arrived back to Basra Palace Bati and I went for our usual after patrol debrief with the Commanders and we left our lads with the Warriors to run down the engines and close them up.

The debrief was done. A quick, twenty-minute chat about what happened on the patrol and what we saw etc, we headed back over to our accommodation, ready to dive into our beds as it had been a very long and exhausting night. I walked into the accommodation to find my platoon missing - except for the lads who just had been out with Bati and I, they hadn't long finished closing down the Warriors. I asked them if they knew where everyone was, but like me they were in the dark. I walked over to Ops room to see who was about and find out what was happening. I bumped into my boss on route and he told me that the platoon had taken over "QRF" (Quick Reaction Force) late last night. I was desperately tired and in need of a cold shower and a bottle of water. My mouth was dry, like Gandhi's flip flops, from the long patrol.

I headed back to the accommodation block, gathered my lads together and we headed the short distance over to the Palace where the QRF base was located. At the same time, the remainder of 'B' Company had left Basra Palace on a re-supply mission to the PJCC. The PJCC was a small command centre located inside the grounds of an Iraqi Police Station. The PJCC had its own camp gates and fence to provide protection from the Iraqis. You couldn't be too careful, you never know if an Iraqi policeman or woman would go rogue and try to kill a British soldier. There are thousands of reasons why, but the most popular and common reason was Al Qaeda had kidnapped a family member and threatened to kill that family member unless they turned their gun on the British or American soldier. Sick as it sounded this was our enemy. They had no limits against us - or their own people.

As we settled into the accommodation in the QRF room, a message had been sent over ordering my platoon to prepare ourselves. Something had just happened to the remainder of my Company who were out on the re-supply mission and quite possibly they had come under attack. Every man in the platoon quickly got their kit together and legged it outside to their Warriors. I got into my Warrior and prepared my map whilst my driver got the Warrior's engine up to temperature. As I stood in my turret, preparing, I could hear my name being shouted

"Locky, take callsign One-Three with you and head out and help the lads. Follow the bulldogs by the back gate, good luck."

What the fuck, I quickly thought? Just me, Bati and the same lads chosen again? We had just spent all night out on patrol and yet once again he was dicking us over his favorites for this mission? Why the fuck aren't you going? There are four Warriors in my platoon, two fresh Commanders and you pick the tired guys?

I told Bati - who was standing in the turret of his Warrior - what our orders were and then he followed me to the back gates. As we approached there was no sign of any Bulldogs, just an officer screaming at me to crack on and the Bulldogs would meet us out there soon. I screamed down at the Officers - over the loud engine noise of both Warriors - and explained my boss didn't give us any brief or coordinates of any locations. The officer told me to head to the thick black smoke filling the sky to the North. We left the camp. As we headed on our way, one of the lads in the rear of my Warrior tugged my leg to get my attention, I bent down to see what was wrong and he told me my ECM had stopped working. The ECM is what protects the Warrior from any blasts triggered from certain IED's. The ECM would help cut any signals out while we passed by. I got on the radio to Bati and told him my problem and asked if his was working. He said it was, so I decided to let him lead. I could follow closely behind and stick within his ECM bubble. We headed for the smoke and arrived only to find a large heavy goods vehicle on its side and engulfed in flames. It was an oil transporter, deliberately attacked and set on fire with the driver burning inside his cab. I looked around and saw no sign of British Forces and got straight on the radio back to base.

"Hello Zero, this is One-Two, confirm the location I am supposed to be heading to, over."

I got no reply, so I tried again. This time I tried with a radio check.

"Hello Zero, this is One-Two - radio check, over."

Again, no reply. I spoke with Bati who was standing in the turret of callsign One-Three and we quickly realised that as our platoon had moved over to QRF whilst we were out on patrol, they had a radio frequency change! Nobody bothered to tell us when we arrived back with the platoon; we were now out in the middle of Basra on our own.

The tanker now started to explode and we quickly realised we may have headed straight into a trap. Just behind the tanker, I spotted a man in a balaclava recording both Warriors with a hand-held camera. I got on the radio to callsign One-Three and told him to turn the fuck around and head back as quick as possible.

We returned to base - still confused by the wrong orders given by the officer on the gate during the chaos. As we headed inside the gates, waiting for us were the two Bulldogs. We turned the Warriors around and I got the co-ordinates of the location we were supposed to be heading for originally from the Bulldog Commanders. My One-Three Commander, Bati, would lead us out to the location, I was more than confident with his ability to lead, he was a switched-on soldier and a guy with a heart of gold who knew the City well from the previous two Tours he had served there. He headed out and I followed closely behind his Warrior due to the ECM problems I was encountering as the lads in the back were, as yet, unable to fix it. The two Bulldogs followed at the rear. We headed out and all we knew was 'B' Company had come up against an attack. They had been ambushed on a bridge and were stuck on the other side of the river. As we got closer to the area, we quickly noticed a large vehicle - one of our Military HGV's – A low-loader as we knew the vehicle in the Military, it sat smoking on the bridge. It had been hit by an IED or RPG whilst crossing the bridge and was now blocking it. The enemy was attacking from the side of the bridge I arrived on and I just drove straight into the thick of the action.

My Company had been unable to move the vehicle off the bridge due to the nature of the attack and the powerful weapons being used against them by the enemy. With the arrival of Bati and I, we were able to take the brunt of the attack long enough to allow my Company to get the vehicle moved off the bridge.

Within minutes of being in location, my Warrior was being smashed hard from all types of ammunition. It had been hit by sniper fire and assault rifle fire; a grenade thrown at my Warrior bounced off and exploded to the side; a Rocket Propelled Grenade just missed the side of my Warrior also. My other callsign One-Three was also having the same problems. My gunner was unable to fire back at one building because the enemy were attacking us with what looked like innocent terrified people next to them. Whilst we were concentrating on the building, waiting for the enemy to show themselves on their own, my driver was engaging the enemy himself from his driver's hatch - without me even knowing.

While the fighting was on-going, a true hero was emerging. One of my friends from Javelin Platoon - who was a big lad - had managed to make his way, under fire, to the low-loader and hitch a tow rope to it, which he then placed onto the front of his Warrior and the vehicle was shifted. The lad was big too and what he did, at his size, showed everyone not to judge a book by its cover.

Back in my Warrior - still being pinged with pot shots and grenades - I heard a Warrior engine pull off to my rear. I looked out to see my One-Three callsign racing off down the street. I had no ECM and decided to race after him to save my vehicle from possibly getting blown up. With the low-loader now moved and my Company in a position to fight the fuckers back harder and faster, I left. If I had the right comms I could have communicated with the Company. I was a little confused as to why my One-Three callsign had not let me know he was heading off, or why he wasn't replying to my calls on the radio, but I raced after him anyway.

His vehicle was flooring it back the way we had come and I immediately knew we were heading back to base. Around two hundred meters from where the vehicle was damaged on the bridge, I saw out of the corner of my eye what looked like a British soldier hiding in a bush. I yelled at my driver to halt the Warrior,

"Stop. Stop the fucking Warrior."

The driver slammed on the brakes - and as the Warrior was designed to - it went up onto its front tracks and slammed heavily back down to earth. The lads in the back were screaming,

"What the fuck is going on?"

I shouted down for someone to open the back door, but they were unwilling after the smashing we just took from the enemy. Eventually someone opened the door when they realised what I was shouting down to them. My instincts were right, running as fast as he possibly could, out from the bush came a soldier. He must have been the driver of the vehicle on the bridge and had legged it when he was hit in the ambush.

None of us could believe what had just happened. The lad was safe and we continued on to catch up with Bati. At this point his Warrior was well and truly ahead of us, leaving us well outside of his ECM bubble, which was nobody's fault. I made the call to continue back to camp which wasn't too far away.

We made it back to Basra Palace, alive and in one piece. As we drove through the gates I was pulled over by a Bulldog waiting at the back gates. The lad in the back of my Warrior who we had rescued, jumped out and disappeared, never to be seen again. My One-Three callsign was nowhere to be seen either, so I decided to drive towards HQ to see if he was over there. To my relief, he was. I still wasn't sure why he had left the area the way he did, but I was relieved that he had got back in one piece.

I climbed down off the Warrior and walked inside HQ looking everywhere for him. He was still nowhere to be seen. I looked in all the offices and again nowhere to be seen. There was one room I hadn't looked in and it was the medical centre. I didn't expect him to be in there, that's why I hadn't bothered to look up until now. I went over to the medical centre and opened the door, to my disbelief Bati was sitting down being treated by the medics with a wound on his forehead. He had been shot by a sniper but luckily the bullet skimmed across his forehead, leaving a small wound.

I walked out of HQ to see my Platoon Sergeant standing next to my Warrior with his kit on - looking extremely pissed off with me. Whenever my platoon went out on a Warrior patrol, the Platoon Sergeant usually deployed with us in the back of the Warrior and during our Tour he would use callsign One-Three. He didn't come out the night before because he wasn't required. During the chaos when we were crashed out and with the boss ordering me to head to the back gates with Bati and his Warrior, the Platoon Sergeant was left behind!

My Platoon Sergeant came running over screaming at me; like it was my fault he was left behind. He had to scream and shout, because he was left behind looking like a daft cunt. Even although it was a mistake, thanks to the confusion, I just stood there and took it because there was nothing I could do or say to calm him down. There were a few high-ranking officers outside the Headquarters, so tensions were high. After my Platoon Sergeant calmed down and I explained about Bati being patched up by the medics, he wanted to get out and join the action. He took over as One-Three's Commander and commanded the Warrior back to the area currently under attack. I wasn't happy about going back either and I tried to explain about the ECM radio problems, but he just said,

"Mount up. We're going - and stay in my bubble."

We headed back out to join the fight. Our radios were still on the wrong frequency and still we had no communication with the lads currently on the ground - or back at base. As we approached the area again - thick, black smoke littered the sky above. As I looked around from the top of my turret, I suddenly realised we were, once again, on our own. My Company had returned to camp using the back gates and without us knowing, we left camp through the front gates. With no communications, we were in the unknown again. Suddenly, from nowhere, thousands of angry Iraqis charged at our Warriors. We had seconds to turn them around and get out of the area. We floored it just in time and with me leading totally forgetting about the ECM bubble, as the crowds were closing and throwing rocks, bottles and anything else that came to hand.

As we returned to Basra Palace using the back gates, sitting outside with its barrel facing camp, was one of Six Platoons' Warriors - it was just sitting there. God could only know why it was there, but I didn't believe in him, so I wouldn't look up to ask for answers. The Warrior was not there to guard anything because if it had been then the barrel would have been facing the enemy, not the camp. I decided to climb down from my Warrior to have a face to face with the Commander of the static Warrior. As I run over to the front of the Warrior to climb up, perched in the driver's seat was Drugs - a dismount Commander at the time - not a Warrior driver. He was sitting in the driver's seat looking like he was pumped full of adrenaline. I couldn't believe my own eyes.

"What the hell is going on?" I said to him.

He just sat there in the driver's compartment looking as confused as I did. I climbed up on top of the Warrior and popped my head into the Commander's side of the turret. I wasn't prepared for what I was about to see. The Commander and the gunner were both okay, but also confused to the point that they did not know what was happening, like the driver. I jumped down, went around the back of the Warrior and opened the door. There were two, half-naked lads laying in the back. It dawned on me that everyone had been struck down by the blistering heat. I myself, at this point, was running on fumes.

My Platoon Sergeant climbed down from his Warrior to see what the problem was. He, like me, was shell shocked. We had to come up with a plan to get this Warrior and its men to the medical centre - and quick. I had no qualified drivers in any of the two Warriors, but Drugs was a Lance Corporal at the time and could be trusted - because this was a matter of life and death, I took the decision to let him drive the final distance. I told him to drive carefully, I showed him how to control the vehicle and stop safely because I was worried he may forget due to his confused state of mind. I decided I would have to run the distance of about eight hundred meters with Drugs following behind. I didn't want him driving fast because he wasn't himself and I wasn't exactly a fast runner.

My gunner would command my Warrior back and the Platoon Sergeant would do the same with his Warrior. We set off, I had to run the distance with my whole kit on; helmet, body armour. Due to the humidity, I was lagging almost immediately, the heat was blistering. I ran like I have never run before. Every now and then, I would glance behind to make sure the Warrior was following behind. We were about four hundred meters - and just passing the American Forces section of the base - when the Warrior drove straight over a US vehicle. I can remember a load of American Special Forces, on the roof of their accommodation all pointing their weapons at me like I was a terrorist. Suddenly, a golf buggy turned up with two Americans on it screaming,

"Hey man!!! What the fuck are you are doing? You crazy son of a bitch."

I explained what had happened and they told me to climb onto the back of the golf Buggy. They turned the buggy around and headed towards the Medical Centre. As we approached, there were a lot of people outside; some trying to order us to move the Warriors away from the entrance as they were awaiting the arrival casualties. I jumped of the golf buggy, sprinted over to the stricken Warrior, climbed up and threw myself into the driver's hatch to ensure the Warrior was correctly parked up. Drugs done extremely well that day. At this point one of the boys from my Warrior climbed straight up onto the Warrior and started to extract the Commander and gunner. I climbed back down and made my way to the back; the back door was closed. I was being yelled at from several people telling me to move the fucking Warrior. As I opened the back door I hurtled the smallest lad onto my shoulders and with every breath I had, I ran him into the Medical Centre and handed him over. I headed back outside to help with the other casualties, but my boys were already on the case with Stretch, one of the more senior lads in my Warrior, carrying the next lad in. I sat down against the wall. Absolutely worn out and I suddenly became an emotional wreck. I started to cry for no reason, shaking like a double ended dildo. My mate from Javelin Platoon - who had risked his life to help move the vehicle off the bridge - had spotted me becoming emotional and walked over to check on me. I passed out from the emotion of the day and woke up later on lying on a medical bed.

CHAPTER ELEVEN
HEADLIGHTS

I opened my eyes and looked around, all I could see was medical equipment. I was laying on my stomach when I woke up. I tried to move but felt a weird sensation in my bottom. I reached down and felt a long, skinny object hanging out of my rectum. I had a thermometer shoved up my bum. The doctor whispered in my ear,

"You collapsed with heat exhaustion, I am a little concerned, so you need to rest."

I was stunned. I couldn't believe what had happened to me. I had no memory of collapsing. I pulled the thermometer out of my bottom and threw it onto the floor and pulled my trousers up. I needed to urinate really bad. The doctor gave me a beaker to urinate in as he required a sample to test. The results were exactly as he thought. I had heat exhaustion and told me that I had to be transferred back to the C.O.B where the main field hospital was located. They were equipped with state-of-the-art equipment to look after me.

I had been on my feet for over thirty hours in the run up to my collapse, with hardly any rest. I had barely drank any water during those hours either, thanks to being crashed out by the ambush. What water I did manage to force down me was warm and unpleasant to drink. I asked the doctor if anyone else was in his care and he said yes, two others. I calmed down slightly and felt relieved that I wasn't flying back to the C.O.B alone.

As the sun went down, it was safe to fly the helicopter into Basra Palace to collect me and the two others. The helicopters flew mainly at night as they were an easier target for ground to air missiles and RPG's during daylight. Most of the troop-carrying helicopters held little resistance towards incoming fire, other than a few flares that could be fired if the on-board missile detection system ever picked up any heat signatures moving rapidly towards them. The flares would hopefully interrupt the missiles and its solidarity aim was to confuse the missile into seeking out the newer heat signature from the flare.

During my transfer back to the C.O.B, our on-board missile detection system had been triggered. I remember seeing streaks of light flashing away from the back of the helicopter. The ramp on the back of the helicopter was down with an RAF gunner kneeling down on it and he was held securely in place with a cable that connected to his belt. He had a general-purpose machine gun (GPMG) fitted to the back and he was behind it. I was in awe of the sight of the flares fired, the sky was alight, it looked amazing and I had, for that moment, totally forgotten why the flares had been fired. Nothing came of it though and we landed safely and I was taken, with the other two lads, straight to the hospital ward where I had a drip inserted into each arm.

After speaking to the doctors, I was told I would be on the ward for around a week, dependent on my recovery rate, as I was very ill. My blood and sugar levels were extremely low, and I required time to recover. I decided not to tell my partner what had happened to me because I didn't want to worry her back home, alone with my two-year-old daughter. I did speak to her every day from my hospital bed and got to listen to my baby girl talking. I can't explain how happy I was to hear their voices again and to be in hospital - regardless of how ill I was - because it was the safest I had felt since deploying to Iraq.

While I was in hospital, the remainder of my Regiment had finally deployed to Iraq to start their Tour. A handful of officers came to the hospital to visit me as they had heard how challenging life was for 'B' Company thanks to the enemy and the mortars that they continuously fired into Basra Palace. They wanted to hear the truth of it for themselves, fresh from somebody who had just come back. I told them the truth, I told them how hard it was.

The mortar rounds and Chinese rockets were landing all around us, up to eighty bombs on some days. The number of IED's we had found already and the RPG's, sniper fire even the grenades thrown. I had only been in Iraq a month and for that month it felt like I was starring in a war film.

As the week passed by, I was slowly starting to feel better. I still had a drip in each arm, so moving about was painful. I was laying on my bed trying to sleep when the mortar alarm started howling throughout the ward,

"Oh for fuck sakes!!! Not here as well?" I thought.

Next thing I heard was the doctors and nurses screaming at all the patients - including myself - to get down on the floor. A drip in each arm and they still want me diving to the floor? But I did, I managed it although painfully, but I got down and took cover next to the bed. The siren didn't last long and before I knew it everything was back to normal.

It was the 23rd of May and Liverpool were playing in the Champions League Final. We had a TV on the ward! I was in dreamland. I would never have got to watch the game back in Basra Palace. We lost 2-1 though it wasn't a bad game and I got to watch it, so I was happy.

The end of the week came and the doctor gave me the dreaded news I did not want to hear.

"Corporal, you are being discharged in the morning."

I started to scream abuse at the doctor in my head.

"FUCK OFF YOU BASTARD. SEND ME HOME, I JUST WANT TO GO HOME!!"

I wish I had the balls to say it out loud and hopefully I would have got my wish. As for the other two lads who came in with me, one was being discharged back to Basra Palace with me to continue the Tour and the other was being returned to the Regiment's Rear Party back in the UK, because it was the second time in his career he had suffered with heat stroke. Lucky him.

So, I left the hospital and eventually flew back out to Basra Palace re-join my Company. After I had joined back up with my Company, I felt like a complete twat after being diagnosed with heat stroke. As a Corporal it was frowned upon to be bedded down on the sick, but I knew what I went through and why I ended up in hospital, fuck their beliefs. Some of the lads in my accommodation were telling me stories about what I had missed while I was gone, and I was glad I had a week away after listening to some of it.

I was given another week's worth of acclimatization training before I could deploy back out of the Palace gates onto patrol. My body needed re-adapt to the heat, because I had just spent an entire week in an air-conditioned hospital ward and away from the blistering heat. I wasn't allowed to do anything strenuous for that week and spent the time catching up with my paperwork and overseeing the maintenance of my Warriors.

The City of Basra was becoming more and more dangerous as the days of our Tour passed us by. The feel inside the City had turned from wanting us there to, wanting us dead. Al Qaeda were pressing the locals harder to turn on us, and some risked their lives to do so.

Every week we had a re-supply mission from the C.O.B, bringing vital supplies that couldn't be flown to the Palace. Truckloads of ammunition, fuel, food, kit. You name it, it was delivered. One re-supply, though, would completely change the basics.

The Commanders within 'B' Company attended the brief on the mission ahead. The mission was to secure the route, as normal, also secure it for our Regiment from the Main Base in Southern Iraq, the C.O.B, to bring in the large convoy of vehicles and trucks. We would be pressed hard by the Company Commander on our drills to ensure we didn't cut any corners with them. We needed to know every fine detail right down to the bone.

This mission was like any normal mission we had undertaken so far out in Iraq, with the emphasis on getting to our position on the ground and holding the area safely, so the convoy could pass through, safely and unhindered.

After the brief ended, we would prepare for the mission. Whether it would be checking kit, preparing the Warriors, cleaning weapons, lots of time and dedication would be spent ensuring every fine detail was prepared for the mission ahead.

With everything sorted and prepared, my Platoon Commander and Platoon Sergeant would now give the boys in the platoon a brief on the mission ahead. The brief would be aimed at my platoon's role during the mission, so everyone knew exactly what they're expected to do when we get out onto the ground.

Brief over and all the admin finished, it was time to chill out and drink plenty of water, ready for the evening's mission. What I can say about the lads in my platoon is they worked hard when they needed to, even if it meant they had little time to chill out at the end. My Warriors would always be in good condition thanks to their dedication on the tank park and most days it made my job easier to know they weren't always forced by me to get out and work on them, because they would think for themselves occasionally and just head out and get the jobs done.

Come the evening, everyone mounted up into the Warriors with the correct kit in hand for the mission ahead. It was time to leave Basra Palace for what we thought would be a normal mission. My platoon would be second in the order of march behind Six Platoon leading the patrol.

As we headed out, everything seemed normal, the streets were empty due to the time of night - most people stayed indoors at night anyway. We made good progress on the route. As we approached the position that I had been given to hold during the Company Commanders brief earlier that evening, Six Platoon in their Warriors slowed to a halt about one hundred meters or so away and the team in the back of the lead Warrior climbed out. When a Commander deploys his section out of the back of his Warrior, it's usually because the area like this one looked likely to be a threat and they deploy the lads out to check the area. The Commander in the back will have a head-set on and will be in communication with the Commander of the Warrior as well, so everyone sitting in the rear of the Warrior would have some idea of what they're expected to get out and do on the ground. The four lads who climbed out were just a short distance away from my Warrior when they set off, clearing the road to the front of the lead Warrior.

Seconds later, a bright flash briefly lit up the sky and then a BOOM!!!. An IED (Improvised Explosive Device) had just exploded in the area the lads had been clearing on foot. The radio had gone quiet, all you could hear in the distance was a daisy chain of explosions being set off further and further down the road. BOOM!! BOOM!! BOOM!! - dust and carnage being blown everywhere. I was terrified, trying frantically to keep myself calm, I had men to keep safe.

I stood in the turret waiting for news to come over the radio to give me an idea of what had just happened - but, again, silence. Suddenly, from the blast area, my Platoon Sergeant came running towards my Warrior. The dust had now covered the entire street. I took my head set off and leaned down to talk to him.

"Locky, between me and you, three dead and possibly a fourth".

I was mortified. Six Platoon were my original platoon, those boys were my friends, my brothers, my family, my life. At this point nobody quite knew who had died and we had to keep ourselves together and focused for the remainder of the mission.

The mission had now changed from a re-supply mission to a recovery mission. When the area was deemed safe, we had to carefully move our Warriors into the positions we were given on the brief to help keep the obvious safe while recovery was ongoing. As I moved slowly into position, my driver had somehow managed to get the Warrior stuck over a path running down the centre of the road and we almost had to run a lamppost over at the end of the path to become free of it. The path had stopped us from turning, but luckily - after a few attempts - my driver managed to free the Warrior from the path.

My driver, my gunner and myself had seen the aftermath of the IED through our night vision sights. I had to tell them to turn their sights off and not to look in the direction of the blast. That was the reason the Warrior became stuck as it was dark and my driver couldn't see where he was driving, we didn't want to see anyway, it was horrific. I still lay awake at night thinking about what I saw that night.

When we moved ourselves into position, a car, a few hundred meters in front, started to flash its main beam at us. Whoever was in the driver's seat started to drive forward at pace towards my Warrior - and in line for a head on collision - before breaking hard and reversing back to do it all over again. We could smell the car's burning brakes, it had started to overpower the smell of the IED.

I was confident the guy in the car was a suicide bomber lacking the balls to carry it out. I got on the radio and told my boss what was going on in front of me. His reply was,

"Stop flapping and making shit up!"

Lucky for him he was on the other side of the street or I'd have chinned him.

A few minutes later this car was still edging closer and closer towards my Warrior and I decided I had to fire a few warning shots in his direction, so he knew that I am watching him and was ready to stop him. As my gunner pressed his foot down on the firing pedal on the floor of the turret, the chain gun jammed. For fuck sakes, not now I was screaming in my turret. Every second delayed was another second closer to death.

With my chain gun out of action and my gunner working hard to fix the issue, I shouted down to the section Commander who was sitting in the back of my Warrior with the rest of the team. I was about to ask him to fire a warning shot from his rifle out of the back of the Warrior, but he was switched on enough to know something was wrong and had been listening in to my conversation with my gunner through his headset. He himself had been looking out of the hatch on top of the Warrior to the rear and watched what was happening, he fired a few warning shots to the side of the vehicle, but the car continued to drive at us and then reverse back again.

A few minutes later, this driver finally plucked up the courage to blow himself into the arms of his seventy-two virgins. He put his foot down and hammered the car towards the Warrior at speed. I tried to pull my rifle out from the rifle holder down below me so that I could shoot the driver, but the rifle holder jammed. As I watched the car bear down on us, I braced for impact. As I braced I heard,

POP! POP! POP! POP! POP!

The Commander in the back had engaged the engine area of the car just before it was about to hit the Warrior head on. One of the shots may have hit the driver as he had slumped over to the side, turning his wheel as he did. The car turned to its right, just missing the back end of the Warrior by a fraction. The car continued off into the darkness, never to be seen again.

Soon afterwards my boss was, again, on the radio raging at me for engaging this car. Then a voice appeared over the radio.

"One Zero this is One-Three. I just traversed my turret in the direction of callsign Three-One to see what was going on and it was clear to me what was about to happen, out."

That calmed the situation - for now.

As the recovery ended and the re-supply was cancelled by the tragic events of the night, a camera was found hidden in the area. It was pointed at the blast area and was on record as the IED set off, killing my friends. We were grateful the camera had been found, because the footage would have - no doubt - been uploaded onto social media.

At the Palace we closed the Warriors down, grabbed all our belongings and personal weapons and made our way back into the safety of the hard accommodation for a brief from our

Company Commander. The brief was horrible. He explained who had, sadly, passed away. Everyone was crying, there wasn't a dry eye to be seen. Hearts had been broken; lives had been wasted and families had just been torn apart and destroyed thanks to a war that should never had been.

CHAPTER TWELVE
THE NEXT FEW DAYS

I made my way back to the accommodation, absolutely gutted from the horror I had witnessed, I joined some of the lads for a cigarette in the small smoking area. The rumours started circulating about the Company Sergeant Major during the mission. We found out that after the IED exploded, the Company Commander had told him to deploy the lads onto the ground to help him recover the bodies. The Sergeant Major had been one of the first men on the ground after the explosion and saw the carnage for himself. He had made the decision not to allow any of his troops to witness what he had just witnessed. The Commanders and the gunners in the turrets of their Warriors would see the carnage for themselves like I had, because we had no choice. Rather than order his men out onto the ground - and have more hands to help him recover the fallen more quickly - he preferred to do it himself, with just my Platoon Sergeant to help.

The scene was utter chaos and carnage; I can't describe the horrors of the sight and I won't write about it either. For me, what the Sergeant Major did with my Platoon Sergeant that night was nothing short of heroic. Both men were great leaders by name and a great leaders by example.

Six Platoon had been given a few crates of beer to help them digest what had just happened on the ground with the lads they had sleeping amongst them. The next day our Company Commander decided to give Six Platoon the full day off to mourn and although we all felt the loss of the lads, Six Platoon felt the impact even harder. The lads had to go back to the same living quarters that they shared with the lads who had just passed away.

The night wasn't completely lost though, news was starting to filter in that the fourth lad was still alive; critical, but alive and fighting. This news alone was enough to keep the spirits of the lads high, they had a tiny piece of hope to hold onto. I can only imagine that if all four lads had passed away that night, then the lads would have required more than just a few beers to help them recover from the tragedy that struck them.

The following day saw an investigation opened into my actions that night. I can only guess that I was reported - by a certain person - for engaging the car that had been acting suspiciously after the devastating IED blast that claimed the lives of three of my mates. Luckily for me, not only had the Commander from callsign One-Three looked over to see what was happening when I reported it over the radio to my boss but my Platoon Sergeant did as well whilst he was on the ground working tirelessly with the Sergeant Major recovering the bodies of my lost friends, he had heard the message I sent over the radio and come across for a look. That was the difference between officers and soldiers, trust.

Each person who provided a statement wrote practically the same thing. Everything I had seen, they had seen it too. The actions I took were correct. We have a "Rules of Engagement" card that we must abide by whilst serving in Iraq, we knew the card as Card-Alpha. On the card it stated the rules and permissions of when we can open fire or return fire. We were not like the American Army who had a less restricted version of the rules of engagement - our rules were totally different, unfortunately for us. We knew that for every round we fired from our weapons, they would require accounting for and paperwork filed. For us though, nine times out of ten, we would be returning fire during a gun-fight with the terrorists. Which is fine as long as it was safe to do so and no innocent civilians could be harmed.

I was cleared of any wrongdoing quickly but the experience left me feeling let down because the people in charge of me had made me feel like they were against me. I had to try and continue on as normal and show them that I wasn't going to be broken by them.

I was in a foreign country, being attacked almost every hour of the day, where fighting back became a fucking issue. It was down to the red tape bullshit created because the witch hunting of soldiers in Northern Ireland was beginning to pick up pace and the Military did not want to give these idiots leading the hunt an excuse to do the same for the Iraq war even though some had tried. It now meant that our lives were even more at risk from the enemy, because it was difficult for some - including myself at times - to recognise the right time and moment to fight back. I can only blame the British Government for standing back and allowing these money leeching lawyers to try and bring cases against British Soldiers for doing their jobs and risking their lives in battle against the terrorists.

I take my hat off to the American President - I do not agree with many of his political views - but when he gave a speech warning the whole world that

"If anyone tries to sue his soldiers they would reap the full force..."

I was literally blown away by the words. I wonder if the British Government would ever grow a pair and do the same? I doubt it, because this Country has lost its identity and the millions of men, women and animals who died in both the World War's, died in vein.

As the days passed and the lads still feeling like shit, we were continuing on with our work as per normal. I guess - in the short term - working through the bad stuff helped us out at the time. Nowadays though, thousands of British troops are sadly suffering with Post Traumatic Stress Disorder. It's down to the Military not having a plan in place, or the resources on the ground, to help the soldiers deal with the bad stuff when it happens. For me, working on through the shit as though nothing had happened sufficed at first, but when the work is finished - usually some years later when one has left that life behind to start a new one - the memories pushed to the side, reappear and twice as intense. Don't get me wrong, every Tour we deployed on, we would have a Padre or a Priest somewhere close that we could talk to if we struggled - but that wasn't a cure. It was merely a side track to be honest.

It was early evening and 'B' Company were called over to the main Headquarters for the repatriation service of our lost brothers. The entire battle-group squeezed into a small area for the service, hymn sheet in hand and the Padre leading the service. I remember how hard it was to try and control my emotions after the devastating events a few nights before. Tears pouring down my face, hands shaking, whilst desperately trying to hold the hymn sheet up and all the while trying to fight off the bad memories with the good ones.

The coffins passed us, one by one, heading to the Helicopter Landing point ready for their journey to the C.O.B base and then home. Everything fell silent. Respect and fortitude being shown in the most respectful way to honour our heroes who had died needlessly for a selfish Government which forced this war upon us.

The following morning, my platoon left for the week-long rotation at the PJCC. The PJCC know as the Provincial Joint Coordination Centre. Its main building sat opposite a much taller building than ours - we would come to know only too well as the wheat factory.

The wheat factory was a derelict building with clear firing positions cut into every wall and crevice, on every floor all over the building. The building easily towered over the roof-top of our location and where we stood to guard the base. Looking left to right from the wheat factory, following it right around, were roads, streets and homes. Looking down into the Iraqi police station, they had some sort of dumping area to the front for their burnt-out, blown-up cop cars. Everywhere you looked you could see the vast amount of likely and possible enemy firing positions. We knew by just looking that the PJCC could be a nightmare of a camp to be housed at, it was bad enough being in Basra Palace with up sixty, seventy and some days eighty mortar rounds landing closely around you, but this place looked a whole lot scarier from the rooftop alone.

After a few days of settling into the base and getting into a routine, Slinky, a Corporal in my platoon, was up on the roof, in the sanger, on guard duty when he heard a loud pop. He immediately dived for cover. On looking around, he noticed a small bullet hole on the inside wall of the sanger, inches from where he was just standing. The bullet was not fired by a sniper hidden up in the wheat factory, or from the many other likely firing positions dotted around the outskirts of the PJCC, but instead it had come from a friendly gun and was fired from the building just behind ours. The building was the Iraqi Police Headquarters, clearly they had a rogue running amongst them and a rogue, to this day, none of us ever knew was caught.

Luckily for us, we had one or two Royal Engineers based with us at the PJCC who were very good at making things and they began to build blocking screens to stop the rogue Policemen having a clear sight of the lads guarding the PJCC via the rooftop. Being the platoon's Warrior Sergeant I found myself regularly as the Guard Commander based downstairs close to my Warrior. I very rarely ventured upstairs because we had a platoon with more than enough Corporals in it who were more than happy to stand upstairs and give the enemy hell. I did, however, get a few shifts up there on the roof, but I never saw any action, only heard it from the desk below.

One day while I was getting inside my sleeping bag, all hell broke loose on the rooftop. I could hear the sound of a serious firefight. This particular gunfight lasted longer than usual. Most firefights would last seconds - just seconds. Normally, a terrorist would take a few pot shots and either leg it away from the scene of the crime or, stupidly, stay in situ and get taken out from our return fire. The enemy would often, crazily, watch from the same firing position they just shot at us from and rather than move positions to get a better look they just stayed there to watch our reactions. However most would be sent to meet their seventy-two virgins.

As this firefight continued, myself and the lads in my room started to get dressed in case we were needed. You never knew what the enemy had planned, so we would always be ready for the worst-case scenario. Next thing I knew, as I was tying my boot laces together, I heard the screams of,

"MEDIC!!!"

the word still haunts me to this day. If you heard the call, then the shit has hit the fan and somebody was seriously hurt. I peered out of my accommodation to assess if I could help in any way, but I was told to keep the lads inside and out of the way while the incident was dealt with.

Flashes and images of the deaths of the lads from the IED circled around my head, I was shaking inside, nervously hoping nobody else was dead. The boys were worried, none of us knew what was going on or how serious it was.

A few minutes later we could hear screams of pain faintly in the distance - not the typical screaming of an angry Sergeant Major either, so we knew something terrible had happened and the screaming was from somebody in serious pain. The screaming drew closer and closer to my accommodation and I had to have a look to see who it was as he passed. As I slyly looked out of the accommodation, I saw my Platoon Sergeant leading a stretcher past with my mate laying on it in agony and covered in blood. One of my mates had just been shot while looking through his binoculars whilst on guard up on the roof. An enemy sniper had spotted him observing and - boom - went for the head shot. Fortunately, the bullet missed my friend's head and hit his hand - which was holding up the binoculars in front of his face - instead, or tragedy would have struck again. The bullet went into the top of his hand and out of his arm, close to the elbow. Bullets were designed to travel through the body and cause maximum damage. His screams still stick with me to this day, I will never forget it, nor will anyone on the ground.

This could have been the work of either a well-trained sniper or just a lucky shot from another scared and drugged up enemy who was forced and intimidated into attacking the very people there to protect them. I am not going to lie, I hated having to return fire on them because sometimes I would wonder if that person is being forced into doing it. Although it's us or them in a firefight, you'd still think about it afterwards when things have calmed down and the adrenaline has run out.

Being fired on is probably one of the scariest things to ever encounter. You would hear a loud, distinctive pop that, because of its speed and size, often meant hardly ever getting the chance to see it fly past. Unless it was a tracer round - that would be lit green or red in colour. The only way you knew for sure that it was in fact a gunshot, apart from the sound, would be if someone was hit by one.

Thankfully, our friend would survive, but sadly, the injury would mean an end to his promising career after a long rehabilitation back in the UK.

CHAPTER THIRTEEN
THE SHIT TRUCK MAN

Days turned into weeks and we continued to rotate between Basra Palace and the PJCC. The attacks had become more frequent and there was a feeling in the air that the enemy was stepping up their game plan against us in the Palace. With each attack, our Tour was becoming a game of survival. We required to be on our A-game with our drills and continue not to cut corners with the skills we had learned from our countless hours of dedicated training before arriving in Iraq, because the attacks were hurtling towards us and could happen at almost any time of the day, whether it was a mortar, a Chinese rocket, an IED being discovered or a random shootout.

My platoon was finishing off its last day of rotation at the PJCC, after a long week of attacks. The PJCC was a base that had to be protected, but it was strangely located inside another base, which was protected by the Iraqi police. I was rounding up the Warrior drivers to ensure they knew what they had to do before we headed back to Basra Palace, because the week had come to an end. Five Platoon had already left the Palace and were on their way to relieve us. It was dark and most of our work is done at night to make it harder for the enemy to track our Warriors and attack us.

As Five platoon, and their Warriors approached the entrance to the Iraqi Police Station which they had to pass through to access our base, the Iraqi police guarding the gates had refused to open them, preventing Five Platoon and their Warriors from entering. There was no good reason why the

Iraqi police were being awkward and our top Commander in the PJCC had been frantically trying to get whoever was in charge of them to sort the idiot on the gates out - before we did.

They were having no luck outside and still being refused entry. My boss had given me the order to command my Warrior over to the entrance to taunt the Iraqis into opening the gates. If they continued to refuse to open the gates, we were to crack on and smash the gates down, including anyone or anything else that got in my way. I was so happy with the order because for the first time in months he had chosen me for something worth leaving camp for. I loved being aggressive in my Warrior, because the Warrior looked like a tank in the eyes of those who knew little about Military vehicles and everybody would be scared of a tank heading towards them - including those refusing to open the gates.

I ordered my driver to start heading forward and there was nobody at the PJCC camp gates to open them in order for us to leave. I told my gunner to climb down to open the gates and just as he was about to climb down an officer based at the PJCC came running over to open the gates for us. We drove out and headed towards the Iraqis who were refusing to open their gates.

As we approached the gates, the Iraqis quickly realised what was about to happen and opened the gates before I had a chance to. I wasn't fully sure why Five Platoon hadn't been ordered to just drive through the gates themselves, but whatever - the decision to send me over to them did the trick and the gates were opened. No sooner had I left the PJCC gates, the base came under attack from mortar fire.

With the main gates now open, I returned to base a few minutes later which was no longer being hit by mortar fire and my driver drove us back through the gates of the PJCC. The Warrior had broken down on me just as I made it back into the

PJCC and about to park it up. I was about to send my gunner over to the gates to ensure they were closed - in case nobody was there to do it - when word spread that tragedy had struck again. As I commanded my Warrior out of the PJCC, the base came under attack by a number of mortar rounds, one of which had struck the Officer who had opened the gates for me. He was killed instantly while trying to make his way to the hardened cover - located next to the gates - as mortars rained down on the base.

When I returned in my Warrior and we passed through the open gates, he was no longer with us and had yet to be found. It was after the last Warrior from Five platoon entered the PJCC that one of the boys in my platoon had been told to head to the gates, to ensure they were closed. That was when his lifeless body was found.

My Warrior was the first of four Warriors under my control to break down on me during the Tour and my night was getting worse. The Warrior had been running smoothly and there were no signs of engine failure; until the damn thing packed in on me. I had no choice but to leave it there, in situ, at the PJCC and take one of Five platoon's Warriors back to the Palace - which was an order I had been given.

My platoon mounted up into the Warriors and I was at the back of the pack (what we knew as being the last vehicle). As we were about to head off back to the Palace, I watched a few men from the other Regiment carry the body of the officer who had died moments after opening the gates for me, being placed into the back of their armoured Bulldog ambulance. His body would be heading back with them to Basra Palace. A number of their Bulldogs had come along on the patrol to the PJCC with Five Platoon as a show of force, as we regularly helped each other out on patrols. Plus, they also had men at the PJCC. One of them was the officer who tragically lost his life after opening the gate.

We left the PJCC - my adrenaline still high from the horror - and drove out of the gates at a rapid pace. I was struggling to keep up with the three Warriors ahead and I had no communication with them either because I had swapped Warriors with another platoon who were on a different frequency, due to my platoon being attached to the PJCC. The list I had with the frequencies on was left inside my turret - the one I had just said goodbye to. The Bulldogs were supposed to be following on behind me as we left the PJCC, but left slightly later than us, forcing a gap well over a thousand meters long. We were going too fast for them to close the distance up.

While making our way back, the barrel of my Warrior would face the rear of the vehicle, because although I wasn't supposed to be last - I was. It was part of the drill to protect the rear of the convoy at all times. My attention was drawn to a minibus following from some distance with its lights off, which automatically set alarm bells ringing in my head. The minibus lights being switched off was unusual because it was well past midnight and the streets were rarely lit. I decided that I should keep my eyes on the minibus and track its movement. As we continued down a quiet street, the minibus pulled over and out came a good-sized number of terrorists. I recall seeing what looked like a rocket propelled grenade launcher in the hands of one of them and the rest were carrying weapons - quite possibly AK47s. I had no choice but to fire warning shots at them and let them know I was watching them. As my gunner opened fire aiming a volley of shots straight down the street into a large wall, the lads in the back had been deafened by the sound. It was totally unexpected for them as they all sat in the back of the Warrior sleeping.

It wasn't until the debrief back at Basra Palace that I was told the men, who I believed to be terrorists and had fired warning shots at earlier on in the patrol home, were exactly what I thought they were. They were about to try and ambush the Bulldogs which were some distance behind our Warriors. The terrorists ended up fleeing, thanks to my decision to send a few warning shots at them. The Bulldogs had seen my tracer rounds passing the minibus and into the wall and then saw what I did. They worked out what was about to happen as they could see the terrorists scuttling away from the area at pace and carrying weapons, which gave them enough time to prepare for the attack if it did come.

I received a 'thank you' from the Unit Commander at the debrief, but once again my boss turned a blind eye and nothing else was ever said about it. Just like the lad I found in the bush on the river bank the day Bati had been shot. Except for one time when we were having a Company drink back at the C.O.B with the other Regiment we had deployed to Basra Palace with and someone from the unit asked about it. He wanted to know who the Commander was that saved their lad. A few of my boys mentioned me and I remember looking at my boss when he responded.

"Don't be silly. Wasn't one of us."

Even though I knew it was me, my crew knew it was me, I am certain, he knew it was me too. I could not be arsed to argue my case so I left it there.

A few mornings later back at Basra Palace, as usual, the mortar alarm sounded - waking me and everyone else up just in time for breakfast. We didn't require an alarm clock because that was our alarm. I heard a massive bang on the roof above where I was laying. The dust on the ceiling and its paint fell down, hitting me in the face as I looked up from of my bunk-bed. There were a few more loud bangs which had landed close to our accommodation. But one particular bang actually provided a much-needed morale boost.

The portable toilets were being emptied by an Iraqi man, his big shit filled tank on the back of his lorry, when it was struck perfectly by a mortar round which landed straight into the tank, sending the shitty mess hurtling towards him. Iraqis would often ignore the mortar alarm because they either believed they wouldn't get hit or they never understood what it was designed for. Unfortunately for this one particular guy, he had no chance, because the first missile was not intercepted and hit his truck. After seeing him and the mess - I think next time he heard the alarm he may shit himself.

When the shit hurtled towards him, it swept him clean off his feet and straight towards the hardened concrete wall of the accommodation block. It was like a tsunami, but a shit filled one. The guy was lucky I guess, but what an interesting story to tell your grandkids - about how British shit took the impact of a mortar blast and theoretically saved his life.

One afternoon I was sitting in our company conference area, next to my room, receiving orders from the Company Commander regarding another patrol, when we heard what we thought was a gunshot. Every one of us in that area found it amusing at first, because it dawned on us that someone had been negligent and fired his weapon accidentally.

"Someone's getting a fine," whispered one of the lads.

Some people make genuine mistakes, especially when they are tired and forget to check their personal weapons are safe and unloaded. Most of the negative discharges occur when cleaning weapons. All weapon systems, no matter who you were, would require to be empty of any ammunition whilst inside the grounds of any camp.

As the giggles settled down and the brief continued on the quick reaction force, a Commander from Five platoon, who were QRF at the time, walked into the room to quietly brief the Company Commander.

"A soldier from the other Regiment has just been shot...."

I heard him say to the Company Commander - people gasped. The light humour about negligent discharging had turned into reality and was now, possibly, an attempted suicide or worse - murder.

The QRF left the room and headed of back to the scene and the brief continued very awkwardly. News had started to filter down about the incident and it wasn't sounding good - however they were just rumours, as those who knew kept the news to themselves for a short time at least. As ever, the truth came out and a soldier had been shot dead whilst sleeping, he was shot using his own weapon that was lying next to him as he slept. One of his friends from his own platoon walked into his room while he slept and picked his weapon up, thinking the weapon was made safe he pointed the weapon at the sleeping soldier and pulled the trigger not realising the weapon was loaded. The sleeping soldier would never wake up and the person who pulled the trigger was sent down for his actions. I will never forget the sound of that gunshot we had laughed about during the brief because it resulted in a death of one of our own. My young friend died in Kosovo - that one sound can link so many others together which stick in the back of your mind and reignite memories you tried to forget.

CHAPTER FOURTEEN
SWEAT

It was early July and the news had just broken that one of the lads from the Regiment based back in the C.O.B, had just been killed by a roadside bomb while driving his armoured Warrior into the Hay Al Mudhara District of Basra whilst on operations with his platoon. The lad who died was a legend within Regiment and his death came as a massive shock and a wake-up call to the ever-increasing threat from the IED's.

Our Company Commander's Warrior had been struck by an IED not long before in another location and this particular IED had managed to penetrate the Warriors armour. The guys in the Warrior were all fine, extremely shaken up from the blast, but no significant injuries or lasting damage other than the memory of it. Although our Company Warrior Sergeant Major did lose a few extra strands of hair off his head and he burnt his trousers, but he lived to tell the tale and stuck around to keep me on my toes.

Thinking back to the IEDs that had hit us so far on our Tour, there's one I will never forget. I was on QRF duty and while sitting in the cookhouse playing cards with the lads - we were most probably playing snap because we were "snapped" and I was useless at the rest of the card games - when suddenly we heard the almighty sound of an explosion going off in the distance, outside of camp. The blast knocked me off my chair, literally. I don't know whether it was the blast itself or I fell, but all I can remember is the loudness of the blast that echoed the hall.

The blast had hit a Warrior from Five Platoon, the Commander of the Warrior had dislocated his shoulder and was sent back to the UK for treatment. He was a lucky guy, to be fair, because a few weeks before the blast his Warrior had been struck by a Chinese rocket where it sat in the tank park. Luckily, when it happened, nobody was around because the force of the impact from a Chinese rocket had cracked the hull of the armour.

The Chinese rockets were a much bigger and more dangerous rocket that the enemy had used against us during attacks on Basra Palace with mortars. Mortars are designed to explode on impact and the blast would travel upwards - not outwards - hence the reason we would dive to the floor and keep low.

The Chinese rockets are designed for maximum carnage. When they land, the blast goes in all directions and it's "goodnight" if you're unlucky enough to be close to the impact zone. We all dreaded the Chinese rockets because they were the only viable threat to our accommodation blocks. Normal mortars would leave marks on the walls after impact, but the Chinese rockets could have penetrated the roofs and ceilings and caused multiple casualties.

With the threat getting stronger from IEDs and mortars, we received brand new armour, designed for the sides of our Warriors, that would hopefully give better protection to the wheels and tracks as the IEDs were being positioned to target them. It was down to the Warrior Sergeants in each platoon to ensure that each Warrior was fitted correctly with the armour. The Warrior Sergeants now had even more work added to their shoulders. Each small block weighed around a ton and then there was the bar armour to sit on top - to prevent the rocket propelled grenade threat - which was just as heavy. With the heat of the summer at its highest temperatures, hitting around one hundred degrees Fahrenheit daily, we had to wear our body armour and helmets while lifting this armour onto the Warrior. It was a massive challenge but, with every available man in each platoon grafting, the job was done. It was no easy job, we had four Warriors in each platoon to prepare and fit the new armour onto and with no time to spare.

Each vehicle would take around a day to fit - providing we had the correct parts, nuts and bolts, because nothing was ever simple in the Army. Most the time, as we started on the next Warrior, the instructions were missing from the boxes. Nobody liked working on the Warriors, but with more missions on the horizon, the work had to be done. The positive that pushed us through was that the Warriors protection was going to be even stronger and more durable now.

With each passing day, the maintenance of the Warriors was still the key priority for the Company. With temperatures soaring higher and no sign of any change, the rubber pads on the tracks were wearing thin even more quickly than at the start of the Tour. The track was a nuisance to work on in those conditions which wasn't ideal. You could guarantee that the sand you were working on would prevent your grease gun from working. All it took was one single grain of sand to block the nozzle and prevent it from working. The grease is used to tighten the tracks, which would always require to be pumped up regularly due to the heat actually melting the grease.

I had a Warrior over the REME workshop, based around the back of my accommodation block. The Warrior was in for some repairs that we couldn't carry out ourselves. The Warrior was almost finished, and I required it for the evening as we had a patrol coming up. At the time the mortar alarm was down/offline, therefore, nobody was supposed to leave the accommodation block until it was fixed and back up and running online. I was being heavily pressed by my Warrior Sergeant Major's merry men to send two of my boys over to finish off the last few jobs on that Warrior, so that it was good to go that night.

I hated doing the Warrior Sergeant role in 'B' Company for that particular Tour. There were far too many stressed and hot-headed senior ranks who were always on my case. I never got much rest, I was always doing maintenance or paperwork, or oil samples, or something to do with those bloody Warriors, just to keep them happy and off my case. But it wasn't their fault because they were pressured themselves and it was a knock-on effect - but nonetheless it made me angry. I got on well with the Warrior Sergeant Major so I had him to seek advice whenever the job was getting on top of me and to be honest I think he helped nurture me into my role.

The drivers and gunners in my platoon absolutely hated me at times because of this pressure from above and I wished the lads could understand why I was making them work outside on the Warriors. It seemed like I was on their cases all the time, but the fact was I had people on mine, pushing me to push them and I was stuck in the middle of it. But fair play my Warriors were always in good health and always ready when we needed them the most and this was down to me being pushed to push them.

On this occasion, I had no choice but to send two lads over to the REME workshop because I was ordered to. I sent two of my best lads who were extremely switched on and good at their jobs, I knew I could trust both of them. One was a driver and the other a gunner. Both looked at me as if I was a cunt when I picked them though, but I had no choice and I think now - later in their careers - they realise how the chain of command works and the pressure you have.

As the lads were working on the Warrior, Basra Palace came under mortar attack. The mortar alarm system was down so no-one had any warning until the mortars started to land. They did start to fall and were landing around the REME workshop. The first one landed, then the second, then the third - hitting all around the workshop. I could hear the rounds landing and the blasts on impact from my accommodation, I was literally shitting myself, in the knowledge that I had just sent my best two workers over there.

As luck would have it, when the first blast landed the lads got themselves inside the Warrior and took cover. As they did they heard screams - screams of pain - a man's voice. One of the REME lads who was in charge of the lads working in the workshop. The "Tiffy", as we knew him, had just been hit by shrapnel from the mortar. My boys ran over to help; there was blood pouring from his nether regions and one of the boys fainted at the sight of the blood. They managed, with the other REME workers, to get everyone under cover and give immediate first aid to the lad hit with shrapnel in an attempt to stem the bleeding. The outcome wasn't the best for the lad, but he did survive.

I was relieved the lads were alive and I was even happier knowing that they were the first on the scene to help give first aid. Their quick-thinking helped keep the injured lad alive. They did a cracking job. With the mortar alarm now fixed, it was back out onto the tank park and back into full swing of daily Warrior maintenance before the evening's patrol.

We left camp as a company for the evening patrol and as I looked out over the river running along our base, the site was a beautiful one. The river was stunning at night, with the moonlight glowing onto it. I often looked at the river because it was calm and peaceful compared to the everyday life within the City. We rolled out of the back gates, Warrior by Warrior and into the City. The IED threat had risen once again and now we knew the IEDs have also become deadlier and more dangerous. Through the intelligence we had gained, we had a rough idea of what streets were laden with IEDs, waiting for us.

We would try and stay away from the high IED routes and often used the back streets, the locals would know where most of the IEDs were planted and would avoid those areas and streets - hence the reason we used the back streets, like them.

It would be difficult as a Commander to spot any IEDs at night by looking through our thermal night sights. Everything would be hot from the days' heat and almost anything and everything you aimed your sights at, would be lit up like a Christmas tree. We patrolled around the city as usual, merely to let the locals know we were still about for them and give them reassurance - not because they needed it - but because they had started to change, the feeling was there that they no longer felt comfortable with us around because it was causing more enemy attacks, which meant their properties were damaged, their livelihoods and everything else they had worked so hard to build would be destroyed.

Iraq was a place of nightmares, you couldn't begin to imagine that the place was once a holiday destination back in the 70's and 80's. If only the world was at peace with each other, because Iraq, with its beautiful culture, history and deserts would be a thriving destination today.

Back on patrol, the streets were very quiet once again. Whenever the streets would start clearing out and go quiet we knew something was about to happen to us. There was very little street lighting, so most areas were extremely dark. That wasn't a problem given our technology. Our sights were clear, especially with everything still being so warm from the day's sun.

Driving down one street, I heard an almighty boom. My driver slammed on the brakes, as, like me, he thought we had just been hit by an IED. I stood up onto my seat and looked outside of my turret to ascertain what had happened - still unsure if the blast had hit my Warrior, but confident knowing we had better armoured protection. There was thick dense smoke and the smell of burning in the air. Seconds after I stood up, we came under fire from the enemy; my Company had just driven head first into an ambush - which wasn't that much of an issue because we had the fire power and the ammunition to hit back harder, which is what we did. Bati's One-Three callsign was the Warrior that was hit by the IED, but fortunately the IED hit the back end of the running gear and the track and wasn't too badly damaged even though the sound of the blast was enormous. I had to compose my myself, the thick smoke took my sights and its vision away and we couldn't tell where the gun fire was coming from.

Within seconds everything just went dead quiet; the shooting had stopped the enemy had fled. The smoke eventually settled down and I saw my Platoon Sergeant once again, outside running about. The guy was mad, fair play to him. He had climbed out of his Warrior callsign One-Three to check on the damage after the IED strike. He quickly gave me the thumbs up and as a company we then headed back to Basra Palace, everybody in one piece.

When we arrived back at Basra Palace, my first thought, as a Warrior Sergeant, was to inspect the damage caused to the Warrior commanded by Bati. The running gear had been hit and would mean that Warrior would be off the road for a few days for repairs.

CHAPTER FIFTEEN
THE DRIVER'S SEAT

With the first half of the Iraq Tour now behind us, the lads were finally starting to find their feet within Basra Palace. It had been emotionally hard living in the Palace and the fear of the mortar threat had started to affect some of the boys within 'B' Company. Simple things like taking a shower, going to the toilet and eating three square meals a day was starting to affect them. The boys would urinate into bottles while inside the hardened accommodation, rather than risk being caught in an attack. They would wash themselves using wet-wipes, rather than risk going for a shower and being caught up in an attack. The lads would skip breakfast too, rather than risk the walk over.

The food had changed from the stunning, mouth-watering selection we had at first - but after the boys died by the IED on the resupply mission - all that changed. We were now practically living on spam covered in flies, for three meals a day. It was easier to buy junk food from the small shop located opposite the cookhouse, skip meals and fill up on the junk food to see us through.

After three months of constant mortar rockets being fired at us, we started to learn the pattern of when they would be fired. With the enemy hitting us with mortars at similar times and patterns every day, we could relax slightly and breathe a little easier.

Being able to take a dump in the outside portable toilet in-between the bombings, was always a good feeling. Don't get me wrong, we still tried to dump as fast as we could though. Quite a few times I had been out taking a dump and the mortar alarm would go off. I'd then have to jump off the portable toilet as fast as I possibly could - with my trousers around my ankles - and dive straight into the filthy ground outside it. Lying on the ground, with my face down in the dirt and my bare backside exposed to the sun. I just laid there, praying that the mortars falling would land somewhere else. I can't even try to explain how scary the mortar alarm was for us, for everyone who experienced it they still panic on hearing any alarm to this day. For me, any bang, knocks or loud noise will force me into cover – something I will never forget.

I had to return to home for a few days during the Tour because my partner required an operation on her cruciate ligament. We had nobody at home to look after our baby at the time, so that was my reason for heading home. My family were complete and utter selfish arseholes who never visited us unless they wanted something. Except for my one brother, David. They knew my partner couldn't drive and was on crutches with a two-year-old child. Not once did they bother asking her if she needed help, except David. He had his own hectic life to live. So, I was forced to return home - not that I required much forcing to be honest - but I did cherish my few days with my two girls. As I was with them, holding them, feeling lucky to have them, I couldn't tell them of the danger I was living in, in Iraq. I had to keep my horrors to myself and I still hadn't told them I had been hospitalised for a week with a drip in each arm.

When I returned to Iraq, my good mate, Winko, had been seriously injured by a mortar during an attack on the base. Our Regimental Sergeant Major (RSM) and the Commanding Officer had finally made time to fly in and visit the lads as well. They chose the wrong day for the visit though. Not long after had they arrived, the enemy sent them a "welcome to Basra Palace" mortar attack and it was this attack that nearly took my mate's leg off. Fair play to everybody on the scene at the time including the RSM, they selflessly risked their own lives to extract my injured mate back to the Medical centre for treatment. That, no doubt, had saved his life and his leg.

The brotherhood of the lads in 'B' Company was showing. Everybody tried to help each other through the bad times. There were a couple of lads who would keep the lads entertained by being the Company Clowns. They could spit out a joke with ease and confidence. I never really had any confidence since my friends death in Kosovo and I would sometimes wonder where I fitted in with my platoon. I had a good relationship with the lads, but I didn't bond like the lads already had with each other. I just put it down to me being from another platoon and ignored the fact that everything I had witnessed during my career was the reason I wasn't myself anymore and had closed myself up into a shell. I am certain the signs were there but nobody ever picked up why I was often so quiet.

As we continued with life inside Basra Palace, the usual patrols would take place amongst the highest of threatened roads – we were now patrolling with our respirators close to hand as a number of Chlorine bombs had been found in the area, making life that little bit scarier. With our intelligence being spot on, we often avoided many possible IED routes. The threat was huge and as real as it ever was. We had little markers on our maps showing where the possible IEDs were and our maps would often be covered with them. We managed to avoid quite a few hairy situations in the City and nobody wanted to return fire unless it was necessary. There were so many locals in the City, the chance of us injuring some of them was very high - and the enemy knew this to well.

It was a common tactic of the enemy to film their attacks on us, in the hope we made that one mistake and hit a local, so they could use the footage as propaganda. Fortunately for us, nobody did. Our lads were very well trained in decision making and - to be honest - when you're sitting in an armoured Warrior and people are pinging small arms fire at you - you had time, as a Commander, to make the decision on returning fire or leaving the area.

It was my platoon's turn on the Rota to head back to the PJCC for another week. The lads always enjoyed being at the PJCC, regardless of the tragedy and injuries sustained there, because we always had regular firefights with the enemy. Mostly they'd fire at us from the small holes over at the wheat factory because they didn't have the balls to knock our camp gates for a fight.

We left the remainder of the Company back at Basra Palace as they had the usual missions coming up. It was the beginning of August and the Tour was close to mid-way through. The lads, myself included, were getting homesick. Being away from the loved ones was a killer, especially living in such a hostile country. The re-supply mission would bring in our parcels and letters from home; also the small shop we had near the cookhouse would be restocked. The shop wasn't huge, sold the basics, cigarettes, cans of pop, crisps and chocolates, but enough to keep us happy.

Some of the PJCC's layout had changed since I was last there. With the death of the officer who unselfishly opened the gates for me that fatal night being a stark reminder of the mortar threat. The small cooking area that the chef had outside, was now inside. Upstairs on the roof there was added protection to make it difficult for the enemy hiding away in the distance. A popular building that often saw attacks on us emanate from, had been flattened. The building was hit by a Javelin missile during a heavy attack on the PJCC one warm evening. Five Platoon had been at the PJCC that week, they fired the Javelin. The first Javelin to be fired on our Tour. What a buzz that must have been. It was a good friend, from my normal platoon back in the UK, who flattened the building and the enemy inside it.

On top of the PJCC roof it had been made safer, the view from the police station behind was now obscured to them. Our sanger was now reinforced and had more camouflage added to it to help protect the guys on watch. The Engineer based in the PJCC had worked tirelessly reforming the roof and mostly doing so alone.

It was the 6th of August and news had just started to filter into the PJCC of another ambush that had just occurred - this time on Charlie Company who were out on a strike operation at the time, along with their Warriors and various other vehicles. They were based at the C.O.B and made their way towards the area they were carrying out the strike op in. As Charlie Company approached they were ambushed and all their vehicles came to a standstill. While the Commanders and gunners in each turret vigorously scanned their arcs for any signs of enemy fire, things took a serious twist. During this, the lad I had taught just before I left for Iraq (who I had warned about cutting his skills) was fatally shot. He was hit by a stray bullet. My friend was killed by a freak shot, nothing more. He had his driver's hatch open, ever so slightly and somehow the bullet made it through.

News, again, filtered down to us at the PJCC on the death, but again no names as yet. The hours passed and listening to the action on the ground - the true horrors of it came to light. While the ambush was ongoing and my friend's Warrior had gone static, the Commander of his vehicle at first didn't realise his driver had been shot. There was no way of telling because there was, simply, one way of communicating with each other and that was by using the headsets we each wore under our helmets. Half the time they would be broken in some way, because the kit was shit.

Some drivers would fall asleep when the Warrior stopped. It is tiring trying to keep focused. We often drove for hours at a time and sometimes we could be stopped in situ for a good few hours. The driver has the engine next to him and you feel the heat from it. Then you have the heat from the sun, I often hated driving the Warrior in hot weather. Not forgetting that the drivers would also have their body armour and helmets on; as well as their clothing. All this, plus the fact you're always working long hours, would make you tired.

The Commander, now unable to make communication with his driver, had to climb out of his turret and head to his driver's hatch. Doing this in a built-up city with a sniper threat and an on-going ambush took balls - and plenty of them. But he did, he climbed down ready to kick the shit out of the sleeping driver, only to find him passed away. He was just lifeless on his chair. The horror going through the Commander's mind at the time must have been terrifying.

With the driver down, the Commander had to try and recover his body to the rear of the Warrior. They needed to get another driver into the seat and get out of the danger zone. Unfortunately, the driver was a big guy who had somehow locked his foot under one of the pedals - the lads who were trying to remove him couldn't. This forced the Commander to take the decision to hitch his Warrior up to another Warrior and get it towed out of the danger area to safety.

With the Warrior now recovered back to Basra Palace, the lads had to keep their emotions in check and pull together to help recover the driver's body which was still stuck in his drivers hatch. I can't imagine what these guys went through that day – just listening on the radio sent visions of it flowing freely around my mind. I often get stopped by people who have never served in the forces before and one of the first things they usually say to me is "anyone can get Post Traumatic Stress Disorder", I agree – obviously, as everyone has their own horrors but I don't need reminding of mine either or who's affected.

Back at the PJCC, I had just come off my stint as Guard Commander during which I had heard the entire radio communication on the ground regarding the ambush and I knew who had died. I headed over to my bed space, sat down on my camp bed and closed my eyes. At this point I just wanted to scream my fucking head off in anger. I just couldn't get the memory of telling him - during the training course - that he needed to start doing the drills I taught him correctly or he would know about it in Iraq. I couldn't help thinking it was my fault, did I not teach him something? Have I missed something on his course? But I had taught him everything, it was a freak shot that added to my belief that when it was your time to die, it was your time to die.

All the reports I heard stated he had become an incredible driver within his platoon and a proud soldier who had loved his new role in the driver's seat.

With the threat becoming ever worse in Basra, somebody high up the chain of command decided to pull all the troops back to the C.O.B from Basra Palace by the end of August. This news was a welcome breath of fresh air. The nightmare was coming to an end. I was leaving for home as it was time for my leave.

When I returned to Iraq for the third time, my Battle-group were pulling out of Basra Palace for good and in less than forty-eight hours, so I stayed in the C.O.B and helped our CQMS (Company Quartermaster) prepare the accommodation blocks for the arrival. Each bed space required a built-up wall of breeze blocks and we had over one hundred bed spaces to make up in a very short space of time. We worked in a small team - it was all the man power we had. We worked together and made it happen. We moved, carried and repositioned thousands of breeze blocks. The bed spaces were finished and I was fucked! Exhausted wasn't the word. The reason behind the breeze blocks was safety, although the C.O.B rarely got hit by mortars the threat was always there.

The day arrived, in a massive convoy of Warriors and Bulldogs, one by one they left Basra Palace. There was motion put in place by the enemy to allow us to pull out of the city in safety. Nobody would attack us as we left. Instead they lined the streets and waved us out. The enemy, as sly as they were, gained a moral victory that day when we pulled out of the City. The moral victory was enough to help them recruit more locals to become murdering scumbags. Propaganda was the enemy's key, they could now tell those locals that we left them.

Our new camp was heavenly. It had warm showers that were cleaned regularly; proper toilets, a volleyball court and to top it off, we no longer had to walk around in full body armour or helmets.

We shared our new camp with the Swedish Air Force who didn't have many servicemen there. They had a cafe which we were welcome to use. The cafe sold Swedish cakes and sandwiches, but for me the fact that it sold ice cold cans of coke was a blessing having come from a Palace with nothing.

We formed up - as a platoon - for a Tour of the C.O.B in order that everyone could familiarise themselves with the new camp. Although we had stayed here for a few days at the start of the Tour, parts of the camp had changed. We walked around the areas we were required to know before finishing at the shop. The shop sold everything we needed, from magazines to cigarettes. In the surrounding area, there was a Sandwich shop, a Burger bar, a Pizza outlet and even an Indian takeaway. These were all American owned and we felt like we were on holiday, I really wished the British top brass looked after us the same way the Americans get looked after. While we suffered in Basra Palace, the Brigade and the rest of my Regiment were living more comfortably. Nevertheless we had it all now, so all our morale was high.

We also had access to computers! We had to pay to use them, but they had a webcam and everything you required to chat with your loved ones back home. I was online one evening, facetiming my partner and daughter - seeing and hearing so much about my daughter growing up while I was away - when the mortar alarm went off. I immediately hit the floor and crawled under the table for extra protection. The siren was loud, it sounded for about two or three minutes but when you're down on that floor, it feels like a lifetime. As the siren faded, I gathered myself together, got back onto my chair and faced the screen; my partner was in tears. She watched the whole thing; the internet room was full that night, so she saw everyone dive for cover and heard the loud echoing sounds of the alarm. Her heart sank and there was nothing she could do apart from sit, watch and pray.

None of us told our families of the true horrors that we were living. There was extensive news coverage due to the number of British Soldiers dying in Iraq, but we always played it down on the phone, in letters and over the internet. The thought of my partner knowing the whole truth for me wasn't possible. She was at home with a leg injury and a young child to take care of, so the added worry was a big no-no. Although my partner was a stalwart who would do anything for anyone, I knew I had to keep everything from her until I got home safe and alive at least.

Whenever a British Soldier was injured - or died - on Tour, no matter where you were serving, Op Minimize would be called. Op Minimize was put in place to blanket all communications available to British Troops. Telephones and the internet would be cut to avoid anyone phoning home and talking about something that had just occurred. Although it was totally understandable, it was also a hindrance at times. We didn't always get time to call home and the phones were not always readily available, but when we did get the time to finally make the call and Op Minimize was on, we would get pissed off. The phone lines would be cut for however long it took for the information to be passed onto the families of the soldier or soldiers involved. There were occasions when the phones were down for a couple of days, quite a few actually.

Op Minimize was introduced for valid reasons. For example; if Private Ryan was killed and his wife lived next door to mine, I might ring my wife and tell her, despite not having the full facts of his death. She could then go next door and tell Private Ryan's wife before the chain of command told her. There would be serious consequences for me, especially if some of the information passed on was wrong. Imagine the heartbreak of being told your husband has been shot and injured - by Pam next door whose husband just phoned to gossip. Then you get a knock at the door from his Regiment's Welfare Officer and he breaks the news that your husband has actually died.

The second half of the Iraq Tour passed very quickly without further serious injuries or loss of life. When the Tour finally ended, the Regiment headed over to Cardiff for our medal parade. Local people came out in force and waved and cheered us on as we marched, proudly, from Cardiff Castle, down the high street and into the Millennium Stadium.

During the ceremony several candles had been lit for the boys who did not make it home. R.I.P boys. Gone but not forgotten.

CHAPTER SIXTEEN
NOT AGAIN

In the weeks since our return to the United Kingdom from the hectic and horrid Tour of Iraq we were based back at our Barracks in Tidworth. I was back with my original platoon - Javelin Platoon - and no longer part of 'B' Company anymore. I had a cracking platoon in Support Company, the boys were a great team and fun to be around. They were always smiling and treated each other with respect, no matter how shit the day was. The senior ranks also respected the lads and this made the platoon work and work well.

I received a message to report to the Platoon Commanders office that he shared with the Platoon Sergeant. I was at the Warrior sheds, instructing on another Warrior driving course. I went down to the office during a break to see my boss as I was asked to do. He greeted me with some fascinating news..

"Locky, next year, February time-ish, you're deploying to Afghanistan with some of the other lads from our platoon and attached to Charlie Company. I will let you know more when the information is passed down the line, ok bud?"

Oh my god, my heart had just stopped,

"Not again - not so soon," I said as I walked out of the office. I skipped all the way to my room with happiness and delight, closed my door and BOOM! - the blood rushed to my head. I was tamping; I punched my locker door hard, threw my kettle at the wall, I was outraged!. I couldn't believe that we were penciled in on another Tour within weeks of returning from a devastating Tour of Iraq which claimed the lives of five of my friends and injured countless others. I had to break the soul-destroying news to my partner. I knew she was going to be gutted, regardless of the fact that the Tour was over a year away. Still, a year is a year.

Since the day that I joined my Regiment in 2000, most of the lads had already served four Tours. The Army had massive numbers of manpower at the time but my Regiment seemed to be deployed more than the rest. Share the fucking love around and use the other Regiments instead of us! Unfortunately, we were one of the most experienced Armoured Regiments in the British Army and for that reason alone we did more than our fair share of Tours. I guess our higher-ranking officers - the guys at the top who no-longer had to leave their warm, cosy offices - were the ones volunteering us. Maybe they were after bigger pay packets - only they knew.

I decided to wait until I got home the following Friday to sit my partner down and tell her the news. She took it well. I was expecting tears and disappointment, but she held it together because she knew I was a broken man from the horror I had lived through on the Iraq Tour. I was a changed man on my return from Iraq, my partner noticed the difference immediately.

I hated leaving the house, any loud noises and I would be shaken. She often tried to advise me to go to see the doctor, but I wouldn't acknowledge her advice. Besides, back in those days, going sick with Post Traumatic Stress Disorder would be heavily frowned upon and would damage your career prospects. I learned to cope with my issues the best I could and quietly - by ignoring them. There was no support offered during or after the Tour and other than 'B' Company Commander sending letters home to our families pre-warning them of the difficulties we might have - that was it.

We did have a pointless two-day stopover in Cyprus en-route home from Iraq which the Military classed as the reinduction back into normal routine. All the two days did, for any Regiment, is allow the lads to blow off steam by beating each other up while under the influence of alcohol. I would have preferred those two days to have been used to provide information and, perhaps, a chat with Specialists on coping mechanisms that we could use to deal with death and the horrors that we had just survived and witnessed. That would have been much more beneficial to us, because later in life we would need it.

With another Tour on the horizon everybody knew what else would come with an up and coming Operational Tour. Once again we had to suck up the fact that we would be spending much needed family time on the plains of Salisbury and Canada; being fucked about in the cold and wet in order to get our tick in the box and clearance for Afghanistan. I had served eight years at that point and in that short space of time my Regiment had deployed on four Tours - 1 x Kosovo, 3 x Iraq – and all lasting six months or longer. This totaled two years away from our families. Two years away from watching our children grow up. Instead they would be left at home with your other half to care for them whilst trying their very best to be both mum and dad, it was horrible not being there for them and comfort them while they were upset but it's our choice to do the job and it pays the bills and puts food on the table. Add the countless exercises - like Batus - together, which last six weeks at a time and two years suddenly becomes three or four.

I know there are critics out there who think we have a choice to join the Army,

"So shut up and stop whining."

Think of it logically; if we didn't choose to join the Army, then the Army would choose us to join them by bringing back National Service. We would have kids back on the frontline fighting wars that we shouldn't even be fighting. For me I chose the Army because I wanted to escape and I knew, full well what the consequences could be.

As the months passed and the Tour fast approaching, Javelin platoon would split up again, but only slightly this time - just as we did in Iraq - but with some of us dispersing to other platoons, some of the lads would stay behind in the UK and being deployed on the following Tour. I would be staying in Javelin platoon and deploying as the Warrior Sergeant for the upcoming Tour of Afghanistan. At this point in my career I was more than happy to take the role as I did the job in Iraq and knew my job. We wouldn't be known as Javelin Platoon when we crossed over to Charlie Company though, we would become Nine Platoon.

We were to meet up with our new battle-group on the cold fields of Salisbury Plain and train together, ready for our upcoming deployment to Afghanistan. Charlie Company, including myself, rolled the Warriors out of our Barracks and headed out to our RV point to meet up with the battle-group for our week-long training package. This training package would give the lads some vital, up-to-date, knowledge of the current tactics being used on the ground in Helmand Province. Plus the lads would get some first-hand tips from the trainers who had just returned from Afghanistan.

We arrived at the training location and headed into our accommodation, ready for the usual Exercise Do's and Don'ts brief. When the briefs finished, Charlie Company's Officer in Command got the Company together and told us we would be leaving this location tomorrow morning. There was no information other than that. Everyone was left speculating - eventually the speculation became the truth. We were leaving to conduct our own training, because the guys in charge of the battle-group didn't have a fucking clue how to use the Warrior tactically as they had never been deployed with an armoured Regiment before. This was bad news for us, we lost the prospect of learning valuable tactics and information that would eventually be pivotal and life changing.

Nevertheless, we left for our new training area - a fair distance away from the battlegroup. We were all grown men, we understood our jobs and accepted any given challenges and responsibilities thrown at us. Within Charlie Company there were a few lads, myself included, with any real operational experience. Most of the lads were new to the Regiment and about to head off on their first Tour, so it was mainly down to us few to really concentrate on drilling the tactics into the younger lads.

Unfortunately though, Iraq is nothing like Afghanistan. Both country's enemies fight differently and use totally different tactics - even when they believe in pretty much the same thing they are fighting for and think they'll become martyrs and get seventy-two virgins upon death. If I thought this was true, I'd have killed myself a long time ago and would be living the dream with my seventy-two. I can see my myself; on my lounger in the back garden of my mansion with seventy-two - no-longer - virgins obeying my every command. That doesn't sound like heaven to me though, as good as it seems. I find it hard living at home with two females and I certainly wouldn't want anymore. Besides, I'd probably end up with all the miserable virgins and my heaven would become my hell.

During training on Salisbury plain, one of the lads, a Lance Corporal and a sniper, was by far one of the kindest and funniest characters to bless this earth. He was loved by all - including those he often pissed off. He would sneak off during the silent hours and meet his wife; she drove him home for lunch and extras and would drive him back before anyone noticed. The balls on someone who did that would have to be massive and fair play, I wish mine were.

Training had finished. I wanted to speak out regarding the disappointment and worry in my mind at the shocking lack of training given to us - which was no fault of our own. I knew if I did, I'd have been told to keep my mouth shut. Everyone else, including the bosses, felt the same. It was written all over their faces. We were expected to deploy without the much needed, possibly life-saving, knowledge. We were expected to use the mine detecting equipment whilst out on operations, yet we never had any real training with the equipment that would potentially save our lives. We, basically, had them and played about with them, but we didn't know what settings or noises we should be using or looking and listening out for. The younger soldiers were the ones expected to use the equipment - and yet nothing but a lack of training on them. We didn't use this type of equipment in Iraq because it wasn't required. Tactics were different over there, so no-one, including the very few of us with operational experience, had ever used the equipment before.

You just shut your mouth and got on with it because that is the way the Army is run. There was no freedom to express yourself without consequences. Nothing was ever said about it for fear of repercussions. The negligence here was massive if anything went wrong in Afghanistan due to the lack of training, but then again, you cannot prove anything against the Army because it's one big cover up. What would I know about it?

Three weeks prior our pre-Tour leave kicking in and I was teaching my last Warrior course before being deployed. I received a phone call from my partner telling me in an upset-panicky voice, that her step-Dad had just died at work of a heart attack. Her amazing mum lived in West Wales, quite far away from our home and she was unable to drive and dependent on him. I had no choice but to run to my Sergeant Major's office, slam my tabs in and explain my situation to him. I wasn't expecting to get any sympathy - you never do in the Army - but to be fair, the guy sent me straight home.

When I arrived home, my partner was waiting with my young daughter, bags packed ready to go straight up to be with her Mum at the sad time but my partner's sister had gone up as soon as the news broke and brought her back to my house where we had a spare room for her.

With the funeral over, it was decided my partner's Mum would move into our home permanently. We spent some time at her home in West Wales, where she had lived with her husband before he passed away, boxing up the life she had with her husband and bringing it all back to my home. I ended up having almost four weeks off, including my pre-Tour leave, the situation at home meant my leave flew by. It wasn't the leave I wanted before I left for war, but I had the slight comfort of knowing her mother was under my roof and my partner was no-longer living alone with my young daughter and had someone to talk when she needed it.

So, with leave over, I gave my partner and daughter a long hug goodbye leaving her with tears running down her face. I was no longer the crying type of person. I had gone through so many emotions during my time in the Army that I became immune to crying. Having no emotions often became an issue - but it was my way of dealing with the horrors I had lived through. Nobody outside of the Military world, bar the emergency services and those caught up in it, could understand the horrors of war. The sight of your mates lying dead in front of you; body parts missing and you're forced to carry on around it and act like it never happened. It isn't easy, but you do get used to it, EVENTUALLY. Not everyone did though, some did crack under the pressure.

When I served in Germany there was one lad who struggled emotionally and wanted out of the Army. He hadn't served enough time to sign off. His only other alternative was to either take drugs and get dismissed or get arrested and be dismissed. Either one would see you leave with a terrible reference for your next employer to read. So, what he did was, he started acting like he was going insane. Not in a bad way. He would walk around pretending to push a bicycle. We would laugh ourselves stupid watching him walk around camp pushing an imaginary bike. But it worked, people had noticed his strange behavior and eventually he was dismissed from the Army on mental health grounds. The day he left - and the way he left - topped it all. As he said his goodbyes to the lads and packed his things into his car, he made his way out of camp. He stopped just short of the gates, right outside of the guard room. He got out of his car and walked around the back where he started fiddling once again with thin air. He then walked over to the Provo Sergeant who was stood outside his guard room and started pushing his imaginary bike. He then placed it against the guard room wall. The Provo Sergeant asked him what the hell he was up to and he replied,

"Just leaving my bike for the next easy cunt wanting out."

That was it. He drove off into the sunset. – Legend.

CHAPTER SEVENTEEN
SICK BAGS AND AEROPLANES

The day had arrived, the boys from my platoon, and myself, headed with Charlie Company to the airport for our flight to out Afghanistan. The flight would take around eight hours. I wasn't the best flyer, I suffered with motion sickness all my life. As a kid I was in the back of my step-Dad's car travelling home and was travel sick. It shot out of my mouth and all over my Mother's new perm which had cost her fifty quid. I hated not being able to see where I was going, because I could use the area to my front to focus on while I travelled.

I hadn't yet been air sick, but I did come close while on my pre-deployment training for Iraq. We were training on the Merlin Helicopter for the first time and the pilots were flying wildly. I was close to being sick, I turned white and everything. Someone passed me a sick bag as a joke and everyone on board was looking at me, waiting for me to be sick. It was horrible, I had like twenty pairs of eyes on me and I knew they were waiting to rip the piss out of me when I was finally sick. Luckily though I wasn't sick, I did gag a few times though and those watching me had started to gag themselves at the sight of me gagging. For those who weren't gagging, it must have been funny watching everyone else gagging at the sight of me gagging. I ended up getting off the Merlin helicopter laughing at what could've happened, thanks to feeling air sick.

We boarded the plane and it took off for Afghanistan. I got my head down on the plane, like everyone else, because we knew we were in for a long six-month Tour and we knew how dangerous Afghanistan had become. As we approached the Middle East, about five hours into the flight, a technical fault occurred with the Air Defense System. It had stopped working and for this reason we had to turn around mid-air and fly all the way back. I was livid at this point of the flight as my backside was numb, I was bored, over tired and I just wanted off the plane. Now we had to fly back and do it all again the next day!

The next day came and as a company of men we made our way back to the airport, but once again there was another problem. The fault that forced our flight to turn around, five hours in and head back to the UK, still hadn't been fixed. The RAF supplied us with another plane. This time, the plane they supplied did not have enough remaining seats on-board for our company of over a hundred strong. The flight was originally scheduled for another group of soldiers who were flying out that day. So, some of us would be staying another night and would fly out the following day. My Company Commander looked at his orbat (order of battle) of man-power, rank and job titles and decided who would be better off flying out to Afghanistan that day. We had fourteen Warriors to sign for and take over; there was another Regiment waiting for us to arrive as they were due to leave for home.

I was picked to fly that day due to my Warrior Sergeant role within Nine Platoon. I was a little disappointed not to stay another night in the UK as I had wanted to phone my partner. I knew from experience that it would be a while before I got another chance. But nope, off I went and boarded the aircraft once again. Up we went, a sweet take off, and within minutes the wheels were up.

We made it safely to Qatar, the first stop before boarding a Hercules plane and flying into Helmand Province under cover of darkness, for safety reasons.

As we queued to board the Hercules, I knew that if I boarded the aircraft last there may not be enough seats for everyone and I could fly another night. The Royal Air Force often overcounted their manifest and got things wrong. Yes, as

I thought, the RAF had in fact overcounted once again by just one seat. I was at the back, the last man to board and there wasn't a seat for me, so I got off the Hercules laughing inside my messed-up brain. The lads were looking at me as I waved my middle finger at them and said,

"See you all tomorrow," as the rear ramp of the Hercules was raised.

One of the ground crew told me to follow him. I thought I was going over to the accommodation to stay the night, but he took me to the cockpit and the pilot asked me if I wanted to sit in the spare seat. "Nope, not particularly...." I thought. I was worried in case I was airsick. It was also dark outside, I couldn't see anything through the cockpit windows.

I was chuffed to sit in the cockpit with the Captain and his crew for the flight. Cockpit safety rules changed after the September 11th tragedy and I never thought I would ever get the chance to travel in the cockpit - high up in the clouds - but low and behold there I was. I was flying into a war zone sitting next to the pilot in the cockpit! The pilot was friendly, very chatty and welcoming towards me. He made me feel comfortable and at ease. We headed down the runway and up went the Hercules for the third time in two days, as we flew higher and higher, we hit a safe height, high enough for the pilot to ask me to press a button. I did - BOOM! - the landing gear started closing away, the wheels were up.

The flight wasn't a long one, about an hour. It did feel quicker having flown in the Box Office of all the seats. The pilot had these amazing night vision goggles which he passed me when we were up in the air. I could literally see everything through them; they were amazing. I'd have loved them as part of my issued kit. I got to turn the plane as well, which was way cooler than anything I have ever driven before. Then the fun was over and reality was about to kick in because we were heading down into Helmand Province to land.

We landed safely and our CQMS was waiting for us as we disembarked from the Hercules. He had travelled over to Afghanistan slightly earlier than the rest of us as part of the advance party, so he could prepare everything, ready for our arrival at Camp Bastion. I was the first passenger off the Hercules plane as I was in the cockpit and I went around the back with the ground crew and waited and watched as the rear ramp came down and opened up the rear of the plane. As the ramp opened, the lads inside were looking at me confused. They thought I missed out on the flight, but somehow I was standing there smiling at them from the back of the plane while they were still on-board.

I told them my story and also told them that I had flown the plane - like you do. We then boarded a waiting coach to take us a short distance to the check-in and into Camp Bastion itself. After we checked into Camp Bastion - passports handed in - we headed to our accommodation. It was late and I just wanted a shower and some shut eye.

As we approached our accommodation, I took one look at it. It was tented, and I thought to myself, I hope it's better than the accommodation we had in Iraq. It did have air conditioning, showers and real toilets, so I was relatively happy. Our beds were the usual camp beds and located inside a mosquito net. The mosquitos in the Middle East were riddled with Malaria and obviously we had to take daily medication for it. We had the same issue in Iraq with the medication, but I didn't see one mosquito over there.

Located in Camp Bastion was a Pizza parlour and a bar that sold no alcoholic beverages. There was also a good-sized shop that sold my cigarettes and a few Afghani locals with market stalls that sold music, porn, gifts and cigars.

The following morning, news got round my accommodation that the lads stuck back in the UK - who had stayed behind to fly today - had a bird strike on take-off and had to turn around and make an emergency landing. My heart dropped when I found out. I immediately felt relieved that I flew yesterday after all. The lads would try and fly again tomorrow. As for myself, I headed over to the Warrior tank park to meet up with the Warrior Sergeant from the Regiment we were replacing and were waiting to hand over to us as they had finished their six-month Tour in Yatminshia, Musa Qala. It was my job to take the four Warriors that he had cared for in his time in Afghanistan off his hands and ensure they were in good working order for my boys.

I had now signed and taken over my four Warriors. They were now my responsibility for the duration of the Tour. I had tens of millions of pounds worth of equipment under my responsibility. When we deploy on a Tour, or on long exercises, it's common to name our Warriors. The last time I went away, which was in Canada, we used the theme of war films, but this time our theme would be Welsh towns. I didn't waste time in naming my Warrior. As soon as I heard the theme, I labelled my Warrior using a box of sticky white stickers that I had found in the iso container used as our Warrior stores. I had named my Warrior, "NEWPORT", after my home City. Thinking back to Iraq, we didn't name our Warriors, not sure why. I think Newport on the side of my Warrior would have suited Iraq, with its striking similarities to the rubbish that is starting to litter the streets and the endless amounts of people living homeless in the City Centre when there are homes and buildings sitting empty throughout the City.

Nevertheless, the Warriors were looking good considering the heat in Afghanistan. We were informed that nearly all the roads we would be heading on - and using - in just a few days' time, would be made up of dirt and sand tracks across the open ground and fields, all the way to our next destination.

We would be heading to a village deep inside of Musa Qala, called Yatminshia, once we'd got round to our acclimatization and training package. We should have started this by now, but the delay meant the packages would not start until the remainder of the lads made it out to Afghanistan.

The lads' delayed flight finally landed three days later than expected, but the main thing was, everyone was now at Camp Bastion together and ready to knuckle down and allow their professionalism and training to keep them safe. With less than a week left until we deployed out from Camp Bastion to Musa Qala, we were running behind slightly on schedule. All hands were now on the pumps trying to get everything prepared for the big move.

The training package finally began. I was looking forward to learning the tactics that we missed out on - vitally - during our pre-deployment package. I had to try and juggle my time driving back and forth from the tank park to the ranges outside the back gates of Camp Bastion, in order to complete my training. I passed my Warrior shoot, which was basically what we do back in the UK, but I was still eagerly awaiting to learn the knowledge and tactics for Afghanistan. We had very minimal training supplied and the training package, in my case, only included the Warrior shoot and an apple shooting pistol contest. I was, again, pissed off at the lack of any professional training.

I guess I was anxious because of how soul destroying my Basra Palace Tour had been and I didn't want to relive it in Afghanistan. Mine detecting training eventually happened, it wasn't much, very basic, but it gave the younger lads some very much needed confidence building before deploying outside the wire to do it for real.

The only thing that would get us through this Tour in one piece was team-work. The lack of vital skills and drills used every day in Afghanistan would have to be learned the hard way. I had every faith in the men working alongside me, regardless of their ages and experience, because as long as we all looked out for one another, we would be fine.

CHAPTER EIGHTEEN
THE MOVE OUT

We completed the acclimatization and training package and now, with our kit packed, our Warriors inundated with supplies of bottled water and spare parts packed into every available hole - wherever we could fit them - we were finally prepared to head out the gates of Camp Bastion and start our Tour properly. There was just one thing on my mind to do before heading over to Headquarters to receive my Company orders on the move out - and that was to call my partner, speak to my daughter and buy as many cigarettes as I could possibly carry back with me. Where we were heading, we wouldn't have a shop or even be close to one, let alone buy any luxuries.

I went over to Charlie Company's HQ none the wiser on the move-out. I had cleaned the entire shop out of cigarettes. I was a little bit nervous and anxious about what was ahead of me I guess, but right from the start of the Tour I had a good feeling and so I had it in my mind that I wouldn't be scared - as I was in Iraq - and this time it was going to be either me or them if I get attacked.

Whenever 'B' Company left Basra Palace in an armoured Warrior, our Platoon Commanders would often lead the way. I'm not sure if it was a tactic, because the officers would usually sit back in their Warrior in either second or third spot in the order of march any other time and place. Therefore, I wasn't the most confident of map readers until we moved back as a Company to the C.O.B, where my platoon was lucky enough to work with the Special Reconnaissance Service.

Working with the Special Forces meant I was then required to lead each patrol. At first I was petrified and absolutely hated the added responsibility. The pressure of reading a map, while communicating over the radio and observing for the enemy threat - and suffering with severe motion sickness - was a lot for me to handle at first. I did finally click and excelled in it. I looked forward to leading every patrol.

It all clicked into place after I threw a bag of crisps off the top of my Warrior towards two young children standing at the side of a road in Iraq as I passed them. I would often do this, because the kids always looked malnourished and hungry. Unfortunately the wind blew the crisps onto the road and the two kids ran out and jumped onto the crisps to fight it out for them when suddenly a large HGV drove straight over them. My heart immediately sunk into my gut; those poor little boys died for a packet of crisps. As the HGV passed over the boys, the driver never once tried to stop his vehicle and just carried on at speed - hurtling down the road like a maniac and past my Warrior. I ordered my driver to slow down and stop immediately afterwards. To my relief the two boys weren't in pieces, dead on the ground, but, in fact, they were still fighting over the crisps like nothing had happened! From that moment on, everything just clicked into place and I understood how and what I needed to do to be a good Commander. It was the day I grew up.

I walked into Charlie Company's HQ more confident in my abilities, but still anxious. I sat myself down next to the other Commanders in my platoon and the brief began. I was hoping - being in Nine Platoon - that either Seven or Eight Platoon would be leading the patrol to Musa Qala which was around seventy kilometers away and a really pressurised job for the lead Warrior Commander. Every route taken and every corner made is down - solely - to the leading Commander. The safety of the Company was in his hands. The brief kicked in and every fine detail was scrutinised down to the bone, so we were clear on everything we were required to do for the move out. Unlucky for me though, I had been given the job I was praying to be overlooked for, Lead Warrior Commander.

When my Company Commander said the dreaded words,

"I want callsign Three-One to lead."

I almost cried inside because callsign Three-One was my callsign for the Tour. I looked at my Company Commander, nodded and acknowledged the responsibility. The brief ended and I walked back to the accommodation with my boss and platoon Sergeant.

Nine Platoon saw a few big changes in the ranks for the Afghanistan Tour. We had a new Platoon Commander in charge as our usual boss was on another task. The new Platoon Commander was different from the other officers I had worked with or had come across during my career. He was an approachable and confident character to be around and the same applied with our newly promoted Platoon Sergeant. The Platoon Sergeant had always been in Javelin Platoon and had it in his blood. I was looking forward to working under both of them because I had a good vibe that I didn't get whilst working in 'B' Company.

Back at the accommodation the boss called all the troops in our platoon together to brief them on what we had just been briefed on. The lads were informed of all the ins and outs - and to be fair - they all acknowledged and recognised the platoon's role and responsibilities for the long patrol to Musa Qala. They also knew it would put us under the spotlight and in the sights of the higher ranks of Charlie Company.

The day came. It was early morning and we were due to leave through the gates at first light. The entire Company came together for a photograph and everyone looked excited and ready. I would be accompanied by a member of the Unit that we were about to replace and he would replace my gunner in the turret for the trip out. His role was to help guide me on the route out and also guide me on the possible threat and ground signs that he had learned to recognise during his time in the country. He had the experience and was almost finished with his Tour of Afghanistan, so he knew what he was talking about. For me though, it would be a steep learning curve because of the lack of pre-deployment training, advice and tactics. This was my opportunity to inundate him with questions - he talked me through a lot of things.

As we left Camp Bastion, I hadn't realised just how big the camp we shared with the Americans and other NATO forces was until we left. The drive out and away from the camp seemed like it took forever. Eventually we hit a road and followed it for a short distance before I turned into the open sandy grounds and headed for a prominent mountain in the middle distance. The mountain was my marker for the trip. If I headed for it, then I wouldn't go far wrong the lad told me as I led the Company.

The trip was scheduled to take around ten hours to cover the distance. The Warriors are heavily armoured yet can easily cope on most terrains they were driven across. They had a decent top speed of around seventy-five kilometers per hour, whether on the dirt tracks and across rough terrain or the road. The Warriors could also continue to match the same speeds whilst towing another Warrior. Each one weighed around twenty-seven tonnes, fully laden with armour and weaponry. It was no match for the Taliban, the Taliban drove about in 4-x-4 vehicles, or on motorbikes.

About halfway through the drive to Musa Qala, one of the Company's Warriors had a serious engine failure. The engine would need to be replaced, which would take all night. This meant we were now spending the night on the ground. I was exhausted after a long drive and leading the Company. Most of my energy had been zapped from the heat and from the concentration required to get everyone to Musa Qala in one piece. Now I had the added job of a two-hour radio and

Warrior sentry on my mind. The sentry would be two hours long and my sentry would start during the earlier hours of the morning. We would be required to keep watch for any enemy movement.

The guard was very difficult. Trying to keep your eyes open when you're shattered is dangerous - you always need to stay focused and alert, as it just takes one mindless mistake and the enemy could be in the camp causing catastrophic and needless damage to life and equipment. The heat coming from the night sight my eyes were drawn to, made me even more tired. Luckily for us it was February and the nights get cold. Nobody would be left on their own during sentry duty in a country like this, there will always be a gunner next to you in the turret. It's not remotely similar to a basic radio sentry, where you could sit in the back of a Warrior, on your own, listening to the communication radio, reading magazines to keep yourself awake.

As a Commander, I was authorised to fire the 30mm Radon Cannon - the main armament of the Warrior - from the Commander's side of the turret. It should only really be fired if something has either happened to your gunner, or your gunner's firing mechanisms aren't working. I have done so though, and many Commanders have also. We can over-ride the gunner and fire at the enemy ourselves. Being in charge, making all the decisions and sitting back while your gunner wipes out the enemy isn't easy to appreciate. You want a piece of the cake, after all, it is your decision for every round that is fired.

My gunner and I had a chart in our turret. We would draw a line for every confirmed kill we got on the Tour. In Iraq, the rules of engagement meant every round fired would be documented and investigated - because of that nobody wanted to fire their weapon because they were worried about any possible repercussions. Finally, though, our Government saw sense and relaxed the rules for Afghanistan, meaning we could now engage a threat if we firmly believed that there was an imminent attack.

With my sentry over, I had two hours left until it was time for stand-to - which was something we did as a Company when we felt we were about to be attacked by the enemy. Again, like Iraq, we had to be prepared to fight at certain times of the morning and the evening. Enemy attacks often occurred during these times, so it was vital everyone was awake and prepared for any outcome. On this occasion, nothing would happen and eventually we set off again. The stricken Warrior had a new engine and everything was sweet and no longer stricken.

The second half of the trip saw us draw closer to that mountain in the distance, but it still remained well out of reach. Some of the terrain became tricky and some of the Warriors, including my own, threw a track in the heavy mud. Throwing a track basically means the track has slipped off the running gear and the wheels and would require to be put back on by hand which wasn't easily done and could be time consuming. When my own track slipped off, it was stuck at an awkward angle and would require every ounce of strength my crew had in them
and anyone else around and available to help that I could muster. The track required dragging closer to the front wheel of the Warrior and then straightened up again. It would need as many hands as possible.

As luck would have it, we had thrown the track outside a compound which was home to an Afghani family. The locals came out and helped us align the track. I instantly sensed that the locals were more pleasant than the Iraqis we often encountered and this immediately felt like it was going to be a better Tour.

With the track back on the Warrior and finally back on the move, the day was passing by quickly. We arrived safely at F.O.B (Forward Operating Base) Eddy where we stopped for a few minutes to rest up ahead of the long drive. F.O.B Eddy was on the outskirts of Musa Qala, so I knew I hadn't too long left to lead before reaching our final destination.

The next part of the drive would be the most dangerous. It required us to travel through an area where many British and American soldiers had been seriously injured or killed by Improvised Explosive Devices (IED's). Fortunately for us though, the route had been cleared and held by the Americans prior to our arrival, so we literally drove straight through but the thought of getting blown up was always on our minds.

We were told about the IED threat; the types and how they were being used, by the Regiment we were to replace. In Iraq they would be set to explode into the side of the Warriors, due to the identified weakened areas and the fact that we were in a built up, more modernised area compared to Musa Qala. So the ground in Iraq was more difficult for the enemy to dig into to lay the IED's - but in Afghanistan the IED became a living horror story for all. With the Country literally made of sand, it was easy pickings for the enemy. The IED's could now be placed into the ground like mines and used in the same way. The threat was huge, and nobody knew where the IEDs were. It wasn't like Iraq. We didn't have the same intelligence that we had access to in Iraq either. It was up to the lads to try and find these IEDs using the limited drills they had been taught with the Valum metal detectors.

We made it safely through the danger zone and to my front, looking down from a high track, I could see our Main Headquarters called DC, (District Centre) based in the centre of Musa Qala and right next to a wady (in some Middle Eastern English-speaking countries, a wady is a dry valley or a ravine - until rainy season). During the dry season the wady would turn into a daily market full of locals selling whatever they had to sell to make a living. We drove down and crossed the large, open wady and then stopped outside of the Main Headquarters. We had made it to Musa Qala, next stop F.O.B Minden, our base inside the village of Yatminshia for the next six months.

CHAPTER NINETEEN
THE FIRST DAY

We finally left the District Centre (DC) and headed the short distance and final leg of the journey, to F.O.B Minden, based in the village of Yatminshia. The light was starting to fade and I was exhausted from the two-day drive to get here. We had a short distance still left to cover and one last obstacle to cross, which was a large area of open ground covered with small stones and surrounded either side of the wady, by old buildings that were made from clay and whatever else the locals used from the ground. The open ground was known for IEDs being hidden amongst it, even though there was an Afghan Army patrol base looking over it. As we approached the wady I was so nervous about deploying my soldiers onto the ground - to walk in front of my Warrior and clear the route with their metal detectors - that I actually felt faint. I could feel myself shutting down and my eyes were desperately trying to close, but each time I managed to fight it off, I had no choice but to stand on my seat and keep my head out of the turret to keep myself focused and awake. Commanding the entire trip took its toll on me. In all honesty, the Company Commander - and even my own boss - could have replaced me with another Warrior Commander during the drive, to give me a break whilst en-route to Musa Qala to help keep me as fresh as they were.

With the dangerous section of the wady now cleared and passed, I called my boys back over and they mounted back into the Warrior. I had chosen to deploy my boys for this stretch because it was ideal to give them more time and experience using the metal detectors on the ground. We continued to our new base and home for the next six months.

As we approached, my Javelin Platoon boss - who was to

be attached elsewhere for the Tour - was standing outside F.O.B Minden awaiting our arrival. It was a bitter-sweet moment for the lads, because the guy was a fantastic boss as well. On arrival, my Platoon Commander was briefed and then told we were to head straight down to F.O.B Yubraj for a week-long rotation. Again, I had to lead the way, the F.O.B was at the furthest point of the enemy line and roughly eight hundred meters away, but out of sight of F.O.B Minden.

F.O.B Yubraj got its name following the death of a Gurkha Soldier. He died during a joint operation with the Afghanistan National Security Force. He was the first Nepalese Gurkha to have been killed since 1999. His unit honored him by naming the F.O.B after him as he had died close-by.

Now under the cover of darkness, we arrived at the F.O.B and pulled our Warriors inside the very small base. We immediately received a brief from the off-coming soldiers from the Unit we were replacing. The brief stated that the Taliban were currently on a three-day cease-fire which had just started.

Cease-fires were always on their terms; they call the shots and usually call them when they have run out of the opium harvested from the wild poppies growing throughout the village. After the brief we finally got our heads down for a good night's sleep. There would be no sentry or radio stag tonight, this was covered by the Unit leaving for home the following morning. My chosen bed would be in the back of my Warrior. I wasn't comfortable with the idea of sleeping on a camp bed in a small, cramped and dark room made from mud. The creepy crawlies over in Afghanistan consisted of massive ugly looking camel spiders and scorpions - therefore I wasn't putting myself in danger by sleeping in their ideal living conditions.

The following morning we were woken up earlier for stand-to. Again, we would have to be ready and prepared to protect the base at certain times of the day, because the base was often attacked during those particular times.

Despite a cease-fire being in place, the goat-raping terrorists were not to be taken seriously. During stand-to, I would be mounted up in my Warrior with my crew. My driver would be sat in his seat, with the engine running, and my gunner would be on his seat scanning his arcs through the sights, with his finger close to the armament switch. I would be listening in on the communications radio and would normally be stood on my seat also observing my front with my binoculars - or smoking my cigarette - stupidly hoping to be a target for a fight.

With stand-to over and the lads we were replacing finally departing F.O.B Yubraj, ready for their long trip back to the U.K, my old boss had also travelled down to F.O.B Yubraj with us for the next few days. We were now, as a platoon, completely alone and into our first real day of Operation Herrick 10.

The entrance to our base was, simply, a piece of sheeting. I didn't like it, I thought it was a little odd and very dangerous considering where we were. I never understood why the place hadn't been reinforced since British Forces took over the compound, given that the base was constantly being attacked. I had my Warrior parked just behind the sheeting to act as protection if anyone fired from that direction. Fair play to my new Platoon Commander and Platoon Sergeant though, they spoke with the Company Sergeant Major about fortifying the base almost immediately.

During the day I would take my Warrior out of the base and push slightly forward of it in a show of force. To show the enemy the new boys in town were here to play. As I was sat out talking away to my crew through the headset, I noticed, far in the distance, two enemy getting off a motorbike. We had tracked them entering the far end of the Village, they had what looked like an RPG (Rocket Propelled Grenade Launcher) and they were running towards us. Monitoring the enemy through our sights, it looked like they were about sixteen hundred meters away, in the far distance.

I knew from all the briefs, that no-one in front of F.O.B Yubraj - and the enemy line that the base sat on - was an innocent civilian. They had all, apparently, left that area of the village when the Taliban arrived quite some time before. I got onto my Platoon Commander over the radio and I gave him a sighting report and asked for permission to engage if the enemy continued in my direction as they may pose a serious threat to my Warrior or the base. He told me to "wait out", meaning he would seek permission from higher and get back to me. A short while afterwards over my radio came,

"Hello Three-One this is Zero, permission to ENGAGE if the threat becomes imminent, Zero out."

Those were words I didn't expect to hear, to be honest. If I had asked that question in Iraq, the answer would have been a stern No!

We lost sight of the enemy due to the amount of derelict compounds and walls forward of our base. Each compound wall had holes in it, purposely made so the Taliban could attack our base from them. Each wall had a name to make it easier for us to identify where the enemy would be firing from during an attack. We had names like Blue door, a lone door - to our front - that was blue in colour and easy to recognise and locate. Then we had other names like swimming pool, this one was a large area which resembled an old outdoor swimming pool. We had others and they all had some easily identifiable themes to them. Some of the other locations that will never leave my mind were, Hell's Gate, Holey wall and the Red iso.

With permission granted, I now had pressure on my shoulders. As I looked back at the F.O.B., everyone in the platoon was up on the roof watching for the enemy and waiting for me to engage. I had the dilemma of engaging and breaking the cease-fire or not firing and hope an attack isn't imminent. Even though I had witnessed the enemy with an RPG - and that is a weapon system not to be messed with. I had no choice but to engage if I spotted them continuing in my direction - because the weapon they were running towards us with could easily cause the lads serious injuries and almost certainly fatalities.

Within minutes of the enemy disappearing behind the walls in the far distance, up they popped again. This time around eight hundred meters away and inside my firing range. The enemy had covered a fair distance in those few minutes since I requested permission to engage - but, to be honest, we couldn't tell what the ground was like further to our front because our sights were nothing like the Hubble Space Telescope. The Regiment we just replaced had never pushed forward past the F.O.B on any patrols, so we had little intelligence other than there were no locals to our front.

With the enemy now firmly in our arcs of fire and with both my gunner and I with eyes firmly on the RPG, it was time to consider whether to open-fire on them and send the fuckers to meet their seventy-two virgins. We did not need to consider too long, because the enemy had clocked that we were watching them. They could see the barrel on my turret pointing straight at them and then they stopped running and started to prepare the RPG - ready to fire at my Warrior - knowing they had been spotted. I gave my gunner the order to engage using high explosive 30mm rounds. He fired three rounds for distance - then I fired three, I wanted some. The lads on the roof did not, at this stage, have eyes on the enemy, but could see the rounds landing - which was weird but likely due to the ground. Adjusting the range slightly, my gunner fired another three rounds at the enemy.

The dust from the impacted area settled and we could no longer see movement. As the enemy were so far away, we couldn't tell if they were dead or in cover because we couldn't quite see how the ground shaped out their end. We required confirmation, via an Apache helicopter. The Apache had the technology to confirm a death. It would be flown over the area of the attack and scan the ground using its thermal imagery system, then either destroy any enemy in that area of interest, or just confirm back to us that there were bodies and they were lifeless. Unfortunately for us though, all the Apaches were deployed on another mission. We never did get our confirmation, so we couldn't draw two lines on the chart that hung in the turret.

All the while I was engaging - back at F.O.B Yubraj, our interpreter was listening in to a Taliban conversation over a scanning radio. The Taliban communicated via their walkie-talkies and the scanner we used to listen in on them had picked up the conversation. The conversation that the interpreter heard went, basically -

"The infidels have broken the cease-fire, prepare to attack."

When I returned to the base and parked up and dismounted off the Warrior, some of the younger lads had glum faces, they had heard what the Taliban had said and it sent shivers down their spines - reality set in. Even my old boss looked uncomfortable and he was a big fucking guy.

It occurred to me that I had in fact broken the cease-fire, yet, if I hadn't engaged when I did the Taliban would have done so. The chatter on the radio was propaganda because they knew that we listened in to their conversations. Anyway, fuck them, with the rules of engagement now relaxed slightly and the fact there were no civilians living to our front, it was game on for me. It was us or them and I was going home in six months' time, but not in a body bag that's for sure.

That was it, the day drew to a close, the first day had been eventful, but tomorrow would be another day and no day is the same on a Tour in a Middle-Eastern country. It was all fun and games that would keep every single man on his toes.

CHAPTER TWENTY
A LONG WAY TO GO

With the ceasefire now well and truly over and the lads within Charlie Company being very inexperienced and young, the Tour was looking likely to become a hard and tasty one for everyone involved. The lads lack of experience meant absolutely nothing at all, with each and every one of them trusted and fully trained. From now on, any attacks or firefights they found themselves involved in, would increase their confidence in their own abilities whilst on the ground - which would only make them stronger, more alert and hungrier to fight the enemy back. The younger boys, like me in Iraq, would quickly grow up and become men.

Now that my gunner and I had taken out the two guys heading our way with an RPG - causing the end to the cease fire - the Taliban were a little more than pissed off with us because they had poppy fields to maintain. Afghanistan has been one of the world's main suppliers of opium since the early 90s. Their poppy harvest alone produces more than 90% of heroin globally and almost all of the heroin inside Europe comes from Afghanistan. Most of the Taliban's cash flow came through the sale of heroin, so it was vital for them to keep on top of their ever-growing supplies. Whenever you see - on the news or read in the papers - that the Taliban are having a cease-fire, you now know why, it's harvest season.

A new Regiment, in any war zone, always makes them a target. Within the first few weeks, the enemy would know all about us. They knew when a new Regiment had taken over a location and they would try their very best to test us, straight from the off and make it difficult for us to settle in. The cease-fire, in my mind, was a way for them to get close to us thinking we would have our guard down being new to the area, so they could slip in close to us and attack our base. This wasn't the case though, because I wasn't in Afghanistan to play nicely. We also knew them, probably better than they knew themselves. I clearly saw them bounding towards F.O.B Yubraj at distance with an RPG to hand. The enemy were set in their own minds to break the so-called cease-fire, regardless, and they could because the ceasefire was set on their terms.

Within the next few hours, the enemy started to attack us from distance using the compounds and walls as cover and firing points. Some of these walls were ten inches thick and extremely difficult to penetrate. With the attacks stepping up on us, the decision was made to hit one of the active firing points - hard. The boss gave the order to one of the boys up on the roof - where we would guard the base from - to prepare the Javelin. The Javelin had been fired just once during the entire Tour of Iraq and within a few days of being in Afghanistan we were about to fire our first.

With the Javelin now prepped to fire, it was in the hands of the Javelin det to lock-on to the target and ensure the enemy were within distance - then BOOM! - off it flew. I was in my turret protecting the base at the gates and all the action was to the front of the F.O.B., so I was missing out - but I had already seen action and was also lucky enough to film the Javelin being fired. The shot itself could not have been any better. I told my gunner, Gollum, to keep his eyes on the area we were covering and I climbed down from my Warrior as quickly as I could, so I didn't get hit by any enemy fire. As I got down, I quickly pulled my camera out and pointed it at the roof just as the Javelin fired. The missile dipped slightly and then rapidly took off, disappearing into thin air. I couldn't see where it was heading as the wall of our base was blocking my view, I did get to hear the Javelin hit its target - and hit, it did.

When the dust from the Javelin's explosion cleared, there was complete silence to our front, the enemy were either dead or had retreated. We were not going to be sitting targets like we were in Iraq; we went there to make a difference for the locals and destroy the scum who were murdering innocent people because of their ideology - which had nothing to do with their faith.

With our first week over, we headed back to F.O.B Minden and joined up with the rest of the Company. F.O.B Minden was a much bigger base than F.O.B Yubraj, Minden's compound was big enough for the Company to reside in, but it was lacking hard cover protection against any incoming mortars, so those who had survived the hammering of Basra Palace felt uncomfortable and unsafe and preferred to live in the back of the Warriors. The buildings were made from hardened mud and well-built, but I doubted whether the buildings would withstand a rocket attack. The accommodation for us though was either eight-man tents or two-man tents. I wasn't sleeping anywhere other than the back of my Warrior. The Warrior was the safest place for me and the back seats were more comfortable than sleeping on the floor or on a camp bed.

The food situation was a complete nightmare for us. There were no chefs provided on the Tour - just a few pots and pans. We were expected to eat ration-packed food for the duration of the Tour. We had the usual ration-packed foods; sausage and beans, beef stew and dumplings and a few other minging meals and I hated the lot of them. We did have a small amount of ingredients which came with the ten-man ration-packs and it contained the ingredients needed to make bread, but no oven to bake it in. There were quite a few Fijians in our Company, who were extremely good at cooking. They taught us how to cook all sorts of delicious and delightful treats - from bread to doughnuts to curries. They certainly knew how to cook. I learned to make naan bread for the lads in my platoon, thanks to Mac-The-Knife teaching me.

As a Warrior Sergeant, I wasn't required to go out on every foot patrol and I would stay back in F.O.B Minden when the lads had left the base on certain foot patrols, with either a driver or a gunner to carry out the maintenance with myself on the four Warriors under my care, so that the Warriors were always in good working order and prepared for battle. I'd also have a tonne of paperwork and documents to go through to ensure the Warriors had their correct maintenance schedules and updated accordingly. I was also required to put in orders for lost or damaged tools, oils and lubricants and anything else like spare parts. I always ensured I looked after my Warriors the same way I did in Iraq, we were dependent on them whenever the shit would hit the fan.

I joined the Armoured Infantry because my theory was.... "why walk into battle when you can drive?..." and I still firmly believe that to this day.

Back in F.O.B Minden, we worked on a weekly rotation of camp guard, patrols and F.O.B Yubraj. Everyone looked forward to F.O.B Yubraj - or fight week as we knew it. F.O.B Minden didn't once get attacked while we were there, it was too far back from the front line to be attacked by the enemy I guess and with F.O.B Yubraj sitting in front of F.O.B Minden it was easier for the enemy to attack that. F.O.B Minden could well have been attacked though, because it was surrounded by other compounds and open fields that had easier access in and out of, but I guess the enemy chose not to – scared of the repercussions.

The guard week on the Rota was a major pain in the arse. Our Sergeant Major was extremely hard on us and all the lads would hate him for it. I understood his theory though, having people constantly whining at you and on your case often got the best out of you, especially when times were hard, and the Sergeant Major was always there to get you through it - and he did. Usually by ordering you to fill the dreaded sandbags that he had a 'thing' for. I understood what it was like to be hated because of the job and the rank you hold and if you weren't hated at least once on that Tour, then you clearly weren't good at your job - or doing it right. Sandbagging became nothing more than a punishment within Charlie Company thanks to the heat.

As the weeks passed, the mortar threat was high, even though we hadn't actually experienced any mortar attacks at this point. The Sergeant Major had gone sandbag mad this particular week; he was like a feminist stuck in a room, surrounded by boxes of man-sized tissues, desperately wanting change. Everything had to be sandbagged and over knee height. As a Company, we must have filled well over a thousand of the fucking things, but it had to be done and he was absolutely right in doing so and keeping us alive.

In Yatminshia there were no flushable toilets and we had to shit in foiled bags. This was a massive inconvenience, but nothing we couldn't adapt to. There were no females with us on the Tour, so the toilet issue was made easier and to be fair to the Sergeant Major, he ensured the Engineers came out and built some basic toilets, so that we could do our stuff into the bags in private. The doors of the toilets became our reading material while peacefully emptying our bowels.

There is an American martial artist called Chuck, who became a legend on our toilet doors as everyone would scribble his best sayings onto the doors like;

Chuck built the hospital he was born in...

When Chuck cuts an onion, the onion cries...

When Chuck crosses the street cars look both ways..

The messages and sayings left on the doors often pissed the higher ranks off due to them losing their morale the higher up the promotion ladder they would climb. To us, it gave us just a little bit of added morale - morale that we didn't have too much off.

In fairness to the lads, whenever times got low and miserable, we always did something to keep us entertained. We built a volleyball court and a gym using things you wouldn't find in your average fitness suite. We also had two laptops that we could use to send emails to our loved ones. This was something new to us - we didn't have these encrypted laptops in Iraq and they were a fantastic boost for morale and so easy to use. A simple log-in and away you ago; the email is printed on the other side, folded and sent as a letter. We knew them as e-blueys and our families did the same back to us making letter sending so much easier and quicker.

We were very limited in what we could do in our downtime and what we had we appreciated. It isn't easy not having a TV to watch, a mobile phone to use or a laptop to access social media, but we got used to it. There was a long way to go on this Tour, but we knuckled down and kept our heads focused on the end goal.

Guard for the private soldiers in the platoon would involve standing in one of the hardened sangers giving over-watch. Commanders would control the guard, ensuring everything ran smoothly. Nobody enjoyed guard, standing in a sanger for two hours at a time - every couple of hours - for a week was depressing and extremely boring. In the day, you'll be on your own too, while trying to stay focused on spotting any enemy activity. Night time would change and we would have two men on guard in each sanger merely to keep each other awake and alert. The Guard Commanders usually sat, bored to death, in the Operations Room while the higher ranks went about their business.

The patrol week was a different story. Every couple of weeks the Sergeant Major would go on a vehicle patrol down to DC in Musa Qala for supplies. Whichever platoon was on patrols that week would go down too. In DC, the main HQ, they had much better luxuries at the base, from toilets and showers, to a television and there was freshly made food. Getting to go down was a definite morale boost for us. The thought of freshly cooked food was enough to put a tear in your eye, after weeks of eating ration packed food.

Other than the patrols to DC, the usual foot patrols would take place with each patrol going no further forward than F.O.B Yubraj. Each patrol would be intelligence led or to gain intelligence. We were trying to gain information on the ground that nobody had yet ventured onto - ready for a planned mission to take the land and push the enemy back, which would happen further into the Tour.

There was always a threat of some kind whilst out on foot patrol - the biggest of the threats being the dreaded IED. We knew that IEDs in Afghanistan had become harder to detect and more sophisticated. Hundreds of soldiers lost their lives to them - or limbs - and suffered serious life-changing injuries because of them. The enemy systematically planted them on ground where they thought we would plan to patrol. They didn't give a shit about the civilians who lived close by. There were lots of young children living behind F.O.B Minden who could easily step on one. They didn't care about their own, they only cared about killing a soldier. There were even children living close to F.O.B Yubraj - not in front - but pretty much level - around 200m away on the same line that we hadn't yet crossed over and those two children and an elderly man were the only known civilians so close to the frontline.

CHAPTER TWENTY-ONE
PENETRATION

As the Tour pressed on, I started to become disheartened about my role within the Company, thanks to the higher ranks making the decisions. I had somehow found myself becoming Charlie Company's lead Warrior Commander and I was always the man chosen to lead the biggest of the missions. It got me down, there were other Commanders capable of leading the missions and all of them were just as good at leading as I was. In a way it wasn't a bad thing, because it would help me to get noticed on my career path but being in a war zone and always the first to lead had its danger. I often thought my Commanders were willing to let me be the first to die because I had led so many missions and patrols.

Being first on any route brought with it a higher and greater chance of being struck by a landmine, a pressure-plate IED, or any IED. A pressure-plate IED is designed to detonate when a heavy object passes over it - like a vehicle. Dependent on how it has been designed, and for what reason and the ultimate objective which would be the weight required to set the IED off. For instance, a landmine will be set off if you step on it but stepping on a pressure-plate IED doesn't always set it off - if it has been designed for a heavy object like a vehicle. Hitting a vehicle will likely result in more damage and cause a greater number of casualties. There are many varying types of IEDs being used against us in the modern world today. Technology and ideology are the biggest threats to this planet and mixing them both together is a recipe for disaster.

For me though, I just got on with whatever was asked of me. I had started to feel disheartened with the sheer amount of work I was doing and the lack of sleep. I had cherished the extra responsibility and gave my all whenever out, on the ground, leading the Company. I knew what it took to stay alive, thanks to the vile enemy of Iraq, they had prepared me to hit every attack and every enemy hard.

It was decided that all the uncovered ground to the front of F.O.B Yubraj - and beyond - would need to be cleared so that the locals who once lived there could return to their homes. In order to start the mission, which would take months of prepping and intelligence gathering, we would require to start slowly penetrating the untouched depths of Yatminshia. We knew, over the weeks of being in Yatminshia, what to expect and what the enemy had in terms of fire power and their tactics. We had some extremely hard fought fire-fights with them and almost every day in F.O.B Yubraj something went down. I would put money on it that almost every man in my platoon had at least one confirmed enemy kill by the end of the Tour.

So, the first objective was given to Eight Platoon. They were given the first major responsibility - to patrol on foot, forward of F.O.B Yubraj and clear the area and the compounds used to attack to us from. As I have said, up until this date, intelligence stated nobody had ever pushed further forward over the enemy line and intelligence also suggested amongst rumors that the compounds were possibly littered with IEDs.

While the patrol took place, my platoon was on rotation and now at F.O.B Yubraj for the week, so we were there to witness the patrol and help if needed. Eight Platoon patrolled over to F.O.B Yubraj before starting the mission, this was their chance to have a quick drink and a piss before moving across. The younger lads in Eight Platoon looked very much up for the mission. Fair play, I was expecting them to be shitting themselves, but they weren't. After a quick stop they left. I was on stand-by for the mission inside the turret of my Warrior in case the shit hit the fan and I was called upon. I had a bird's eye view from my turret. Our Company Commander was also at our location, he was on the roof watching the patrol take place. On the roof was also the FSG (Fire Support Group) - their job was to call in accurate fire support from the artillery based in F.O.B Eddy, they also had the power to bring in aircraft and helicopters, dependent upon the situation on the ground.

As Eight Platoon prodded into the compounds, I stood in my turret, with my headset on, listening in to the action. Within minutes of the lads entering the compound, IEDs were being identified. It wasn't possible to get the specialist EOD (Explosive Ordnance Disposal) teams in to clear the IEDs. EOD are the bomb squad, they are a team of selfless and courageous individuals who risk their lives, getting extremely close to the IED's and disconnecting them - rendering them safe and hopefully allow our intelligence to identify who made them and how they were made. Disabling the IEDs, rather than destroying them, is vital. The intelligence gained from inspecting one IED was unbelievable, but it wasn't my cup tea, I'd prefer to shoot the hell out of them instead as it was a much safer and quicker option.

EOD were unable to make it to Yatminshia and the decision was made to destroy the IED's using a Claymore. Claymores are not designed to be used for destroying IEDs, but they are so dangerous and effective they had to be used because we had nothing else that could destroy the IED effectively. The IEDs were hidden inside of the compounds, so we had to rule out the use of my Warrior's firepower to destroy them.

Claymores are extremely dangerous weapons. Each Claymore is filled with deadly ball bearings and when set off, the blast would head in one angled direction, causing devastating damage to anything within fifty yards of it. The user dictates the direction of the blast by placing the Claymore into the ground using a picket and aiming it at the area required. A wire is placed into the Claymore and then the operator is required to get to cover, as far away as the wire will allow. The wire has a clicker on the end that is used to detonate the Claymore.

With the Claymore set in position, everyone else - bar the lads with the clickers - were told they had to retreat to cover. The order was then given by the Company Commander positioned on the roof and the clickers were pressed. BOOM, the Claymores exploded and destroyed everything in the set direction, including any possible IEDs.

As Eight Platoon retreated from the area, another possible IED had been found. This time outside, in the open and in the ground. They were told over the radio to mark the area and head back to the F.O.B. Over the radio I heard,

"Hello Three-One this is Zero. Over."

I was being called by my Company Commander, I quickly replied,

"Zero this is Three-One, send. Over."

I was then given the order to destroy the possible IED using fire power from the turret of my Warrior.

I told my driver to head over to the area with the flagged, possible IED and we stopped short. I then had permission to engage the possible IED using a 30mm high explosive round. I looked at my gunner when the order came across and he looked at me and we both said out loud,

"What?"

We are trained to fire rapidly into a minefield, using the chain gun, 7.62mm rounds. Taking a shot at a very small object and hitting it with a 30mm round would be some shot, but my gunner always had a good shot in his bag. He once put a 30mm round through the chest of an al Qaeda terrorist in Basra, so I had every faith in him. I gave him the order to fire and he sent shots of three rounds at the target. Each round hit the area - and the possible IED itself - and then bounced off into the wall of a compound right behind it.

When the mission ended, my boss came back from the usual debrief with the news that the IED I had tried to destroy was nothing more than a cap from of a rocket, but I was not to be disappointed, because both the gunner and I had effectively had extra fire practice, which helps to keep on top of our skills and drills in the turret. There is a lot to remember sat in that turret, so keeping on top of things and running through your drills when you can is pivotal.

With the first of the many penetrations into Yatminshia over, it was back to routine for Nine Platoon. We were still over at F.O.B Yubraj on our rotation. F.O.B Yubraj has started to change for the better. A lot of manpower had been used to spruce the living conditions up for us. We had Hesco Bastion barriers placed in front and around the F.O.B giving a meaner look from the outside, but primarily added protection. We also had more protection placed in front of the entrance.

Attacks were still taking place on F.O.B Yubraj. It was early evening and my platoon was preparing for stand-to, as we do every morning and evening, and I had just climbed up onto the back of my Warrior when an RPG was fired at the base. The missile whizzed within a few meters of my face, hitting the upper right sanger on the roof which was manned at the time by one of the more senior lads. Luckily, Stretch - the lad in the sanger was alert and saw the missile hurtling towards him, he immediately dived for cover and survived with zero injuries somehow. Luck was on his side that evening, not many people could survive that, but he did, and he loved it, the usual British soldiers' sense of humour had kicked in but to be fair he was the type to enjoy shit like that.

As the RPG hit the sanger, the force from the blast threw me into the outside of my turret head first. I had to quickly gather myself and re-orientate. My hands felt like they were burning from the heat of the passing missile. I dived inside of my turret, feet first, where my gunner was waiting with his eyes on the sight, I told my driver, Sheep's-Teeth, to pull out at quick speed and head around the rear of the base, then turn left and come up directly in front of the F.O.B. The sheeting which covered the entrance was low enough for our turrets to see over, was still tightly pulled across, blocking our exit. I wasn't in the mood to jump down and move it, my base was under heavy small-arms fire and I wasn't sure if the lad in the sanger was dead or alive. I told my driver to drive through it - and he did, ripping the sheeting clean of the walls and dragging it behind us caught in the armour on the back of the Warrior. We hurtled around the base as fast as the Warrior would move and headed out to the front of the base, passing the spot I had fired at the day before. We pushed forward of the base about 50m. I couldn't push any further because I wasn't sure what may be hidden in the ground, nobody had ever pushed this far forward.

My driver at the time, was serving on his first Tour with my Regiment. I had taught him to drive the Warrior in the build up to the Tour. I had every confidence in him because I had trained him. He was a character and-a-half and no matter where you were, he always had a can of coke in his hand, even in Afghanistan. I wasn't too sure how he would react to the threat from the enemy or the thought of possibly being hit by an IED, but like my gunner, he just kept his head high and got on with it and I was totally confident he was by far the best driver I could have been given. My gunner was the same, he was a little weird in his own way - plus he looked like Gollum from the film Lord of the Rings. He was renowned for falling asleep in the turret and he often mumbled things like ..."my precious..." before being screamed at for sleeping. He was a cracking gunner though and by far the best in my Regiment. This lad had hit things at distance with a 30mm round that would make you think it could only be hit in a Hollywood action movie, he was that good.

As my driver slowed to a halt, the sky was dark, little streaks of light flashed over my turret and into the Hesco Bastion walls surrounding F.O.B Yubraj, those streaks were tracer rounds being fired at us. I still wasn't sure if any of my boys had been hurt in the Missile attack that hit the sanger or if anyone had been shot from the amount of ammunition being fired at the base. The lads on the roof were firing back and giving as good as they received; I was in position, the Warrior was now static, my driver had his hatch closed, my gunner was ready and primed and locked onto a likely firing position that we could see muzzle fire flashing from and then I gave the order to fire. The enemy were about to meet the wrath of callsign Three-One, again!. We hammered round after round of 30mm high explosives and 7.62mm chain gun at them, destroying everything in sight that flashed. I took the initiative to destroy a few compound walls while I was engaging. The area in front of F.O.B Yubraj was littered with rat-runs, blocked by these compound walls, so to take them down limited the enemy's protection. Fuck the enemy, it's us or them.

The attack was over and it all happened in just a few short minutes, time would almost certainly stop when you are engaged in a firefight with the enemy.

Nothing had been said over the radio regarding injuries, so I knew all was good back at the base. I stayed outside in position for a further twenty minutes or so, acting as a sitting duck, hoping for another attack that never came. I returned to our base, the sheeting that once blocked the entrance still caught up in the armour and still dragging behind my tracked vehicle. As I reversed into the base the lads were gathered around a table in the forecourt of F.O.B Yubraj telling their stories of the battle we just had. Stretch, was there looking in great shape after being inside the sanger that got hit by the RPG. Our Platoon Sergeant was frantically working away inside the ammunition stores, counting his ammo and restocking the weapons on the roof and my Warrior.

The battle was a great experience - totally different to the ones we had in Iraq - this battle brought out the team bond within the platoon and the toughest to date. As the days passed, the action slowed, almost to a halt. Some of the lads were asking the interpreters if the enemy were back on a cease-fire. We all hoped for another attack before we switched back to F.O.B Minden on the rotation. The last evening, we were fucking about with a few cylumes, (cylumes are glow sticks) and ended up with one leaking. Suddenly all hell broke loose with them. The entire platoon, bar the lads on the roof, had engaged in a cylume fight. Lads were being covered, head to toe, in luminous poison from the sticks. We had become walking torches and we could probably have been spotted from space, even though we lit ourselves up for the enemy, they chose to stay away, replenishing themselves after being given another kicking.

That evening held so much morale for us but was also dangerous.

CHAPTER TWENTY-TWO
THEN THE LEGEND WAS GONE

My platoon were given the task to patrol down close to the wady, just forward of the enemy line. Recceing the area and the compounds that hadn't been searched yet. The boss had called all the lads in the platoon together, to give his orders for the upcoming patrol. We congregated inside the same tent we used to eat our food because it had tables and chairs, for the brief on the mission which was to take place the following morning. He allocated everyone their jobs for the mission and as usual left me and a driver off the patrol. This was something each platoon did with their Warrior Sergeants. My tasking was as normal; prep the Warriors while carrying out all the required weekly and monthly jobs, then go through the paperwork for each of the Warriors. I always had loads to do and it worked well. It saved the lads having to come back off a long day's patrol and be forced to start working on the Warriors.

Once the brief ended, "H" turned the radio on while one of the lads pulled out a pack of playing cards. The platoon had always bonded closely, compared to other platoons I had worked with. Everyone in the platoon, bar the Platoon Commander and Platoon Sergeant, had stayed within the tent. The band Oasis came on the radio playing their hit Wonderwall, "H" started singing along and the entire platoon joined in. We sung the entire song, start to finish. We weren't quiet either and I was shocked the Sergeant Major, of all people, did not come running into the tent with sandbags to hand shouting,

"Fill these fuckers up as punishment for bonding so well."

The boss actually came back into the tent and told us the Company Commander and Sergeant Major were really pleased to finally see a platoon that had bonded within the Company.

Usually, most of us walked around the place with our heads down low. There wasn't anything to look forward to or do, we were always working, the food was terrible, the drinking water was warm, we had to shit into foil bags. What could possibly make us want to walk about all happy and pretend to be chirpy?

Anyway, later that night I was sat on Noodle-Arms' bed talking to him and Tuna when "H" approached us. "H" had just joined us for the patrol week as he was one of the few snipers within the company. He went from platoon to platoon, on patrol after patrol, week after week. "H" sat down next to Tuna and told Noodle-Arms that he had just been briefed by the boss and he had been asked to pick one lad from the platoon to assist him in carrying out a belt-buckle crawl behind enemy lines and - if required - post a grenade into the enemy's position in the following day's patrol. "H" was always coming up with some crazy conversations, but each one - and the way he would tell us what he was planning - always made us laugh. The guy's imagination was unbelievable but he always said each word with a straight face that had you believing he was being serious about what he was telling you.

At the start of the Tour, I was in the smoking area of our accommodation in Camp Bastion smoking a cigarette and chatting with "H", when two younger boys from Charlie Company - who were on their first operational Tour - came over for a cigarette. "H" told them that the superstore, Tesco, delivered your shopping to Camp Bastion and he was taking orders. He pulled out his notebook and literally started taking food orders from these two young lads, I was in tears, I played my part too, I ordered a few things. It was little things like this that "H" would do that kept your morale up on the Operational Tour.

The morning of the patrol arrived, "H" came to the back of my Warrior where I was sitting filling in paperwork. Ready for my day on the Warriors carrying out maintenance with a driver. "H" handed me his wallet and said,

"Do me a favour Locky boy. If I don't come back, use the money inside to buy every man in the platoon a drink at my funeral."

Those words were fucking harrowing to hear and he just stood there at the back door, with a straight face as usual, telling it how it was - but you always saw the funny side of what he would say. But this time it felt different, like he knew something. I just took his wallet from him like he said and placed it on the side, in the back of my Warrior and continued sorting the paperwork out in the file I had across my lap.

The guys left the base and headed out on patrol while the driver and I started work on the four Warriors we had to maintain while they were gone. Enough work to keep us both occupied for a month. As we cracked on with our tasks, I was in the middle of taking an oil sample - one of our monthly tasks involved taking an oil sample from each Warrior and sending them for tests and analysis - when I heard a loud blast, far in the distance. My heart immediately sank . My boys were out there, in the direction of the blast.

After the initial blast, there came the sound of a massive gun battle taking place around the same area. All hell had broken loose inside the F.O.B Minden - people were running around panicking; the ops room door was firmly closed, and had a sign placed on it telling everyone to stay out and stay away. Something wasn't right. Nobody knew what had happened out there, all we did know was a bomb had gone off and a gun battle was in full swing - and my boys were right in the middle of it.

With no information being leaked, I decided to listen to the radio from my headset in the turret. I was now listening to a massive ambush on my platoon. The enemy had ambushed my platoon, leaving them trapped in a few different locations, but all within distance of each other. One of the Nine Platoon lads had been killed by an IED, but that was all I was hearing over the radio. No names or any real info on what had actually happened. I probably missed the most important parts of the conversation and the chatter was now firmly focused on recovering the body and extracting the lads from the ambush area without any more loss to life.

Spanky, who was serving with Eight platoon at the time, overheard a conversation in the ops room before the door was firmly shut. The initial "H" was heard. Spanky had walked over to my Warrior and told me that someone with that initial had been mentioned as the deceased. I didn't really know Spanky all that well up until that day. He was a forward-thinking lad who always said what he thought, and I liked that about him. He was honest and didn't give a fuck about hurting someone's feelings by telling them the truth. I told him who I thought they were talking about. We both sat on my Warrior, gutted. The "Legend was gone". We were still listening in to the action taking place on the battlefield. We decided that we were going to mount up in my Warrior and head down there to help the lads out. Spanky was going to be my gunner as I had a driver, but no gunner.

The ops room door opened and out stepped the glum Warrior Sergeant Major. He was as white as a ghost, but he quickly briefed up and motivated the Eight Platoon lads who had now stepped up as the Quick Reaction Force. They all mounted up into their Warriors and headed off out of camp in the direction of the fire fight. I couldn't go, I had no gunner, I was gutted. I wasn't allowed to go or gun the Warrior myself.

"It's too dangerous on your own," I was told.

It was wasn't hard to gun on your own if you were confident enough and had a switched-on driver who could think for himself and I didn't need to fire anyway as there was enough fire power now headed to the area, I could have gone as a taxi and collected my boys who would at this point be fighting purely on adrenalin.

So, I was left back at camp. I was stood up high on my turret, like a meerkat on a rock, with my driver continuing to listen and watch what was taking place in the far distance. I couldn't see much, just smoke. A lot of heroes were born that day, but most importantly, a LEGEND was lost.

Eight Platoon, in their Warriors, hammered towards my platoon and successfully recovered "H". His body was collected; brought back to the helicopter landing zone directly outside of F.O.B Minden and laid down on the floor inside a body bag. I could see the body bag from my position. I was heartbroken, everything "H" had been saying overnight as a joke and then when he handed me his wallet, was almost as if he knew his time had come.

With the Warriors now in the battle and smashing the hell out of the enemy, my platoon made a successful withdrawal. They patrolled back to F.O.B Minden with all their might and courage somehow - and I don't know how - but they did. As they entered camp, each and every one of them looked shell shocked and lost, their faces white as a bed sheet. I had tears pouring down my face, I couldn't talk to them, I couldn't look at them, I was gutted I hadn't been on the ground with them but most of all, I felt guilty for not being there with them.

Later that evening I decided to try help the lads stay strong by cooking them a curry - like I often did. I wanted to make sure they had food inside of them because they were still in total shock. With all the adrenaline they had used that day, the lads would need food in their stomach. As I was cooking, one of the lads who was there at the time of the blast and witnessed the death of "H" told me what happened. "H" had, selflessly, put himself in the face of danger trying to get into a better firing position as the platoon came under attack. He stepped on an IED and instantly looked up at the lads, acknowledging what he had just done, and then a Legend was gone.

R.I.P "H"

That night I was sitting in the back of my Warrior alone, trying to forget the horrid events of the day, when I saw the wallet lying there in front of me. I didn't want to touch it, but with all my might I did. I picked it up and headed for the Ops room. The door was still firmly shut. I knocked the door and handed the wallet over to the Sergeant Major. I couldn't really speak, I just said,

"It's 'H's, he gave it to me this morning before he left on his last patrol and said to use the money inside to buy every man a drink if he didn't return."

I then turned around and walked away - weak with emotion, heading back to my Warrior where I stayed until the following day.

During the night I struggled to get comfortable, all I could think about was all the lads that had passed away since I joined the Army. It was nine deaths and all, bar two, was either a member of my platoon or attached to it. It felt like I was being cursed in life for something I had done in a previous one. We still had no help after "H" passed away although there were now improvements put in place that saw certain people being trained to help you after a tragic event, "Trim Trained" we knew it as, but again the lads wouldn't want to open up to them because we all worked together and people would talk regardless of confidentiality. We would be left to push our feelings and compassions to one side for the remainder of the Tour. Because a few of the lads had attended a week's course, it does not make them qualified to be stepping up and giving advice that should be given by experts. Don't get me wrong, advice is exactly that and we all learn to deal with situations differently anyway, but I still think in this day and age the MOD should be doing more on the ground with soldiers after a death, because having the right professional people around you, giving the best help at the time of the incident, would cut down dramatically on lads cutting short their Military careers and being left to struggle in life with the horrors they have witnessed. Possibly taking their own lives, like the SEVENTY-PLUS who passed away in 2018 alone.

It's time for change, soldiers and veterans alike - are being let down by the very people they sacrificed their lives for. Charities are left with the strain, some pick and choose who to support and others are simply overstretched and overwhelmed with the burden.

CHAPTER TWENTY-THREE
THE POLICE STATION

I was awoken in my pit while out cold, dreaming of my beautiful partner. It was very early in the morning and I hadn't long gone to bed, nights like these occurred all the time. You never knew how much sleep you would get from one day to the next. As I opened my eyes, one of the lads on guard at the time kneeled over me.

"Corporal, you're wanted in the Ops room for a brief."

I was still half asleep. All sorts of things rained down and spun around the inside of my head. A brief? I thought to myself. I'd gone to bed having just left a brief. I started to worry, maybe I was being called into the Ops room to be told some bad news from back home - or I fucked up maybe. I gathered my myself and headed over to the Ops room.

As I approached, my boss was outside and several other Commanders were also there waiting. My boss asked me if I was alright and I said yes. He said something had happened in a village some distance away and we may be heading up there to help and that was all he knew. I'd have probably been more up for the mission, but I was still exhausted from the long day before.

My Company Commander walked out of the Ops room and talked to us about the ongoing events in this Village. A Police Station was attacked, leaving everyone inside dead. This wasn't uncommon over here. The Taliban would often attack their own people. We were then told by the Company Commander that we would be travelling to the Police Station at first light - as a Company - to take the building back and provide a show of force in the area to reassure the locals. Eight platoon got the chance to lead the patrol.

First light came, and we mounted up inside of our Warriors and left. I had a good team under me they were a real good group of lads and I couldn't have had any better. My Dismount Commander, Skender, was a mad fucker who would always be smiling whenever you saw him. He had shit-hot skills and knowledge of the ground. In the back of my Warrior, working as my dismount team under Skender, I had a Fijian called Tuna, Wiggy and then there was Neish - we named him "Thursdays" because every Thursday the local Afghan Army would stand outside their base asking us for sex as we passed by - and finally, the last man in the team was our very own scouse wannabe, Noodle-Arms. The lads worked together as a great team and did everything I asked them to do. They just got on with it without moaning. They were the very best I could ask for whenever I called them out from the back of my Warrior to make a safe route through a dangerous location. They did the best job and with my guidance and their skills, we would end up finding numerous IEDs throughout the Tour.

Off we went, one by one in a snake of Warriors twenty meters apart. The dust from the ground rising high enough to irritate us even though we had goggles on. We headed into the heart of Musa Qala and out the other side across the hills, through the mountains and across barren lands. The journey took forever. The ground, although it was firm, had many possible areas that looked like it could be booby-trapped with IEDs.

The longest part of any journey was always down to the lads mine detecting. It wasn't a go-fast solution. If you choose to rush the very drills that you had used since day one, then you would need a long hard look at yourself. You were still alive because of them... It takes one simple mistake out there on the ground and you, or your men, could be going home in a wooden box.

The day wore on, the trip was slow. It wasn't anyone's fault, it was the way of the land. Better to be safe than sorry I often said. We persevered and eventually reached the location late into the afternoon. This was the first big mission I hadn't led the Company on, it was nice to sit back and follow.

As we arrived, I positioned my Warrior at one end of the compound and immediately started guarding a rear entrance to the grounds using my Warrior, all the other Warrior Commanders had similar tasks - all basically securing the building and the compound. I didn't get a chance to enter the building for a nose, but the lads who did told of the horrors they saw,

"There was blood everywhere and it smelt of death,"

one said. The bodies had been removed and buried by the time we got there as it was part of their faith, but the blood was left there, untouched crawling with insects and smelling of death.

Nobody knew exactly what we were expected to do at the Police Station because the attack was over before we had even arrived. I think the message came across that the Police Station was still being attacked and needed support. A message from the Company Commander came across the radio - we were to close all the Warriors into the centre of the grounds and make an all-round defense within the compound itself. Word spread that we would be here for the night and a sentry list was made up to keep watch. While this was happening, I asked a friend to take a photo of me sitting up on my Warrior, my binoculars in hand, watching the most beautiful sunset I have ever seen.

Evening fell, and my sentry came, it wasn't as dark as I was expecting thanks to the low moon shining away in the distance. I had my gunner with me and the conversation didn't really flow as we didn't really have much in common - even though we went to the same high school, but studied in different years, we never really spoke. We always worked well as a team though and I also taught him how to drive the Warrior.

During the guard I was hoping for something to kick off. I thought the enemy would be back to try and kill us - like they often tried back in Yatminshia. They had already killed many people in the building behind me and given where the building and its ground was located, I honestly expected an attack. The enemy dodged us like the cowards they were. I had just travelled an entire day to be here, only for them to hide like goats in the mountains, high on drugs.

The following morning the Company Commander decided there was no point in hanging around any longer - nothing was happening and the enemy was nowhere to be seen. F.O.B Minden and F.O.B Yubraj were both under-manned because of this call out and stretched to their limits. Staying away any longer was pointless and dangerous. Nothing was happening here, so let's fuck off. That's exactly what we would be doing, but this time I had been given the job of leading the Company back. I was asked to get us back as quickly as possible.

I studied my map to work out a route. Do I head back the same way we came, I thought? Is it safe? What will the enemy be thinking? Is this the only way back? Can I make best speed on another route? I chose to go with my head and picked a different route. We didn't have satellite navigational systems to get about - like the ones you have in cars - we used a compass or a GPS handheld device, whichever was your personal choice. I had both, but used the GPS, it was accurate enough with the map, but I ensured that I always had my map in hand.

We headed off through the gates and led the company back to Yatminshia. The drive back didn't take long at all, the longest part of the route was at the edge of Musa Qala, where I had to stop and deploy my boys out onto the ground to mine detect a hundred-meter stretch of road. The road had areas that looked suspicious to me and safety was always on my mind. My lads deployed out, they spread out and led the way. There were plenty of locals about, so I knew there wasn't going to be any threat. If there was, the locals would quickly disperse. They knew if an attack was coming and the sight of them dispersing was a dead giveaway for us.

As the lads on the ground went about their job of clearing a route, as I had asked, I was being pestered to hurry up. I had received a message over the radio asking me to call my lads back to my Warrior and mount up and to make best speed back to F.O.B Minden. We weren't too far away from it either, this was and could well be a deadly route if we choose to ditch our drills. I replied back over the radio knowing full well all the Commanders in my Company were listening,

"This is Three-One, I am the Commander leading. The route ahead doesn't look safe and my team WILL continue until I say otherwise, out."

I had a reply of the Company Commander.

"Three-One, very strong, well done, out."

Again this was over the radio and everyone heard the reply, including the officer trying to rush me and my team through our vital drills.

Eventually I was happy with the ground and the lads had worked hard to clear it. I called them in and we set off for home. We arrived back at F.O.B Minden around fifteen minutes later and half a day early. As I dismounted from my Warrior the officer came over to me and apologised for trying to rush me on the patrol. I explained that even though he felt I was being slow - or over cautious - maybe he should take note of the fact that I had got him back to base much quicker than it took getting there. When I am tasked with leading, I will lead at my pace.

We then continued with the usual taskings following a trip, starting with the maintenance of the Warriors, then crack on with the personal admin which would firstly be to clean our personal weapons. The Warriors always needed love, care and attention, they were big scary monsters to the enemy and if we wanted the enemy to keep being scared, then the Warriors needed to be maintained. After the Warriors were worked on, closed down and all the tools accounted for, I headed for the shower. My weapon I would clean afterwards because I had the rank to do own my thing.

The showers were solar bags that hang up on the wall and were heated up by the sun. It wasn't a pleasant shower, but it was manageable. We just got on with it and sucked it up, because out there somewhere people, have it worse than us.

With the trip over I could finally get my head down and catch up on my much-needed rest. This Tour was becoming a pain in the arse due to the lack of sleep.

CHAPTER TWENTY-FOUR
THE MOVE OUT

Back in F.O.B Minden, the Charlie Company Commander started to get bored in camp with the lack of anything to do. He decided that a mission was required to stem the boredom and capturing the whole of Yatminshia was the one for him. Taking the Village of Yatminshia would not be easy for anyone, a major offensive, requiring hundreds of troops would be required. It would take weeks of planning. If he got permission for the mission and it went well, he would for sure fly up the rank chain faster.

Some of the lads in my platoon hated the thought of taking Yatminshia. Don't get me wrong, we loved a fight, but not a needless fight. If it's not broke, then don't fix it as they say and there was no real need to take the village - there was little benefit to be gained because we hadn't seen one innocent person or family past the enemy line, like the Regiment before us. No other Regiment had previously attempted the mission either. To the lads in Charlie Company it felt like a price was being put on our heads by the Company Commander so that he could get where he wanted in life - and that was up the money tree with the rank. The officers always took the praise whenever the missions went right, yet we were the ones who end up taking the bollockings and the shit when it all goes wrong.

We often left messages on the walls of the toilets, knowing full well the officers would read them. Some examples read :

"MBE's over soldiers' lives..." and

"Soldiers are just pawns on an officer's chess board..."

That's exactly how I felt. I had a family back home that I wanted to return to. I wasn't happy about fighting these needless wars anyway. I am a firm believer that we should be protecting our own Country before invading others - for whatever reasons. I know September 11th was one of the worst and most horrific days in history and the worst terrorist attack ever on allied soil, but invading for one man? Really? Turns out he wasn't even sat in the cave they thought he was hiding in with his five wives and seven goats, but actually living the high life in Pakistan. It beats me how they can find frozen water on mars thirty-three million miles away from the earth, yet between all the intelligence forces joining together - they could not find the most wanted man on earth - who was sitting in his back garden, eyeing his goats up for lunch. I had more sympathy about going to Afghanistan though, the twin tower attack was horrendous. Iraq I did not believe in, not one bit, an invasion dreamt up by two corrupt idiots of power — which has now left the world unable to walk down the road safely without fear of a terrorist attack.

When an officer goes on to do well in their career they usually end up being awarded an MBE, Member of the Order of the British Empire of the Queen, yet we go on and get nothing but grief and bullshit. Most of the sandbag punishments came about thanks to the messages on the toilet walls. They never found out which lads wrote those messages, so every man in each platoon would be punished. If only they had been clever enough to check our marker pens.... My pen loved that toilet wall, it sadly died having run out of ink.

The decision was made to cross the wady on a two-day mission and try to penetrate the village on the other side. Intelligence gained so far suggested that the enemy were, in fact, living comfortably in this particular village and they would attack us by crossing over the wady into Yatminshia. The Company Commander wanted us to push as far into the village as possible and gather as much intelligence as we could. The plan sounded reasonable and very much do-able. At the brief for the upcoming mission I was almost certain I would be leading the mission and was prepped and ready for it; however, I wasn't leading. The job to lead the Company was given to Drugs who was attached as a Warrior Commander to Seven Platoon who would come across from Javelin Platoon to fill the manning gap. For once I was actually looking forward to leading this mission. I had led so many missions up to this point that it had become natural to me to be given the lead over everyone else. This mission could be tasty as well, so everyone wanted the lead. There was every chance of being in a fire fight and being the first vehicle into any area you had more chance of a piece of the action.

The day of the mission arrived. Seven and Nine Platoon would be heading out with two vehicles from HQ carrying the Company Commander and we had a recovery vehicle and the Sergeant Major's Ambulance. We had enough Warriors for this patrol to scare any enemy. There was a problem though - with a large number of Warriors this big and long - noise pollution from the engines. One Warrior, alone, is deafening - but imagine twelve? Even Bin Laden could have heard the engines from his home in Pakistan. Eight Platoon would stay behind in F.O.B Yubraj and some soldiers from another unit would arrive to take over and protect F.O.B Minden while we were away.

We headed out of F.O.B Minden with Drugs leading the Company. The journey was potentially a long one, it required good leadership to cover the open ground without allowing the enemy to click on to what we were up to. Fair play to Drugs for stepping up to the challenge, he led the Company through Musa Qala, across the Wadi, past F.O.B Eddy and into the open desert. The route he chose would have looked to the enemy like we were heading back to Camp Bastion.

This was a diversion tactic. The enemy knew when we were due to change over with the new unit after our Tour finished. So to head in that direction after only a couple of months would confuse them.

Having travelled across the desert for a few hours, we came to our stopping point - known as the "RV" point (rendezvous point). At this point, we would break off in our platoons and use the high ground overlooking the villages to conduct some intelligence gathering as we had been instructed during missions brief.

I led my platoon onto some fantastic high ground that gave views as far as the eye could see and we stayed in position for a short while observing. I then decided to head for another area close by. We penetrated deep inside another village with myself in the lead position. Nothing happened, I was expecting to encounter resistance or hostility. We drove into the village and did what we were instructed to do and again nothing happened. The enemy were once again lacking the balls to fight face to face, mind you, I wouldn't want to fight me, not in a Warrior anyway.

The first part of the mission was more than successful. After a few hours of probing, we headed back to the RV point and met back up with the company, ready for the next stage of the mission.

I wasn't sure what the next mission would be, I was half expecting to chill in-situ for a few hours as we had been going non-stop all morning - since first light to be precise. We weren't going to be chilling for long as it was go, go, go for the next mission. The next objective was to push on deeper and get an over-look of another village - which was next to the village in question - from higher ground – we would be entering that village tomorrow. Again I was given the mission to lead. I looked at the map and the ground looked extremely challenging to get around safely and out of sight.

The idea is to keep the vehicle on low ground as far as possible by sticking to the bottom of hills, mountains, dried out ravines or anything low enough but out of sight of the enemy in the hope of confusing them regarding where we were actually heading and how big we were as a Company of men and Warriors.

I studied the map long and hard. I couldn't find a route through the area without exposing myself and the other Warriors. The terrain looked tough, but this was the sort of mission I cherished. I headed off and the remainder followed on. I drove for hours; heading in and out of the hills, up and down dry river beds, I didn't want to give this mission away. The noise was the biggest give away but if you can't see where the noise is coming from or what the noise is then it's harder for enemy to act and therefore we win the element of surprise.

Around two hours into the journey I could tell that my Company Commander was getting annoyed with my route choice, I had no other option but to use the route I had chosen as it wouldn't expose the Warriors. The tone in his voice had changed over the radio, he was getting frustrated with my route. Any fool could tell the journey would be difficult. I, for one, was not a short-cutter and they knew I was solid with my decisions. I told him - numerous times - over the radio, that we were heading for the best location and we would be where we needed to be shortly.

Finally, all my hard work paid off. I found an opening through this maze of hills and we came out to the most amazing view I saw during my time in Afghanistan. The village in question was below us, we could see everything we needed to see, the spot was fantastic, and I was very proud.

We stayed in-situ for a few hours observing the locals going about their business from above. The locals, I guess, must have seen us sitting on the high ground, but nothing happened. I was always anticipating the worst to happen as

Iraq had scarred me for life. I guess looking back, I was suffering from post-traumatic stress disorder, but it wasn't something I could tell anyone, not in this line of work. After nine deaths and having carried two of their coffins - there was no wonder.

We left the area after a few hours and headed for a piece of ground just outside the village we had just over-watched. We would hold up for the night at this location and prepare for tomorrow's mission. When we arrived at the night's location, the ground was very rocky and again the lads had their reservations about staying here sleeping on the ground. The ground was hard, we would need to dig a shell scrape by the side of the Warrior for the lads to sleep in.

The shell scrape should give them some protection in the event of a mortar attack. We dug the shell scrape out - each Warrior doing the same - time was passing and it was getting dark extremely quickly. We managed to get the job done in time for food because when the lights go out at night, they stayed out. For the smokers like me it was a pain in the arse, although it wasn't too bad in the turret because you could get away with using a lighter and puffing away without anyone seeing the light.

The usual routine kicked in. Warrior sentry for the Commanders and ground sentry for the lower ranks. My duty - again - was in the shit hours. I had thought I might get a decent shift, considering I did my share of the leading that day. But it didn't work out that way. Everyone did a shift, including the Company Commander and Sergeant Major, so fair game. My shift was a nightmare though, again I had my gunner with me for Warrior sentry. Around half way through the precious - small - amount of sleep I had before my duty, the heavens opened. Pouring rain hammered down onto the lads sleeping outside the Warrior and into the freshly dug shell scrapes. I had to wake them and tell them to get inside my Warrior they were that tired they hadn't noticed themselves becoming soaked; we were all drenched top to bottom and I no longer had a bed. Everyone squeezed tightly into the back of my Warrior and we slept side by side.

I was awoken for my sentry duty; the rain was still hammering down and there was no sign of it easing up. The sentry Warrior was about fifty meters away, so I was definitely getting wet. I headed over with my gunner, I couldn't run, it was too dark, and the ground was unsteady under my feet. Also, the rain which was running away under my feet felt quite strong, I didn't want to get washed away by taking the wrong step. I ended up sitting in the turret for two hours, freezing cold. I sent my gunner across to wake the next team up for their shift ten minutes before theirs starts and ours finishes. He was gone over half an hour because he had got himself lost and struggled to the find the Warrior with the next team in. When he finally returned with the next Commander and Gunner - over twenty minutes after our shift had ended - the rain had finally stopped. It was still extremely dark and we still couldn't see. We had around an hour and a half before the sun started to rise, so we didn't have much time left to sleep. We walked back to our Warrior, but we struggled to find it, my gunner was lost again and so was I. We became a little disoriented due to the darkness and ended up walking into the recovery vehicle which was located centrally. Luckily for us, from there, we were able to work out where our Warrior was located and managed to find our way back to the Warrior. By now, we'd lost over half hour of valuable sleep.

CHAPTER TWENTY-FIVE
THE FIRST

As the sun rose, I had been given the task to lead the next mission into the very heart of the village in question. The village overlooked Yatminshia from across the wady, all the current intelligence we had gained over the months of our Tour pointed to this particular village being the main location of the enemy.

"This isn't going to be an easy mission," said the Company Commander. "It will take only the best leadership, command, team work and determination to succeed."

I wasn't worried about the mission though, yesterday I had led the Company into the surrounding areas of the village without even a sniff of action, why would the Taliban try anything today?

After a quick look at my map I decided to swing into the village using the low ground as best I could. I wanted to give the locals and the enemy the element of surprise. We weren't going to the village for a fight, we were going to gather intelligence, ready for the big push to take control of Yatminshia, our own village, in a months' time.

I set off into the hills, the ground was ideal for the Warriors to drive on, the weight of the Warriors lifted the dust off the ground high into the air that could be seen for miles. I continued snaking in and out of the hills, keeping to the lowest parts of the ground. Every track I took and every turn I made, the remainder of the Company's Warriors would follow. The Warriors behind mine would stick to the same tracks made by my Warrior, because my tracks were safe to use. Going off track could be dangerous. IEDs were cleverly hidden and the enemy had a great understanding on how to best use them against us. They knew the land better than we did, they knew the ground, they knew every track and hill top too, they had the upper-hand on us. For us, it was a game of minefield and chance, you had to carefully look at the ground as you headed towards it. You would be looking for ground signs that did not look right to the eye; like fresh soil sitting on top of old soil; objects left in places you wouldn't expect them to be, wires protruding out of the ground - anything that stood out was a risk and would require clearing.

I hated the thought of sending my boys out on foot from the safety of the Warrior, but the possible threat had to be checked, it was part of their job and a proven tactic that has saved countless lives. One type of IED - the command wire IED - was purposely made to be set off by hand, from a distance, like the Claymore. Whoever placed the IED could then set it off whenever they wanted to, or when the target was positioned closely to it. The IED would be set into position and a long wire placed into it and dragged as far away as needed. The IED would then need to be well hidden, including the wire, because a wire on show from the ground is a giveaway. I always worried that if my team ever found a command wire IED, then the enemy may well set it off on them if they were watching.

The lads were well aware of the IED threat, they also knew their jobs and what it took to stay alive. I continued to snake in and out of the hills looking for threats and every time I come across a threat on the ground that I wasn't comfortable with - on the route I had chosen - I would deploy my lads onto the ground to check the area in question. My lads had already found countless IEDs inside the Village of Yatminshia and most were found hidden between F.O.B Minden and F.O.B Yubraj thanks to me spotting the ground signs from my turret in the armoured Warrior. Nobody had yet found a command wire IED though, the easiest of the IEDs to find using the equipment we had.

As I made my way towards the village, I had only one narrow track with a small bridge left to cross. The bridge was the only way into the village. It wasn't a bridge you would see in everyday life, it was a very small bridge with a rhyne running underneath it. It was a possible rat-run for the enemy, who could use it to move about unnoticed. I deployed my boys onto the ground and gave them the order to sweep the bridge for any possible mines and IEDs that could compromise the mission. They went to work clearing the bridge for my Warrior and the rest of the Company to pass over safely. Thursdays, Noodle-Arms, Tuna and Skender were my team on the ground for the mission. When the sweep was complete, the boys mounted back up inside my Warrior ready for the final push into the village.

I quickly took another look at my map to be certain that there wasn't another possible route out if the worst was to happen whilst inside the village - there wasn't one. It was exit the way I had come in. As I moved off, nervously, I was aware of people sitting up on the high ground, watching my every move. We knew these people as "dickers". Dickers would sit on the high ground and watch us pass by, then they would pass on the information to the rest of the enemy. This information could be used to spring an attack on us, or simply to make the enemy aware we were advancing and giving them time to escape the area or hide any weapons.

There was nothing we could do about the dickers, other than carry on with the mission. I continued moving forward, the ground opened up as I turned the first corner and soon I was in the centre of the village. Our interpreter who was sat in the back of our Company Commander's Warrior during the mission, had a scanner to listen to the chatter and activity over the enemy's airwaves as we passed through. The enemy were now talking and the dickers I had spotted as we made our way into the village, were indeed passing on our details. They could be heard giving us away to the enemy. The enemy now knew what was heading towards them and how many Warriors there were.

Over the scanner, the enemy were trying to devise a plan. They had not anticipated us turning up without their prior knowledge and the order was given to fire the rockets. We took this as a mortar threat, but also with a pinch of salt because they were known to say things over the radio that never materialised.

I continued pushing forward and soon enough I was at the village's furthest point. I was at the edge of the wady and I could see F.O.B Yubraj in the far distance. I was extremely high up overlooking the wady, it would not have been possible to drive down into the wady if anything happened. The enemy were still talking about the rockets, yet nothing was happening.

I had successfully gained access to the village and all the Warriors were now in. We hit no snags on the way in and it was easier than we had anticipated, but things were about to change - drastically.

The rockets the enemy had spoken about started landing around us, one narrowly missing one of the Warriors in my platoon. The mortar almost hit callsign Three-Two. The rocket landed inches from the rear of the Warrior sending mud, stones and debris from the impact hurtling towards the Warrior. We had to start moving and get our Warriors to cover. We needed ground where the enemy couldn't see us, but it was impossible because we had too many Warriors in the same area. We were sitting ducks and too close together. We were, however, safe inside the Warrior; the armour would protect us if struck, but we didn't want to take the chance.

Being the Commander furthest forward and with eyes on the whole of Yatminshia, I was now desperately trying to pinpoint the location that the mortars were being fired from. The enemy required a good amount of distance between us and them, so the only real alternative for them was to cross the wady back into Yatminshia and fire the rockets at us from there giving them an increased chance of hitting us.

I couldn't locate the firing point, the lads in F.O.B Yubraj had also been trying to spot the firing point from their location on the other side of the wady. They, themselves, soon came under direct fire from the rockets. I wasn't convinced the rockets were coming from Yatminshia, but looking at the map, it was the only viable location. My Company Commander radioed his decision to withdraw all our Warriors from the village. I was furthest forward, so it would be hard for me to lead from there. I got on the radio and told him to let me lead out, but I was told a stern no, there wasn't time. Seven Platoon were the closest Warriors to the bridge and to safety and were given the task to lead us out.

While I was waiting for my call to leave the area, I noticed I was surrounded by landmines protruding out of the ground - everywhere I looked. My driver had driven straight into a minefield while trying to find a safe area during the mortar attack. Neither of us had spotted the mines due to the dust that had risen from the exploding rounds hitting the floor all around us. Luckily, we hadn't hit any, otherwise God knows what would have happened to us or the Warrior. With the Warriors being so heavy and the ground being pretty much dust, they left track marks and this was my lifeline. I had to stand up with my head on show to the enemy. I had no choice, I had to get a better view of the ground behind so I could command my driver out of the minefield, safely sticking to the tracks we made on the way into the minefield.

I had a different driver for the mission - Onion. My usual driver had left for home on leave (R&R), each man would be granted ten days' of leave during the six-month Tour and the lads leaving for home had already left when our Company Commander decided to carry this mission out. The Company Commander knew we were short of man-power but decided to take the mission on anyway because he was confident in the men he had. My new driver was experienced enough. Again someone I had taught shortly before the Tour had started. It was easier for me to have the boys I had taught, because they knew how I worked and what I expected - which was high quality performances.

We managed to reverse out of the Minefield safely and headed out of the village in the same direction by sticking to the tracks that we had made. The bridge was now in sight and I knew after crossing over it we would be back in the safe zone. As I was heading out - last, but one Warrior - the mortars were still landing around us. The sky had again opened, rain started pouring heavily down on us. My sights were dirty and clogged from the dust, mud and debris that had hit my Warrior from the impact of the mortars, so my vision was extremely poor. I stood up once again, putting the top of my head slightly on show, as I helped direct my driver out by guiding him along the tracks. As we neared the bridge, there was a small queue of Warriors waiting their turn to cross. I told my driver to slow down leaving enough distance from the Warrior in front. For some reason, I started singing,

"It's raining men...." because it was the only rain song I could think of at the time.

The bridge was now clear to cross and we headed towards it. As we drove over it - still singing - an almighty "BOOM" sounded from below, followed by the rapid shaking of the Warrior. I was being shaken and thrown about my turret with extreme force and there was black smog everywhere you looked. I instantly realised that I had just been hit by an IED - the first.

CHAPTER TWENTY-SIX
NOT AGAIN

My Warrior was badly damaged by the IED. The first thing I was required to do as a Commander was to send a contact report over the radio to alert all of the other Warrior Commanders of my IED strike. Although the sound of the blast gave it away, not everyone would have heard it or realised what it was.

"Charlie-Charlie-One, this is Three-One. Contact IED wait out,"

I said in a calm manner.

With the contact report sent and everyone now aware of the IED strike, I had to check my boys to make sure they were okay and not injured. I had my driver, who I couldn't see, sat forward left of me in a hatch. My gunner was sat next to me and also a four-man team sat in the rear of the Warrior. I was responsible for their safety. I screamed down to the rear of the Warrior asking the lads in the back if they were okay. They were, they quickly replied thank goodness. I looked across at Gollum and he was okay, but shaken up like me, I heard Onion, my driver, shouting up from his driver's compartment to make me aware he was okay. Relief flowed through my body.

My next job was to send a sit-rep over the radio.

"Hello Zero, this is Three-One, over."

Zero quickly replied, "Zero send, over."

"Three-One roger, Reference IED strike, damage currently unknown, NO CASUALTIES, over."

With the sit-rep sent, I was not able to dismount my Warrior and check for damage until I had protection from all the other Warriors on the ground. Unfortunately for me, there was only one Warrior behind me and being hit on the bridge prevented the other Warriors re-crossing it to give extra cover and support from the enemy side.

As my adrenaline cooled down, I started to feel a sharp pain in my neck, I wasn't sure why, but I was thrown around extremely hard. My gunner was also starting to ache, then Noodle-Arms started to feel pain and discomfort in his shoulder. Our adrenaline had kicked in the moment the IED struck, so our injuries were hidden and it was only after things had started to calm down that we started to feel uncomfortable within ourselves.

I stood up on my chair, with the top of my torso out of the turret. The dust had settled and I could see the full damage caused to the top of the engine area by the blast. There was now a large crater in the earth underneath where the engine is located, on the front right-hand side, from where I was looking. The IED had hit us hard, but luckily the engine took the full impact of the blast. I was listening over the radio, waiting patiently for a plan to be drawn which would give me and my Warrior protection, in order to start prepping the Warrior, ready to be recovered. I was desperate to climb down from my stricken Warrior and assess the damage but couldn't do anything until the protection was put in place. Everything seemed to be moving slowly - almost like time had stopped.

The plan was finally given. Seven Platoon were ordered to move up to the high ground, to ensure a good, clear view of the ground around my Warrior whilst also giving everyone lower down protection from above and keeping one eye out on any enemy activity from the village we had just left. The remaining two Warriors in my platoon had spread out, one behind me and the other to the side of me in the best position he could achieve despite being on the other side of the bridge. My Company Commander and the Sergeant Major both moved their Warriors as close to mine as they could. Again, to give me and my Warrior more protection so that as soon as everyone was set into position, I could dismount my Warrior and finally assess the damage.

As I waited for the Warriors to move into position, I sat silently in pain, suddenly I heard another BOOM!. I instantly thought to myself,

"NOT AGAIN!!!"

This time the sound came from the high ground where Seven platoon were heading. Seven platoon's Commander had just driven over another IED and the Warrior was totally destroyed. I say another IED because he was the lead Warrior for the withdraw from the village and the first one over the bridge. His Warrior - and all the others out on the mission that day - would have also driven over the IED that took my Warrior out. His driver was injured in the IED, the blast ripped a hole through the armour underneath where the driver's feet were located. A message came over the radio that the driver had suffered serious legs injuries and a rescue helicopter was called in to evacuate him back to Camp Bastion for treatment. He was lucky that day as there was nothing seriously wrong with him.

Now there were two Warriors badly damaged, but only one recovery team. I wasn't too worried though because our REME lads were the best I had worked with during my time, so I knew they could sort this problem out quickly and calmly. The plan had to change for a second time. While I was waiting for plan B, I was looking at the blast area around my Warrior trying to figure out how I was hit, when I realised the IED was actually a command wire IED - some of the wire from it was still on the track. The remaining wire headed down the rhyne, roughly a hundred meters away. At the end of the rhyne there was a small hut with a hole - smaller than your average window - directly facing and in line with the bridge. The bastard who set the IED off did it from that hut and was probably still hanging around inside it. What made things worse for me was the fact Seven platoon had just led the company out over the bridge and physically stepped over the wire, missing all the ground signs of an IED that had probably been laid minutes before. The mine detector would have signaled the wire, the IED should have been found. The boys, through no fault of their own, had missed all the clues.

Prior to the start of the Tour we had missed out on vital training. My team and I led almost every mission, my team and I were the only ones to find any IEDs.

Thinking it through, I was relieved the boys didn't find the IED for many reasons. Firstly, the person who caused the explosion had eyes on the bridge and if he saw the lads find the device, he could well have set it off - killing them. Secondly, the EOD would have to be called out, meaning we would be stuck in-situ for as long as it took them to arrive. On my previous IED find, we had to wait for them to arrive for over twenty-four hours, so this, for me, was out of the question. I would prefer to just shoot the thing and be done with it, fuck waiting in a dangerous location so they can save the device for clues.

The new plan was put in place, this time the effort was to drag my vehicle off the bridge and leave it - with myself and my boys still inside - on the open ground with no engine, damaged tracks and no fire power other than a few hand grenades and our personal weapons. But we would have the other Warriors forming a defense in the area, so the recovery boys could get to work assessing the other damaged Warrior and get it moved before returning for mine.

My track was blown upwards and jammed amongst the road wheels and my engine had been forced upwards sustaining further damage from the heavy decks that protected it. The damage was very noticeable and I could clearly tell the Warrior required some serious work done to get it back up and running again. The work couldn't be done on the ground, on location. The Warrior was too badly damaged, and the enemy threat was real, so the Warrior would need to be towed back to the closest camp to be repaired if it was possible, which would be F.O.B Eddy.

I had to help the recovery lads figure out a way of freeing the jammed track before the Warrior could be towed off the bridge. I wasn't in the best of health due to neck pain, but I got on my hands and knees and helped remove the track. We broke the track down into small parts and placed them up into the Warrior wherever we could fit them. The track is extremely heavy, so had to be broken down into small sections. With the track sorted we attached the tow ropes and we were dragged off the bridge. We were dragged around fifty meters and left on the open ground. The recovery section then left for the high ground to start again with the next stricken Warrior.

My Warrior's back door was damaged in the blast and having no power it was difficult to open, so the lads struggled to open the door for a breather. They had to manually open it using a turning handle which took a lifetime to open. They did get it open, but not for long because no sooner had the door opened we came under attack from small arms fire and a sniper. The recovery lads now had to try and recover the Warrior on the high ground while being shot at. They were in the open too, but higher up. There was no cover for them to work on their own vehicle and the shooters knew it.

The enemy would move locations; pinging shots one after another at them. My Company's Second in Command (2IC) came onto the radio telling everyone where he thought the enemy was firing from. He told us to watch his "tracer", which meant he would be firing a tracer round at the target that we would all now be able to see and identify. The round is covered with a burning powder for this very reason. However he wasn't shooting a tracer round - which he would have had loaded into his 7.62mm chain gun ammunition trays with one tracer to every four or five rounds - instead he fired a fucking flare which tend not to fly in the direction you fire them.

Back down at my location, all the Warriors surrounding and protecting us were engaging into the likely firing positions hoping the shooters were in them. They did this because the sniper was well hidden and nobody could identify his position. My Warrior was a sitting duck, my engine was fucked, my weapon system was fucked and all me and the lads could do was watch and hope we get recovered quickly.

The hours were now passing by and I was desperate for a poo. I had no chance of getting out of my turret without being shot. I couldn't hold my bowels any longer and had to have a shit inside my turret knowing my gunner was sat next to me. I grabbed a shit bag, apologised to the lads in the back and emptied myself. Instant relief. With the dump over, I sealed the bag and slung it out of the turret as far as I could throw it without showing myself to the sniper. The lads in the back were trying not to be sick from the foul smell of my arse. They couldn't open the back door wide enough to let the smell out either.

The guys up on the hill assessing the damage to the other stricken Warrior sent a report to the Company Commander basically saying that due to the damage, it would take all night to prepare the Warrior to be towed back to safety. With the sniper still taking pot shots at us, an Apache Attack helicopter was called in to help identify the sniper. I can't remember if the sniper was killed, but I remember the Apache firing a few times and I know those bad boys don't usually miss. Everything went quiet when the Apache arrived, they are scarier than a tank when they are hovering above your head. The enemy would be super stupid if they attempted to take one of these down without the right equipment.

As the hours passed, darkness fell and my Warrior was still a sitting duck. We wouldn't be moving tonight, so we had to come to terms with that fact. We were stranded. It was a horrible feeling being left in the damaged Warrior. I know we had other Warriors alongside us, but we were still left feeling nervous. Both mine and the gunner's night sights were working thankfully, but the turret was fucked, it couldn't turn at all, so we just sat there all night looking in one direction, preying we weren't ambushed.

The next morning the Warrior on the hill was finally ready to be dragged back down to safety. All that was needed was to hitch my Warrior up and off we go. With both the stricken Warriors suffering serious damage it wouldn't be as simple as just hitching up the Warrior to another one - like they are designed to do - the Warriors required as much pulling power as possible to drag the vehicles out of the area.

Overnight, the Company Commander had asked to have the stricken Warriors destroyed rather than recover them, but permission was denied. In the end four Warriors hitched themselves together to tow my Warrior and another four did the same for the other Warrior and we crawled back to F.O.B Eddy at a snail's pace.

Back in a safe camp and feeling lucky to be alive, I was interested to know why the lads didn't find the command wire that resulted in my Warrior becoming the first in my Company to be blown up. One of the lads in Seven Platoon - who was attached from Javelin Platoon for the Tour - told me straight when I asked him. He said,

"We didn't see any wires, the detector did make a noise, but we weren't too sure what the noise setting was."

This was an instant giveaway that the lack of training could have been fatal. I went across to moan at my Company

Commander, I blamed him for not letting me and my team lead back out, but he told me to wind my neck in and get on with it. Who was I to moan when he's the guy in charge and making the crucial decisions? His job was hard enough without me moaning at him and I respected him for it because he was damn good at it and had made the right call on the day. I was too far forward to lead the Warriors out. I would have needed to head back the way I had come in - overtaking at least ten Warriors, creating new tracks and possibly forcing my boys out onto the dangerous ground from the back of my Warrior to clear the new tracks we would make - which was time consuming - and time was against us as there were mortars being fired and landing all around us.

I was later told that both Warriors were written off, so I had to remove all my possessions and kit from of my Warrior. My baby was dead - NEWPORT was dead, I was gutted, but at least it wasn't my fault and nobody was seriously injured either – so we thought. I transferred all the kit over with the help of the lads in my platoon. Noodle-Arms had gone across to see the on-site medic about his shoulder pain and I was hoping to do the same, but I didn't get the chance.

My team had gone through hell the past few days. Trapped in the back of the Warrior, no way of seeing what was going on around them, they had very limited information relayed down to them as I didn't want them panicking or freaking out. I guess they managed to cope so well because they knew the reason they were trapped and they were switched-on enough to stay focused. We worked well together as a team and they had trust in me as their Commander and I trusted them back equally. They were my boys for the duration of the Tour, every patrol I led, they played a pivotal role alongside me.

CHAPTER TWENTY-SEVEN
THEY WAVED

After we returned back to F.O.B Minden, my neck had stiffened up to the point where I could no longer turn my head in comfort. I would need to see a doctor. We had limited medical care at either F.O.B with just one medic looking after each one. There was access to a Doctor, but he was based back at District Centre in Musa Qala and again he had limited equipment and resources. To have my neck properly checked out I would need to be flown back to Camp Bastion - which wasn't going to happen. I had a job to do, I had become a valuable asset within my company. The Yatminshia mission was on the horizon and we would require every man we had available.

I did travel down to DC thanks to the Sergeant Major and his usual resupply trip. The Doctor examined my neck, said I had minor whiplash and gave me a box of co-codamol tablets to help keep the pain at bay. He agreed that I would be fine to continue patrolling outside of base, but as a Warrior Commander only. Noodle-Arms was in a similar position to me. Both of us were taken off foot patrols for the rest of the week and left behind to recover. We felt useless. Although I did not go out on foot patrol that often normally, it was still a kick in the teeth because after "H" passed away I wanted to be out with them.

My leave wasn't due until mid-July but a good mate of mine in the platoon, Will, who was one of our Javelin Det Commanders and the same rank as I, had asked me if I would like to swap leave dates with him. I could not say no to his offer and I was now going home a month and a half early. I would be home for my 27th birthday.

I boarded the helicopter with Spanky, my boss and all the other lads flying home together on the same leave. We took off for the twenty-minute flight back to Camp Bastion and took in the beautiful scenery as we flew in a Sea-King helicopter. We landed safely, and I flew back home to the UK forty-eight hours later.

When I returned, ten days later, to RAF Brize Norton for my flight back out to Afghanistan, all the lads had also arrived back looking re-energised and fresh. We flew out to an American Military base in Abu Dhabi for our connecting flight. The base was massive. The sun was the hottest I had ever felt it. We were held in a holding room before our flight into Helmand and the air-con in the room was nonexistent.

I was sitting with Spanky at the far end of the room chatting about our leave, when an Australian officer - who was attached to our Army - came into the room. Out of the corner of my eye I could see him eyeing people up, I knew what was coming. The RAF didn't have their own baggage handlers, so the lads on the flight would be chosen to do it. The officer was on the hunt for slaves and I, for sure, wasn't going back outside into the heat. He marched across the room and stopped in front of Spanky and I. He looked at Spanky and told him to go outside to help with the baggage. He had spotted my rank slide on my chest when he marched over, so I was ignored. Spanky wasn't happy with him, he told the officer that he wasn't going anywhere and to fuck off and pick someone else. Spanky explained to him that he felt deliberately picked on because the room was full of soldiers and yet he chose to ignore them and walk the length of the room over to him. I was crying inside at Spanky saying it how it was. He was right though, he did single him out. The officer took Spanky's name and then asked for mine. I asked him why he wanted mine and he said that as a Corporal I should have backed him up. The stuck-up prick wrote a letter of complaint to our Company Commander.

Back at Camp Bastion, we had our usual brief on return from leave and I was told I would be commanding another Warrior to F.O.B Eddy with the Royal Logistic Corps, who would be travelling there in a few days' time on a resupply mission. The Warrior was for my Company - and possibly for me - as mine had been badly damaged by the IED. I didn't want any other Warrior, I wanted my old one back.

Spanky was warned that he would be my gunner for the trip and Bey would be my driver. The Warrior itself was in shit state; all the armour was on pallets next to it and it would need a hell of a lot of work carried out to get it prepared for the journey. We worked almost every spare hour over three long days, trying to get the Warrior ready and we just about succeeded before we left on another long journey.

I had attended numerous briefs with the Royal Logistic Corps who I would be Commanding the new Warrior with, but none of them sounded confident at their own jobs. They kept repeating the same mission over and over again. I think I attended three briefs on the move out and it was the same brief, repeated each time. Anyone would think this was the first time they had ever left the safety of the base. I had confidence in my abilities - as I had already proven. In my old turret was a tally that was almost full. I explained to the Commander of the mission what protection my Warrior could provide them with, but he wasn't interested in me and my Warrior because this was his mission and he wanted his own men to shine.

The time to head back and re-join my company had arrived. I mounted up into my Warrior and switched on my PRR (Personal Role Radio), then I gave a radio check to make sure it was working. On the morning of the patrol, I had to meet the RLC in their vehicle park at 04:45hrs with my Warrior packed and ready to leave. At the vehicle park, there was a totally different feel to ours. The RLC's stores Sergeant was there with a table set up giving away crisps, chocolates and cans of drink. My boys and I emptied the table, we were like that greedy fat kid Augustus Gloop from the Chocolate Factory. We mounted back up into the Warrior ready to leave. I had set the radio frequency with the settings given to me during the three briefs, but I heard nothing on the radio. I climbed down and spoke to the officer leading the mission to find out what was going on. He told me that there were a number of problems with the radios in their vehicles and we would now be switching to our personal role radios (PRR), which only had a range of around five hundred metres. These guys were out of their depth, the patrol should be delayed until they fixed their radios and I told him straight - but once again I was told to wind my neck in, which was becoming a familiar theme on this Tour.

I had already fallen out with the RLC Commander over my ammunition for the Warrior, I had none. I was expected to command a Warrior seventy or so kilometers across terrain that was riddled with enemy with no ammunition, bar the rounds I had for my rifle.

We left the vehicle park on time with, as we warned in the three briefs, no ammunition and just a personal radio with limited coverage. All the RLC's vehicles were wheeled, mine was the only one tracked, so I was worried that these cowboys would drive too fast and leave me out on my own with no way of contacting anyone if the shit hit the fan. My Warrior was last-but-one in the vehicle order of march, with a recovery vehicle at the rear! Madness, the recovery vehicle had no major fire power and should be, at least, the centre vehicle.

As we left the park, instead of turning left towards the gates leading out of Camp Bastion, we turned right - which wasn't mentioned in the three briefs. As we followed on, it became clear why we had turned right. We were heading on a lap of honour, so that these cowboys could be waved at by the remaining members of their unit. Hundreds of their troops lined the road, most still wearing their sleep wear - it was the most bizarre thing I had encountered in almost twelve years of service. Spanky and I were bemused; gob smacked with it all,

"What the fuck is going on?" Spanky said.

"Fuck it," I said. "Let's join in."

Up rose my middle finger, Spanky's followed.

"Fuck you all, fucking dipshits!,"

we were shouting as we passed by the waving crowds.

We hit the main road just outside Camp Bastion like I had done when I led Charlie Company a few months prior and immediately these cowboys floored their vehicles, leaving my Warrior eating their dust. I got on the PRR radio - fortunately they were still in range - and I demanded they slowdown, which they did. The recovery vehicle was even slower than mine. When we hit the open ground the story would change, my Warrior would become the fastest and most resilient. I was tempted to head off on my own and let them eat my dust.

Half-way through the long drive and making good progress, one of the vehicles to my front had started to forget the dangers of the terrain. We watched from the turret of our Warrior as the vehicle started to snake off the track they should be sticking to. The driver of the vehicle was driving erratically and dangerously and I actually wondered if he was having a seizure of some kind. I was constantly keeping one eye on the recovery vehicle behind, as well as one eye on them. The recovery vehicle was struggling with the terrain too. At one stage we lost visual with it and when I got on my PRR to make the vehicles in front aware I heard nothing back. They had moved too far ahead and out of range. I had no choice but to tell my driver to stop. I had to think fast, something could be wrong, yet the idiots in front hadn't noticed I had stopped. I had flares in my turret and decided to fire one up towards the patrol, hoping they see it and work out there as was a problem. I had little faith that they would though, because the patrol had become a fucking jolly for them. As I reached for my flares the recovery vehicle came around the bend, they were okay. The crazy speeds we were doing trying to keep up with the vehicles in front, didn't match theirs. The Commander of the recovery truck messaged me over the PRR, thanking me for waiting.

I moved off at my pace now, we had lost the idiots in the desert. I was confident I could get us to F.O.B Eddy safely, it wasn't too far away at this point. As I patrolled on, luckily for them, they had stopped about four miles ahead for a break. Nobody had noticed the armoured Warrior and the recovery truck were missing. I pulled up behind the last vehicle and jumped down. I went over and blew my trumpet into the Company Commanders face. I told him his boys were fucking cowboys and somebody was going to get killed if they continued driving the way they were. They were missing potential IED areas, they were rushing, it was clear what they were up to! Again, I was told to wind my neck in, but I made myself clear. From then on they drove at a slower pace and we finally arrived in a pack together at F.O.B Eddy, seven hours after leaving Camp Bastion.

As I commanded the Warrior through the gates of F.O.B Eddy, my Company were there. All the lads from Yatminshia were in F.O.B Eddy working on a pre-arranged Warrior maintenance schedule. I was greeted by the lads as I entered the gates - then I spotted my blown-up Warrior, which was still there, looking miserable and dead. I was told the Warrior was looked at by a specialist team and then given the okay to be used again after repairs. My Warrior still hadn't been repaired though, it was left to the hard-working REME boys attached to us for the Tour. They would repair the engine and all the minor work to the track would be left down to me and my lads to fix.

I wasn't best pleased when I was told my Warrior could be used again. A couple of the lads had told me that they hadn't seen anyone important arrive to inspect the Warrior during the time they had been at F.O.B Eddy. The lads from the REME and I had first looked at the damage to the Warrior when it was recovered back after the IED - none of us thought the Warrior would ever be used again. I had it out with the Company Commander over it and he told me to "...wind my neck in..." again. As per usual, I did. I continued working throughout the night and into the following day without any much-needed rest, we had to take parts from the other damaged Warrior and put them onto mine. I wasn't happy about this, we had now bastardised my Warrior with parts from another seriously damaged Warrior, in my eyes, was insane. Again, "wind your neck in." I had no authority to hold my ground over it even knowing how highly trained I was on the Warrior. We had only taken the road wheels and other parts of the running gear, but they were still parts taken from a Warrior that had been written off for good.

With the Warrior now back in my hands and the engine roaring sweeter than it ever had, I was back to leading the Company from the front again. While I was on my leave, the lads had continued to get attacked at F.O.B Yubraj and they had also come face to face with the enemy who were trying to use one of the many rat-runs to ambush them but ended up running straight into the lads and meeting their seventy-two virgins.

The weather had turned too, the wady was turning back into a river and crossing it was a challenge, but luckily the Warrior is amphibious to a certain height. The rain continued to pour, turning our base - F.O.B Minden - into a scene from a wet Glastonbury festival. We were now walking through piles of thick mud that weighed you down with every step. The Warriors loved the mud, the thicker the mud the better the performance and for those commanding, we tried not to rag the Warriors about too much to stop the tracks getting too dirty because they would need to be cleaned.

The track between the two F.O.B's, Minden and Yubraj, became a challenge for my team to clear on foot thanks to the mud. I often made Thursdays and whoever was beside him walk through the deepest parts of the mud just to film it for my own entertainment. Thursday was stuck deep inside the boggy mud during one of my patrols and required the help of my new dismount Commander - who had just replaced Skender as the Commander for the patrol. He had to crawl on his knees through the thick mud over to Thursday's position to help him escape. We often fucked about out of sight of the enemy in an attempt to stay normal even though it was wrong and dangerous. Back in F.O.B Yubraj, one of the lads, Eyebrows, had a blow-up doll sent out to him in a parcel which we all found amusing at first, but then we decided it wouldn't be fair to shag it, so we dressed it in some old uniform and positioned it up on the roof in full sight of the enemy in hope of a firefight by confusing the idiots.

I was tasked out of F.O.B Yubraj to a possible threat not far from where "H" had died. The threat was spotted by one of the lads on guard duty up on the roof of F.O.B Yubraj. One of the Commanders in my platoon followed me out in his Warrior, callsign Three-Two, and we drove the short distance for a look. As we approached, we saw a couple of guys a few hundred meters away moving in the direction of F.O.B Yubraj with weapons. I think this was the route they had been using to travel between Yatminshia and the village across the wady - where I was blown up. I'm guessing they were coming over to attack us, but the eagle-eyed guard on the roof had spotted them carrying weapons before they had chance to attack the F.O.B. yet again. Me and callsign Three-Two unleashed hell from our turrets, we annihilated everything in our way, we took down more walls that covered their rat-runs, we took down anything blocking our vision - but most importantly we took down the enemy and stopped them in their tracks. The enemy were going mad on the radio like they usually did.

"What's going on, are you attacking" they said.

When we headed back in to the F.O.B, the interpreter said to me that he heard the enemy saying that,

"Newport had risen from the dead."

I'm guessing one of these idiots had something to do with my IED strike at the village on the other side of the wady and hearing what was said made me even more determined to defeat them.

I was no longer that scared little boy that I was back in Iraq. Iraq broke me and made me weak, but it also made me. I was now a man, a man who no longer feared the enemy. I was prepared to fight the enemy whenever they attacked or tried attacking. I wanted the enemy to fear me like I feared the enemy In Iraq. I wanted them to live a life of misery in their heads, like I was, if they survived long enough to see an end to the war. My life up until then had been seriously demanding and strenuous. I had lost one-too many friends through war - Seven at that point – Nine altogether. I was also slowly losing my mind thanks to that Iraq Tour and I could no longer sleep a full night. I wanted the enemy to suffer but suffer more than just death. Death was the easy way out.

In my perfect little world everyone would be equal, all religions would be respected, the colour of your skin would be respected, those with disabilities would be respected, people with weight problems would be respected. Nobody would live rough anymore. Everyone would work if it was possible to work. I would ban social media too. I think social media has become the biggest enemy to this world with the amount of fake news and propaganda spreading wildly across it like Japanese knotweed. For me though, all these reasons in my perfect little world are the reasons why I will never believe in a god of any kind.

My Company Commander was still eyeing up the mission to take full control of Yatminshia. I am not sure if the enemy knew or heard anything about the upcoming plan that was still in progress, because the attacks from them had become more frequent. We had two more Warriors blown up days apart, both hit by IEDs along the track we used every day to commute between the two F.O.B's of Minden and Yubraj. Nobody was injured in either attack, but the threat was there, the threat was real, and the threat was becoming more dangerous. Luckily for me though, both of the blown-up vehicles belonged to the other platoons within Charlie Company and not mine. The Warriors weren't too badly damaged either and our REME lads worked quickly to get them back up and running, those guys were miracle workers out in Afghanistan. We were lucky to have such a great team of men working alongside us. I wouldn't have the Tiffy or bally on my case either and they would leave me to look after my Warriors by myself. They were always there if ever needed and just an arm's distance away if ever I required advice, or a problem fixed and that was the case with all of their team.

CHAPTER TWENTY-EIGHT
THE PREPARATION

With my platoon now back at F.O.B Yubraj on our usual rotation at the platoon house, it was nice to have a break from the hectic few weeks of being back in Afghanistan. The past two weeks had been exhausting for us, we had carried out numerous foot patrols and with the weather starting to get warmer by the day the patrols were taking their toll on us. The Sergeant Major was also becoming more and more power mad, his obsession with us filling fucking sandbags while he watched continued on, so the week in F.O.B Yubraj was more of a holiday away from him and a break from the rest of the company, it was the only thing we had to look forward to other than a parcel from home.

My boss was called back to F.O.B Minden for a brief. Nobody knew why, and rumors were circulating about the reason for the brief. On his return, he gathered us all together for a chat. He told us that the mission to push into the depths of Yatminshia had been granted and the final plans were being put together before a date was confirmed. He then looked at me and I knew what was coming. He told me that the plan was for me to lead the battlegroup into Yatminshia with my platoon following closely behind me. Being thought of first - out of all the Commanders - to lead such a daunting mission was a privilege for any man and one that I deserved.

We had just a few weeks until the day of the mission. I had been shown some aerial photographs, taken by our British Drones high above the parts of Yatminshia that we would be heading into. The photographs were taken to help us plan out the mission. I couldn't just rely on my map to get us in as the route into the area required plenty of thought, it had to. I had lives to protect. The pressure I now had on my shoulders was huge, my body was already worn out from the years of stress while serving my Country and I was only twenty-seven.

Being based in F.O.B Yubraj for the week gave me the perfect opportunity to find the right location for the drive into the depths of Yatminshia. From the rooftop of Yubraj the routes in looked extremely tricky and challenging, the ground looked like it was full of manmade rat-runs and the streams could cause a problem for the Warriors to cross. The Warriors can cross most types of ground and tackle most obstacles in their way - including steep ground - but some holes, gullies and streams would need the use of specialist equipment to help them over. I wanted to push forward of F.O.B Yubraj and use the week to prepare my route in. One of the two routes I thought may be good enough was my first port of call. The first location looked ideal from the rooftop, but until I pushed my Warrior over for a look, I couldn't tell.

I got permission to push the Warrior out and carry out some reconnaissance and off I went. I got over to the first location and immediately realised that the route was no good, yet even from the rooftop at F.O.B Yubraj the ground looked passable. Unfortunately there was a gully that wasn't visible from the rooftop. In an ideal world, the Warrior would plough straight over this gully, but I was concerned the gully was extremely damp and boggy from the amount of rain we had in the first few months of the Tour. I decided to test it out just in case. I wasn't going to use the route if it wasn't necessary because it would be time consuming for each Warrior crossing over it on the day of the mission and the enemy would surely know we were coming and would have time to either flee or prepare to fight.

As my driver slowly dropped the front of the Warrior into the gully and began to drive down into it, we immediately became stuck. This was the worst possible situation for a Warrior Sergeant to be in, not because of the danger around us, but the embarrassment of getting stuck.

Luckily my Three-Two callsign was close behind and young Puppy and Taylor hitched the tow ropes onto the back of my Warrior as quickly as they could. I was pulled out in seconds and we headed back to the F.O.B. With route one tested and a definite no go, I had one possible route left, but this route was slightly further afield, so I would have to wait until my platoon were back in F.O.B Minden to plan the recce.

With another week of countless enemy attacks on our location at F.O.B Yubraj, everyone was looking forward to the mission. Because the attacks on our base were becoming more and more frequent and more dangerous for us, we now had a GMG (Grenade Machine Gun) and a .50 Caliber Machine Gun on the rooftop. Both these weapon systems were not to be messed with, any enemy that attacked us would have to be mentally retarded or high on drugs. Up until we had the new weapons brought in the Javelin missile was our number one deterrent, thanks to its range and precision, but the Javelin wasn't cheap - coming in at around £60,000+ each. Back in Iraq we had only managed to fire a single Javelin but so far, midway through the Tour of Helmand Province, the Javelin operators in Charlie Company had fired over thirty and the enemy still returned.

Back at F.O.B Minden with just over a week to go until the mission, my platoon was now back on patrols week. This was again the perfect situation for me to get up close to my second route without giving the mission away. My Company Commander wasn't happy with me pushing up too close, but knew we had to do it when the time was right and for his plan to work it had to be recced. A message came over the radio that a local man had turned up at F.O.B Yubraj claiming there was an IED planted a short distance away from the base, but he didn't know the exact spot. This was my moment, I now had a reason to push as far forward as I would need to get good eyes on the second route. My platoon would head out on foot patrol and sweep the area of interest looking for the IED that had been reported and while this was happening my callsign Three-One and my boss's callsign Three-Zero would push out in front of them acting like we were giving the lads on foot patrol cover while they search the ground for the IED.

I left F.O.B, Minden leading out, with the boss following behind and headed to the area of the second route. As I approached the ground looked easily accessible and wide enough to push through. I was excited, I had found the ideal starting position and immediately let the Company Commander know over the radio. As I was scanning the ground ahead and around the route of interest, my platoon had spread out, searching for this so called IED. The lads failed to find the IED after searching the area for quite some time, it was possibly a hoax from this local to gauge our response, but we could not be certain. My Platoon had finished the search and headed over to F.O.B Yubraj where I would meet them shortly.

I had done what I set out to achieve and got my plan for the day of the mission. I was happy with the ground and so I decided to pull my Warrior back over to F.O.B Yubraj and meet up with the lads for a chat about the patrol before returning to F.O.B Minden when I spotted what looked like a freshly dug hole about twenty inches long. I wasn't happy with the ground sign as it stood out like a sore thumb, so I positioned my Warrior to block any view from the danger area in case we were being watched. I told my boss over the radio what I thought I may have found and told him I was going to put one of my boys on the ground to give the area a once over with the metal detector. I shouted down to the back for one lad to dismount and come around the side with the metal detector for a chat. Skender was back with us and headed the team as the dismount Commander. I explained to him what I had found and he immediately went over for a look. It was clear after the initial first swipe of the metal detector that something was lurking under the ground. Skender hit the ground and on his belt buckle, he crawled close to the suspected IED, kept an arms-length distance from it and stayed as low as he could possibly get. He started carrying out the drills we had been shown during that shambles of a training package. I called Skender and told him to stop, I wanted to blast the ground with my chain gun and blow the IED up myself. I got on the radio and asked for permission to shoot the area of interest but, sadly, I was told NO. I now had to allow Skender to continue on his belly, sweeping the dust away and prodding the ground until the device was visible and confirmed. Fair play to Skender, he kept his nerve and he provided the confirmation I required to send the sit-rep over the radio of the IED find.

The IED that was reported by the local man was actually located over at the second route I had chosen. With the area around the IED now marked up, I was told to pull my Warrior back to F.O.B Yubraj and wait for the IED specialists to fly in and recover the bomb for evidence. Usually we would wait in-situ, at a safe distance, with our eyes on the IED but with the lads on the rooftop of F.O.B Yubraj, a short distance away, they could see the location well and it made sense for them to keep eyes on it should the enemy return to remove it.

I told Skender to mount back up inside the Warrior and my driver pulled off. No sooner had my driver pulled off I spotted yet another IED.

"What the hell is going on?" I said to my gunner.

This second IED wasn't even dug into the ground and must have been the one that was reported earlier in the day. The IED was less than a hundred meters from F.O.B Yubraj and my platoon must have walked past it while searching. My boss commanded his Warrior over for a look and quickly agreed with my second find, I threw a marker bottle down in the area of the IED to help the EOD team spot the position when they arrived, then I sent a second sit-rep back to my Company

Commander on my second IED find of the day. I returned to base astonished at my finds. I couldn't believe how the enemy had managed to get so close to F.O.B Yubraj with the IED. I'm guessing the enemy had planted that IED a long time before we arrived in Afghanistan. As for the second IED, it could have been dropped by someone who was spooked.

Several hours later the helicopter came in with the EOD team on board, they arrived in record time. Usually they can take around a day or so because there aren't enough of them in theatre. My boss escorted them on foot to the location of the first device, close to my second route. After a little while they patrolled back to the second IED and spent a short time there before moving back to our location. Then BOOM!, followed by a second BOOM!. The EOD team had just blown the two devices up. What evidence had they gathered before the blast? It would have been far safer and easier for me to have just shot and destroyed them in the first place.

With the devices gone, it was time to head back to F.O.B Minden for a debrief on the day. As I left Yubraj and Commanded my Warrior back down the usual track to and forth the F.OB's I spotted another IED. This time it had been placed while we were busy dealing with the other two IEDs. My day was getting longer. Fortunately for us the EOD hadn't yet left for Camp Bastion.

I had to confirm the latest IED located, before calling in yet another sit-rep. Again, Skender got out and I briefed him as always. No Commander would send their men out for a task, blind. Skender made his way to the area of interest and confirmed what I could see, wires protruding out of the ground. For me this was all I needed to know, I wasn't going to make Skender start digging away at it on his belly again, because we had the EOD at hand and the confirmation was there in front of us. I got Skender to mark the area and get back in. I reversed the Warrior to a safe distance and radioed in the third find of the day.

"Hello Zero, this is Three-One over," I said over the radio.

"Zero send over," replied.

"Three-One roger, one times possible IED found at my current location grid reference 12341234, can you send the EOD over?"

The EOD team had already made their way back to F.O.B Minden with my platoon on foot, so I could not contact them over the radio myself.

Around half an hour later the small EOD team arrived on foot with my platoon and they set to work once my lads had withdrawn to a safe distance. The EOD had to throw caution to the wind, there was one too many IEDs discovered today. Something wasn't right. The enemy had stepped up their game - maybe they know the plan on the upcoming mission into Yatminshia? Maybe there is an inside man leaking the information or maybe they have just decided that their best weapon against us is the IED?

The ground had to be swept clear before the EOD could begin looking at the area containing the possible IED. Once the sweep was done and the EOD had again got down and personal with the IED, the Commander of the EOD team walked over to me and passed me the wires that had been sticking out of the ground,

"There's your IED," he said.

"Looks like a few wires to me, but I'm no expert,"

I replied. He laughed and said that this was becoming a common theme. Wires were being placed into the ground to look like an IED and he believed the enemy were doing it so they could watch our reactions and drills, to keep themselves updated on our tactics. Needless to say he did say well done for calling it because there was only one other option open to me - to destroy it myself. The fake IED was deliberately placed in a spot between the two F.O.B's knowing we couldn't fire at it in case a round ricocheted towards any one of the two bases. The enemy were clever in some ways, but thick in others.

Back at camp after an eventful and long day, I had my debrief on the second route I wanted to use. The Company Commander had every faith in my abilities and was happy with my decision. Everything was going right for me on this Tour and at that moment I didn't want it to stop. I had been told that my performance so far had been excellent and beyond what they expected of me. I was then told that I was to be recommended for promotion to Sergeant when we finished the Tour and arrived back in the UK.

This was a massive boost in confidence for me. It wasn't often you get told your overperforming. In Iraq the 'B' Company Commander never once said anything positive to me, often telling me that I was quiet or lacked leadership qualities. Despite the fact that I had been thrust into battle for the first time and had excelled. The positivity went to his own guys; I was attached to them for that Tour, so no surprise. I thought that finding the driver of the vehicle hit on the bridge in Basra, piss wet through some distance from the bridge or the day I fired on those arseholes I spotted at distance with weapons - preventing their ambush on the Bulldogs lagging behind in the distance - on the same night the Major died at the JPCC opening the gates for my Warrior, was worth a well done from him, but I never got one – nor did I receive a thank you the day I investigated the Warrior parked outside of Basra Palace whilst the remainder of the Company drove blindly past it. I ended up on a drip for a week after that.

CHAPTER TWENTY-NINE
H HOUR

It was still some time before the sun would start to rise on this warm June morning. I hated working the early mornings, I never really understood them to be honest. I knew tactically we had the advantage over the enemy in the dark, but with the loud engines of the Warriors roaring away, it wasn't impossible for the enemy to realise we were up to something.

Leading the Company into Yatminshia was now down, solely, to me. The Charlie Company Commander had given his orders to every man taking part in the mission the previous day. Each person had to know their job in fine detail as there was no room for error. The threat was massive, nobody really knew what to expect - just to expect something. I was slightly nervous about leading. I was heading into unknown territory; the ground could be laden with IEDs and booby traps.

I had the usual psychological thoughts running through my mind. What if this happens or that happens, or if I get blown up and then ambushed? I was heading in first, my life and my lads' lives were at risk, the risk was higher than it had ever been on the Tour so far - we knew what we were heading into. I had a full team in the rear of my Warrior that day. Skender was about to leave Afghanistan early, so he was attached to another Warrior for the mission. I now had a new Commander leading the team in the rear, five of the seven lads I had in my Warrior - and under my control - were all young men around the age of twenty and younger. They were just pups.

Having witnessed my friend's tormented face in Kosovo before he killed himself - a picture I cannot shift - I promised myself that I would protect every one of the boys with everything I had.

I stood in my turret talking to my gunner and driver while waiting for the signal to move out to come over the radio. I was trying to get them in the right frame of mind - ready for the long and possibly drawn out battle of Yatminshia. My previous gunner, Gollum, had been replaced with some young chav from Cardiff who hadn't been a gunner for long and was lacking confidence in the turret. I did not have the time to talk him through his drills on the weapon systems in the turret considering everything else I had to do as the Commander. I would be the one firing the 30mm cannon, so he had the simple task of firing the chain gun and loading my 30mm rounds for me if the enemy attacked.

I was given the call over the radio to move to our pre-arranged line of departure, close to where I had chosen the route into Yatminshia. Callsign Three-One headed out of the gates of F.O.B Minden for possibly the final time. We would be abandoning F.O.B Minden and moving into a new base inside the very heart of Yatminshia, providing the mission was successful and there was a suitable sized compound capable of holding one hundred plus men and a large quantity of Warriors.

At the line of departure, I was sat in my turret nervously waiting for the order to start the mission. Up until the morning of the mission I hadn't had time to think about the dangers that lay ahead or had the time to be nervous about it. The fact was, I was leading my company into a dangerous area - first in the order of march. I knew the biggest threat to me, my team and the Warrior, in the unknown, was most likely to be the IEDs that might be lurking in the ground. The IEDs may be totally unnoticeable to the eye and well hidden. Nobody knew how long they may have been in the ground. Any ground signs from the IEDs being dug into the ground may well have disappeared by now and the earth above it may have settled back down to how it was before.

The big hand on my watch finally struck twelve, "H" hour had arrived, go, go, go. This was it, the moment everyman had been waiting for. The past month or so had passed by slowly for us. I told my driver what points on the ground to head for and off we went. We headed for my first planned location; I had smoke landing on each side of my Warrior, the smoke was being fired by the lads from Mortar Platoon back in F.O.B Minden. The smoke was accurate and gave me a smoke screen from the enemy as I powered through and across the open fields, deep inside of Yatminshia.

The second location I had pinpointed was a road cutting through the field we were crossing. I wanted to stay off any tracks and roads as these were ideal locations for IEDs. As we approached the road, I gave the order for my gunner to fire the chain gun at a Warrior's width across the road. This would save precious time and the need for me to deploy my lads out of the back of the Warrior to clear the road. The road was clear of IEDs and we moved on. I was, at this point, expecting some kind of fight and resistance from the enemy, but nothing was coming my way as I continued Commanding my Warrior deeper into Yatminshia.

We had been briefed countless times over the Tour that there were no locals inside this end of Yatminshia. The locals had fled the village when the enemy arrived. However, as I pushed further inside of the village I could see women and children. I quickly got on the busy radio and sent a sighting report of the civilians up the Chain of Command; the mortars had now ceased firing to prevent any locals becoming casualties. I had a slight sense of relief at the sight of the locals. I knew that they may well be the wives and children of the enemy, but they were the innocent parties caught up in this needless war.

My Warrior had continued to plough through the depths of Yatminshia without any enemy activity. The enemy were communicating over the radios as always, threatening to attack us, but nothing came. I had made it through Yatminshia in one piece with no resistance. I positioned my Warrior at the furthest edge of the village and dismounted my lads from the back of my Warrior to provide cover on the ground.

The entire drive-in lasted less than thirty minutes. We had anticipated that the mission itself could take a day or so to complete as we expected a wall of resistance from the enemy.

With my Warrior now safely inside the village and the remainder of the Warriors also in position, it was time to send the lads in on foot. We had large numbers of soldiers attached to us for the mission and we also had reporters from the media here to report on the mission itself. The lads on foot were now clearing each and every compound in the village.

The mission was going swimmingly, nobody expected the enemy to just withdraw and leave us to take their land without a fight. Something didn't feel right to me. Was this a ploy or a trick? Had the enemy pre-planned this mission and did they have their own plan in place? Was I a sitting duck and a possible target? All these thoughts were running through my head. I had tremendous stress on my shoulders from the horrors I had already lived through during my time in the Armed Forces.

Word came over the radio that one of the compounds being cleared was full of IEDs. An IED factory maybe? Whoever was running the factory had left behind numerous bits of intelligence including a notebook containing English names and addresses. This factory would now require clearing and we had the EOD team on the ground with us so there was no waiting around. The EOD team went to work clearing what they could and blowing up the rest. BOOM! after BOOM! could be heard as each IED was purposely blown up. Still the enemy stayed away. The lads continued their charge from compound to compound.

My Platoon Sergeant had taken a number of the dismounted boys from the back of the three Warriors after we made it through the village and they had cleared quite a few compounds themselves. Each compound they entered that had dark suspicious rooms - they had to consider throwing a grenade into it first, in case the building was laden with enemy or IEDs. The grenade would either kill the enemy or set the IED off destroying it and making the building safer - as opposed to just walking inside it blind. My platoon had reached the last compound in the village and cleared it. They were now close to my Warrior and the job was pretty much done in just a few short hours rather than a day or so, as expected.

With all the buildings now searched and cleared, it was down to the Company Commander to draw up his next plan and decide where he wanted the new F.O.B Minden to be located. As he was doing his work, my boss and I were Commanding our Warriors around observing and taking note of anything that may be a hindrance down the line - like tunnels and gullies - whilst also looking for routes out of the village from the unknown side of the village. We would look for man-made routes that weren't on the maps we had.

I had a large compound wall in my way, it was blocking what I thought was a good view out from the other side and I decided to ram the wall down and flatten it with my Warrior. My driver slowly powered into the wall and down it went. We then drove into the compound and the size of the land inside was pretty big. After the wall fell, I continued ramming down other walls, clearing a new route through this compound when my Company Commander arrived in his Warrior. He shouted loudly over the noisy engines of both our Warriors,

"What are you doing? This compound was going to be our new base!"

Shit, I instantly thought to myself.

"Oh, fuck," I was laughing hard inside.

I just made a track through this compound and all along the Company Commander had it set in his mind as the new F.O.B. Minden. Luckily for me there wouldn't be enough room to house the entire company, so it wouldn't have been used in the end. As he drove off looking for the next possible base, the crew and I burst out laughing. Finally, we had something to laugh about on this Tour.

The mission was complete and a new base had been found. The entire Company had now been called to the new base and warned to stay alert, just in case. We would spend the next few days guarding the new base from outside in our Warriors while the base was set up. We needed to fortify the base, including the rooftop, where the views over the village and the wady were exceptional. Ideal for our lads to guard the camp from. There was a massive hill about three hundred meters away, on one side of the base and that was the only negative thing about the location of the new base.

The hill could easily allow the enemy to sneak up onto it and attack us from and we were within distance of an RPG attack. This particular hill sat next to another hill, slightly smaller in size, which could not be seen entirely from our base. The smaller hill had become a burial site and a shrine to the dead that the locals had used to mourn their loved ones - before they were forced to flee the village. The best route into this side of the village for the locals to use also ran alongside both of the hills.

As well as guarding the base, I was also tracking back and forth helping the engineers make a new track through the entire village. The track was being built from F.O.B Yubraj right up to the new F.O.B Minden. I was playing my part in choosing the new route. I was continuously roaming around the area looking for the flattest and safest ground that would eventually be used by all types of wheeled and tracked Military vehicles once life in Yatminshia had settled down.

Due to the hill overlooking F.O.B Minden, a decision was made to place two Warriors on top of it as a show of force and to give the guys fortifying the new base a sense of protection. The hill was easy to access for the Warrior and easy to climb, but it was the summer months and the track was dry. My platoon had been given the task of guarding the hill, which gave us a break from the sandbag filling tasks.

With every new base came the need for thousands more sandbags to be filled, they were everywhere you looked. I'm pretty certain that if the number of sandbags filled during our time in Afghanistan were laid end to end it would circle the earth - as long as the earth isn't flat.

The majority of my platoon had now left or were home on leave, including our Platoon Sergeant, whose role would require filling. It was no mean feat stepping into his boots, the guy was by far the most confident Sergeant I had worked with during my career and I had some great Platoon Sergeants during my time. It was a tossup between Will and I, as the only Corporals left in the platoon, to step up as acting Sergeant. I did have seniority over him, but I wasn't stepping up, I had enough jobs to do without taking on Platoon Sergeant as well. Will was more than capable of stepping up and he did so and did a bloody good job. It would not have been fair if I had stepped up, because I had not been out on as many foot patrols as Will, with me being the Warrior Sergeant.

I was up on the hill with my boss and his Warrior observing from our turrets, taking in the beautiful scenery and the peace, when I could hear one of the boys from another platoon who was in the turret of his Warrior and new to Commanding - a Warrior Commander in his Platoon had gone on leave - which meant he had to step up because he was qualified. I could tell by the sound of his voice that he was nervous in the turret. Every Commander has been in his shoes. He was out of camp with just his Warrior and team and he was positioned overlooking the wady and the village where I was previously blown up. He had the Afghan Police, who had a Mitsubishi 4x4 parked close to him and on the back was a 50-calibre machine gun.

I told my boss I wanted to go and have a look to see if he was okay, his location wasn't too far away from mine at the hill. I was given clearance to leave the hill and head over to his location.

As I approached, he had deployed his team out of the back of his Warrior, they were out on the ground and looking at a target across the wady, preparing to fire a Javelin if the threat they could see required it. They were being told by the Afghan Police where the enemy was. The lads were struggling to understand them due to the language barrier. I wasn't convinced either, so I headed back to Minden to have a face to face with the Company Commander who was preparing to leave the Tour as his time leading the company was coming to an end. I told him that I thought the Afghan Police were making up fictitious enemy and trying to get the lads to fire the Javelin for their own amusement. So I asked him if I could replace him. He agreed and I headed back and told him the good news and he made his way back to F.O.B Minden. I positioned my Warrior and left my lads in the back of the Warrior as I felt they did not need to be out.

Within minutes of replacing the previous Warrior, the Afghan Police started firing the 50-calibre machine gun into the wady. I grabbed my binoculars and stood up out of my turret to see what they were shooting at. As I stood up the Afghani Police were cheering the shooter every time he fired into the wady. Something still wasn't feeling right to me. As I scanned down into the wady, just out of sight of my gunner - who was also scanning using the sights of the turret - I saw what looked like innocent locals crossing the wady with their livelihoods. Alongside them they had animals, including donkeys and cows and the animals were jumping about like they were scared, probably from the powerful gun fire being aimed at them. The Afghan Army were shooting at them for fun; they were forcing them to run for their lives' across the wady and this was the reason the Afghan Police were cheering. The 50-Calibre is a monster of a weapon, it's capable of causing catastrophic damage to anything it hits and these idiots were shooting at innocent people for their own pleasure. I immediately started yelling at them to stop but they just couldn't understand the word "STOP" ... I had no choice but to send a message to my Company Commander warning him what was going on and for him to contact the interpreter and tell him to get them to stop shooting immediately.

I had all sorts of scenarios running through my head, it was already tortured and fried as it was. I really didn't need the possible murder of innocent people on my conscience as well. What do I do if they hit someone? How do I stop them? I'm furiously waving and screaming at them to stop, but they just kept firing and ignoring my screams.

I had to be aggressive, they had to stop. I pulled out a flare and shot it at the floor in their direction. It did the trick, everyone now turned towards me, faces with evil written all over them. I screamed again and again,

"STOP FIRING YOU FUCKING IDIOTS. STOP FUCKING FIRING."

Finally, they stopped, it was madness. Nobody was hit whilst fleeing the wady.

Shortly after the Afghan Police left the location, I returned to my base and found out the Afghan Police had told their senior bosses that they had been firing at enemy hiding between the animals. They weren't, it was clearly lies, I witnessed everything they had just done and told my boss, who thanked me for putting a stop to it.

CHAPTER THIRTY
THE ARRIVAL

Our new home had been fortified and was now looking like a base, all our hard work over the week had paid off. Sandbags were filled, Hesco Bastions filled and placed around the outside of the base, we had new toilets built for privacy with nice clean walls ready for the marker pens, the roof had camouflage nets placed across it and sandbagged up for added protection.

Nobody at the new F.O.B Minden was allowed to sleep in the Warriors as I had previously been doing. This new rule pissed me off. I had to sleep with five other men in a dark room made from mud and shit. During the evening the ceiling would be crawling with scorpions and spiders, it was disgusting.

With everyone now in a routine - and so many lads still at home on leave - the Company were working together for the first time out on foot patrol and for the camp guard duties. It was good to work with the other lads and get to know them more. I would still go out on Warrior patrol with my Boss and his Warrior. We didn't have far to patrol either.

Now we had another enemy line that was untested ground, similar to the one we had just forward of F.O.B Yubraj, but my Company Commander was not going to leave the land to our front untested as the previous regiment had done with the half of Yatminshia we now controlled. We were out most days on foot patrols walking as far as the eye could see, visiting compounds. The locals were starting to return to the homes they once fled, so it was vital that we made ourselves visible to them to give them peace of mind.

The village was slowly coming back to life. There were now people living back in the compounds we had cleared during the mission. We could never tell if any of the locals that had returned were actually innocent civilians or in fact the enemy, but we would try and keep an open mind, we had to. We could not afford to let our guard down. The locals in the village of Yatminshia would wear traditional clothing like the Pashtun dress with flip flops. We started to notice one or two guys in expensive running trainers. This was a giveaway and a clear sign to me that they were either enemy or dickers, yet we couldn't do anything about it because we had no proof. We had the power to stop and search them, unlike the British police on British streets.

We hadn't encountered much resistance from the enemy since taking full control of Yatminshia. I had a few firefights from distance with them, but that was about it. The previous evening I was up on the hill with the boss and his Warrior, when we spotted, in the far distance, a number of individuals running between compounds carrying what looked like weapons. We couldn't be too sure because even though it looked like enemy activity to us, the activity was happening around eight hundred meters away and it was very dark, with limited moonlight.

Between our Warriors we put up a number of Schermuly rockets (the Schermuly is named after a British born Dutchman who invented a rocket that would light up the night sky). They lit up the sky over the enemy like daylight. The Schermuly would slowly come back down to the ground via a parachute. One of our Schermuly's came down and landed on top of a freshly cropped pile of wheat that had been prepared the day before, causing the crop to catch fire and burn like a bonfire. As the sky was lit up, the guys we could see running about were carrying weapons. They instantly fled the scene when the first Schermuly was fired into the night sky. It was easy for them to flee from where they were, because the ground had many deep gullies in it. With the crop on fire, undoubtedly, somebody was going to be cross in the morning. It was a freak shot, but it did prove those guys were shifting weapons about. It was easier for me to send a fire mission back to the ops room back at base and get the Mortar Team to fire a few of their light mortars into the sky - over the burning crop - and blame them if any angry locals turned up. So I did, I sent the fire mission and the mortar bombs were launched, lighting up the sky for a second time. Nothing would have come of it anyway, the Army would have just handed over money to reimburse the farmer for his loss. The farmer never arrived to complain though. Maybe he was one of the guys with the weapons that night?

The next day I was getting ready, at F.O.B Minden, to relieve my boss who was up on the hill. During the day we would cut down to just one Warrior and switch back to two at night. He had been up there for nearly two hours and it was my turn on the hill. As I was mounting up with my crew into my Warrior, I heard an almighty whistle in the distance, followed by a loud bang. Suddenly, there were shots being fired from the hilltop. My boss was up there. Out I went, my driver was flooring the Warrior as fast the engine would go. We made it up to the top of the hill in a very short time.

My boss had been ambushed; they used the gullies and compounds to creep up on his Warrior then they fired an RGP at him, but luckily it whizzed inches past him and exploded in the distance. My boss whipped out the pistol he had holstered on his body armour and sent the enemy home, riddled with gunshots. I could see from my sights that in the far distance two guys were placing what looked like a body onto the back of a motorbike. I could have hit them with my 30mm, or even got the lads to take them out with a Javelin, but we left them to get away. Hopefully they will have learned their lesson and realised we won't be messed with.

Following the attack, my boss went back to base to chill out and I continued to guard the hill. I was even more alert and on edge in case they returned. This was the first real attack like the ones we had everyday back at F.O.B Yubraj. Was this the start of the enemy's fight back for Yatminshia? My guard duty on the hill was boring as usual and I was slightly disappointed that it wasn't my Warrior which had been ambushed. I hadn't fired my pistol at the enemy yet either. I had only shot a few apples on a picket stick back in Camp Bastion at the start of the Tour.

To be honest though, in the number of engagements I had with the enemy, I either forgot I had my pistol with me or the fight was that fierce you wouldn't dare stand up out of your turret to return fire. My boss's quick reactions saved his own life that day.

My two hours on the hill were almost over and soon my boss would be relieving me from the heat that was blazing down on us. The sun was piping hot and baking me and my lads like cakes inside of an armoured oven. We had minimal man-power left in the platoon because the lads still hadn't returned from their leave. We were only capable of manning two Warrior's at any one time, meaning we had to rotate on the hill every two hours or so during the day. This wasn't a problem because it got us out of the camp and away from those fucking sandbags.

I heard my boss roaring towards the hill. The Warrior was approaching the bottom of the hill and as I turned around to wave at him - from out of absolutely nowhere - a man appeared and started running behind the Warrior as fast as he could, trying to keep up with the Warrior's speed. This was a massive no-no for us. Stupidity at its best. We could easily shoot the man dead as a suspected suicide bomber, but this, youngish looking man, he was wearing his traditional thin dress and nothing more. I gestured 'behind' at my boss, warning him that he had someone chasing him, in case his Warrior struggled up the hill and rolled back down over the man. My boss saw the man and instantly reached for his pistol. He was about to take aim, when suddenly he turned to me and said,

"What the fuck is going on? Look!!!"

The man obviously had learning difficulties. He had managed to slip out of his compound and follow my boss's Warrior the short distance. Within seconds the man's relative came to fetch him home. The Afghani man waved as he was dragged back to the compound he escaped from, kicking and screaming like a child who had dropped his sweets. I couldn't help but laugh, the scene was frightening but also amusing.

Back at base it was my Company Commanders final few days, he was leaving soon on a helicopter. His replacement would arrive on an incoming flight a few days prior to his departure. It was my job to collect the new Company Commander when he arrived.

The helicopter landing spot (HLS) was still located outside the old Minden base. The ground would need clearing first, just in case, as we no longer had eyes on that ground. The ground around our new base was considered too dangerous to create a new HLS due to the mortar threat. Since my boss was attacked on the hill the previous day, we encountered numerous mortar attacks from across the wady in the direction of the village where I was blown up. The mortars were hitting our base with precision as usual. We had patrols set up alongside our side of the wady, hidden in cover and trying to spot the location of the idiots who were firing the mortars at us.

It was early evening and the sun was disappearing, the HLS had been searched and cleared and was now awaiting the incoming flight. As I was waiting for my new Company Commander to land, I was talking to a high-ranking officer who was leaving on the flight back to Camp Bastion. We chatted about the village, the locals, the mission we had just taken part in and then we spoke about the enemy. I told him I thought the enemy were cowards, as the attacks we had been encountering before we took over the full control of Yatminshia were aimed at F.O.B Yubraj, but when I led the mission into Yatminshia where were the enemy?. I told him I hoped for more action, doing the same shit everyday was getting boring now and the days were starting to drag. The enemy were happy to call us out over the radio saying they are going to do this and that to us, yet when I rock up looking for a scrap they are nowhere to be seen.

The helicopter arrived carrying my new Company Commander and he climbed off it and then made his way into the rear of the Warrior waiting behind mine. It was now complete darkness; the moon wasn't shining tonight. As I started leading the two Warriors back to F.O.B Minden, the base came under attack. Charlie Company were being attacked heavily from the hill. We had pulled the Warriors off the hill to collect the Company Commander. I am assuming the enemy had thought the Warrior's had left Yatminshia and seized the opportunity to attack using the advantage point of the hill. As I got closer to the base I could see streaks of light flashing back and forth across the sky. The lights I could see were tracer rounds and the sky looked amazing once again – I found it almost therapeutic.

I told my driver to head for the hill. I hadn't been given permission to head there yet, but I wasn't waiting for it either. We got to the hill and immediately hit resistance, this was my gunner's first real test. I gave him his orders and told him to go to town on the enemy. He did just that, firing the chain gun round after round, the enemy at this point were bounding back, trying to escape. They hadn't realised the Warriors were just a short distance away – I guess that was the beauty of working in the dark. As they were moving back, some of the enemy hid in amongst the goats roaming the fields. I wasn't sure if they spotted the goats, got aroused and ran over to eye the goats up because they were known as the goatfuckers. Those hiding were no threat to me now and there certainly wasn't any need to risk the lives of the animals either, although it probably would have been a blessing for the goats knowing what the Taliban would do to them.

Some of the enemy had decided to hang around and fight back, but with the Warriors fire power it was the wrong decision. My boss was alongside me now with his Warrior and he was also going to town on them. My gunner started flapping at his drills; the pressure was too much for him. He kept having issues with the chain gun, I told him to use the 30mm instead, but he was that hung up by his adrenaline he didn't have a clue what he was doing. It was as if he had forgotten everything he had learned on his gunnery course. I was screaming at him to get a grip; we were sitting ducks and open to RPG attacks.

As luck would have it, the enemy didn't really have any fire power left as they had fired the bigger weapons before I had got back to the hill. As my gunner continued to maul at the chain gun, Blade, who had replaced Skender as my Dismount Commander, shouted up to my gunner telling him to get the fuck in the back of the Warrior. The Warrior had a cage protecting the guys in the back from the turning turret. The cage could be moved left or right, allowing access to the turret. Blade squeezed up the gap and into the gunner's seat while still clutching his shotgun that was almost glued to his hand. He immediately started fixing the chain gun back together and set about to finish the enemy off.

After the attack - and back at base - it was a big welcome to Yatminshia for our new Company Commander. It was almost like the enemy knew he was coming and set about to make his spine shiver, not that it would, because our new Company Commander was a gem of a leader. The guy wasn't here to fuck us about as much like the last one. He knew what he wanted from us and what he expected, and everyone did what he asked. The sandbag filling had stopped as the Sergeant Major had fortified the base immensely, making life that little bit easier around the base.

The next day saw me push out of the base and head back to the location where the Afghanistan Army were firing into the wady in the direction of the locals trying to cross. I was located there with my Warrior on lookout for this phantom mortar team that we still hadn't identified. The mortars were still coming down and the shots were landing closer and closer to the accommodation. Earlier in the day we came under attack from a nasty barrage of mortars near the ops room. As they landed outside and on top of the building, I had no choice but to dive for my life to the ground and pray I wouldn't be hit.

The noise and the sound instantly gave me flashbacks of Basra Palace. I couldn't shift the horrors of Iraq, they had scarred me for life. The mortars hit all around the ops room where I was seeking cover. Myself and two others - one of whom was the Warrior Sergeant Major - had managed to crawl between two doorways. We wouldn't dare crawl any further in case the shrapnel from the blasts hit us. Thankfully the attack passed without casualties and the new Company Commander had another welcome. This is the reason I was back overlooking the wady.

A few hours after arriving at the location, I was scanning my arcs and spotted movement in the area that we had assumed the mortars were being fired from. It became clear we were about to be attacked again. I called in a fire mission on the area and the lads hit the position with accuracy. Within minutes, one of the other platoons engaged at another location further down the wady. They were down there on foot, doing exactly what I was doing. They engaged with a Javelin missile which shot out across the wady straight at the target. As the missile crossed the wady, an F18 jet whizzed past cutting across the path the missile had just used. The Javelin is a heat-seeking missile, so the jet which appeared from nowhere was very lucky it wasn't hit by the missile - that's how close it was. It was that close enough to be classed as a blue on blue; friendly against friendly incident.

Any movement at my end of my area had stopped completely after my mortar team gave them some much needed medicine of their own. Fighting fire with fire. I stayed in position, hoping for more attacks. My head was so fried from the shit that I had witnessed and been involved in over the years, that I just wanted to keep fighting. I wanted to kill every last piece of shit out there who was making this world a bad place. I had become angry and miserable thanks to what I thought would be a good job when I first joined up as nothing more than a young kid.

There were no wars being fought by the British at the time. Ireland had settled down and the Bosnian and Kosovo wars had become nothing more than just peace-making operations. Had I known back then that my life - after nine and half years' service - would leave me with anger, hatred, flashbacks, no sleep and not wanting to wake up any more - then I might well have taken another route in life. Even if it meant staying in the City I hated as a young kid and possibly living rough.

CHAPTER THIRTY-ONE
TWO TIMES

After the battle on the hill the previous night, things in camp had settled back to normality. Almost every attack, including the mortar attacks, had become almost natural to us at this stage of the Tour. It was hard to stay focused some days. The heat was becoming a factor, it was now the hottest I had felt it in Afghanistan. Life inside my Warrior was becoming unbearable. Wearing full kit and having no access to cold drinking water was an absolute soul destroyer for me, the water we had would be warm. I was never a tea or coffee drinker, so water was all that I had. I would leave a couple of water bottles outside of my Warrior at night and if I wasn't working that night I would set my alarm clock to wake me up in the early hours of the morning because my water would be cold enough to enjoy. I would drink enough water to get me through the day ahead.

We hadn't long received the new ration menus that we got our hands on just before the mission to take Yatminshia. The new menus were amazing. No longer did we have to endure the shit we were forced to eat since the day I joined. My favourite meal out of the new menus was the Thai green curry. The flavour was out of this world. I wasn't sure if it was enjoyable because I hadn't eaten any decent food in such a long time, but I did know that this curry tasted better than what the poor lads are being served in their camps today. Also, in the new ration boxes was a powdered squash; the powder mixed into your water to make an energy drink and the flavours were stunning - the warm water it was added to, didn't seem that bad. Finally, things were looking up for me as the pain in my neck had started to settle and I was no longer taking pain relief.

On the other side of the hill was the Memorial Hill that we had renamed from burial ground as it seemed more fitting to those resting there. Now that the locals were back in the village of Yatminshia and living alongside us, it was pivotal to show them that we wanted to help them move forward. One of the ways the Company Commander had decided to help the locals was to clear the Memorial Hill of any IEDs, then the locals could visit their loved ones once again. Almost all of the locals had fled the village soon after the Taliban had stormed in, killing man after man for no reason other than power and deluded beliefs. The memorial ground was large in size and the task would be huge. Apparently, the Taliban had cruelly hidden IEDs amongst some of the graves, undoubtedly, to kill more innocent people. What a nasty way to kill someone and their weapon of choice was worse. These guys have no limits, pigs of the earth. I could never understand why anyone would want to hurt another person for no reason. You only get one life on this earth, everyone should be trying to live it as freely and peacefully as possible. Power, Corruption and money are the three biggest enemies of world peace.

Nine Platoon were given the task of clearing the Memorial Hill. I guess with the amount of IEDs I had found so far on the Tour, it made sense for my platoon to carry out the mission. The mission was scheduled to start in the morning and the brief for the mission was simple; I would lead the platoon to the Memorial Hill and the lads would use their equipment and skills to locate any potential IEDs. I was praying that the IEDs rumoured to be hidden amongst graves were exactly that - vicious lies and rumours - and the task would be over in a few short hours. We would not have the bomb disposal team with us either, so anything we found would mean an extremely long wait.

I was hoping for an easy day, the sun is a nightmare and the days were long. I didn't want to sit and wait for the bomb disposal to fly in. I would rather shoot the IED's, but obviously - under the circumstances - this wasn't possible. It was a burial ground.

The mission had come around. It was early morning, but not as early as most of our previous missions had started. This mission required to be carried out in daylight to make it easy and safer to identify the IEDs in the ground as the lads walked amongst the graves - nervously and cautiously - hoping not to tread on anything that might go bang. The lads were young, they had the rest of their lives to live as long as they can get through this next mission and see out the Tour.

As most of the senior lads were still away on leave, it would be down to our younger boys in the platoon to step up and see this mission through. I had no doubts in my mind whatsoever that the boys would shine, like their older, more senior colleagues often did. In my Warrior for the mission I still had Sheep's-Teeth, my usual driver, and the Cardiff chav as my gunner but the team in the back had changed due to my lads being on leave. I now had Thurdays, Wiggy, Youngy and Blade - who was now Skenders replacement as my Dismount Commander.

The time had come to start the mission and the first thing was to get to the hill a short distance away. We left F.O.B Minden and I Commanded my Warrior towards the hill without any issues. The ground was looking solid with no signs of any freshly dug earth. I headed past the hill that overlooked our F.O.B using the only road into that particular part of Yatminshia. As I headed along the track I told my driver to stop the Warrior. I had a small obstacle to my front, about thirty meters away. It was a small man-made bridge with a dry stream underneath it. I had a problem; I could easily drive my Warrior over the bridge but if the weight of my Warrior buckled the bridge and caused it to collapse, then the local people of Yatminshia wouldn't be able to enter or leave the village in their cars. Under the bridge was a dried-up stream so it made sense for me to cross the stream and stay off the bridge - leaving it well alone. My mind was made up, the stream it was. My next consideration was any potential threat within the stream itself. The stream was dry, so the enemy could easily bury an IED within it if they thought the same way that I did - that the bridge could force us into the stream. Again not an issue, I had my lads in the back who were more than capable of clearing the ground.

I shouted down to Blade and explained that I would need him to make a safe route through the dry stream and back up onto the track for me. The Warriors back door opened and out he popped with his shotgun in one hand and the metal detector in the other. There was no real need to get all my boys out for this short clearance, the area was out of sight from the enemy thanks to the surrounding hill which gave us cover, so the only threat would be from any landmines or IED's. Thursday was the second man to climb out behind Blade for the tasking. As he climbed out I had visions of the time I made him clear a route through some wet, boggy mud for a laugh and he got stuck, losing his boot. The other two, Wiggy and Youngy stayed in the back of my Warrior. The day would be long for everyone if we found any IEDs, so the thought was to just use my guys as sparingly as I could while I had cover from the enemy.

The lads patrolled slowly, walking forward, swiping the metal detector left to right to check for any hidden IEDs. They needed to stay within a short distance of the Warrior because it had internal equipment which intercepted certain signals and negate enemy equipment capable of sending that signal to detonate certain IEDs. The lads made their way up the track and down into the stream. They spent a few minutes clearing the dry stream - ensuring they had covered every angle. With the dry stream cleared, they continued on. I told my driver to take it easy down into the dry stream as he drove in.

A week later, I awoke from an induced coma. As I opened my eyes, I saw doctors and nurses hovering over me. My hand was being squeezed tightly by my beautiful partner, who was by my side. I didn't have a clue what was going on.

The last time I blinked, I was heading into the dry stream, commanding my Warrior to the Memorial Hill and now I am lying in a hospital bed with my partner beside me and a there was a doctor looking into my eyes whilst shining a small light and asking me questions that I could not answer. It took some time for me to come around from being roused from the coma. I had tubes feeding into my body everywhere I looked, including my penis. I remember hearing the doctors asking me who I was and if I could remember anything. I couldn't talk, I was too drugged up and weak, I didn't know where I was and wondered if I was in some crazy dream.

Every time I opened my eyes and looked around, I could see stuff that you wouldn't think was possible. I was hallucinating from the drugs being fed into my body. I could see my gunner dancing on an empty bed next to me; he was wearing what looked like African clothing and was holding a small metal vase in each hand, both of which had black smoke pouring out of them, he was looking at me as he danced on the bed. I was trying to act normal, I was trying to figure out if I was alive or dead.

My step-Dad bent down to talk to me and I could see insects crawling all over him, it freaked me out. The ceiling was covered with Disney Princesses and between the lines of the ceiling panels I could see my own pee flowing which was coming from the catheter inserted into my manhood.

The hallucinations from the drugs - which were relieving me of pain and fighting my infections - had started to calm down after a few days. My partner had been at my side since I arrived in the UK. It was still hard to accept as the days passed, that I had been involved in an accident. I couldn't take in anything that I was being told because my brain wasn't functioning properly. My partner kept trying to explain to me that I was blown up AGAIN and all my guys were alive and safe. I just cried and cried. I just couldn't understand anything she - or anyone else - said.

I was just heading into that dry stream, I had told my driver to drive into it carefully, I have not been hit by an IED. The only IED I have been hit by was well over a month ago and I only hurt my neck. I can remember that for fuck sakes because I had been living on pain killers for it. I kept repeating this to myself over and over, but nothing was making sense. I wasn't sure if I had problems with my brain or whether I was just in shock or maybe the first time I was blown up on the bridge over a month ago - whilst heading out of the village caused me these serious injuries and I have been dreaming everything since? I was very confused.

It started to become clear that I was in a bad way; I was in a lot of pain all over my body. I had been told numerous times what injuries I had, but I just couldn't remember them. What I did remember though was my partner telling me that I was flown back from Afghanistan - straight to Birmingham Airport, where I had numerous police vehicles escorting me under blue light to Selly Oak hospital. At the hospital my partner and family were awaiting my arrival. I was in a coma, fighting for my life. The doctor who flew back to the United Kingdom with me as my carer, had told my partner and family what injuries I had sustained, but one of them had stuck out.

He told them that I had a healing fracture to my neck which was about a month old and had not been caused by the second IED. My partner instantly mentioned that I had hurt my neck in a previous IED - a month before - which was a massive shock to the family as it was unknown to them until my partner spoke out. I had broken my neck in the first IED. I had continued on the frontline for a further month with this injury, completely unaware. I thought it was a case of minor whiplash. What would have happened if I had been sent to Camp Bastion for a medical examination straight after that first IED? There was no way on this earth I would have been allowed to continue on that frontline if I had, but nobody knew the truth.

My Partner and my Family were fuming with the Army for not acting after the first IED, although I could have argued my case to be sent back to Camp Bastion for a medical check-up, I did not. I was happy with the advice I had received at F.O.B Minden and later down at DC. I hadn't long lost a good mate from the platoon and I had felt guilty that I wasn't on the ground at the time of his death, so I wanted to stay and continue to do what I could for them. Unfortunately for me though, now it has become clear that I had a broken neck and continued serving on the frontline - that would be the last anyone heard about it because the Military squashed all knowledge of it, as it was due to negligence. Don't forget, the boys and I were ordered to take parts from that damaged Warrior and place them onto my - apparently cleared to continue - Warrior.

As the days passed and I was becoming more alert, I had become verbally abusive to the staff caring for me. I was nasty, I didn't give a fuck what I was saying. One young, female nurse was trying to give me the critical care I desperately required and I was nothing more than vile to her. The drugs were turning me into a monster and it wasn't just the nurses I was being vile to. My own partner, the Regimental Sergeant Major and the Commanding Officer who had visited me with the Padre got it too.

The visions I saw on the ceiling made me think that my pee was dripping onto them from the ceiling. The Padre was at the bottom of my bed when I lifted my legs showing my naked behind, I then farted. The noise was extremely loud, but the smell was worse and it headed for the Padre. I would now need to seek redemption from the guy in the sky, if there was one? I was still alive after surviving two IEDs and countless ambushes, but I still don't believe in him. If there was such a force up there, then the world would be a beautiful place, we wouldn't have idiots ruling the world and we certainly wouldn't have any wars, or murderers, paedophiles and rapists living freely amongst us - or idiots holding placards demanding the name "man" is removed off a box of tissues because it hurts their feelings or certain tv presenters moaning that men showing affection to their young children is morally wrong and weird.

I was finally starting to talk and recall what injuries I had after being told numerous times. I had broken my skull, fractured my right occipital lobe and had a brain haemorrhage. I also had a traumatic brain injury, broke my right shoulder and shoulder blade - leaving muscle damage to my rotator cuff and other tissue and muscles in the area. My spleen was badly ruptured, requiring an emergency operation. All the way down the right-hand side of my rib cage I was covered in big nasty looking red and black bruises. I had broken my back, my Thoracic spine was seriously damaged, I had a wedge fracture to my T4 vertebrae which was so badly damaged the nerves around it were fucked and required another operation, nine months down the line, to insert a cage around the damaged vertebrae.

The prognosis was short and sharp. Your injuries are worse than losing a limb, you may never walk again, you certainly will not be doing any physical activities again and we doubt that you will work again.

The brain injury was being squashed - like my neck injury. The Military and the Government easily made things appear to be different to what you thought they were or were advised by the medical experts. My brain injury alone would have cost them thousands in compensation, as would the negligence around my neck injury. I was told by the medical experts that if I had lost my legs, then they would not be capable of covering up the seriousness of my injuries, because the injuries were visible. Non-visible injuries are unseen by the eye, that's why most charities concentrate on the limbless and promote their charity using them.

We are all the same, we all hurt inside, we have all suffered the pain, the nightmares, the physical and mental effects of seeing your friends die in front of you. Having to pull the trigger and possibly take a life, nobody is any different and we should all be treated the same and not frowned upon like I was - and am to this day, almost ten years on.

I was making a decent recovery, more than enough to get me moved out of critical care almost a week after arriving. I had argued hard with the doctors to move me. While in critical care I was only allowed visitors to see me for up to two hours a day, three at a push. I wanted to be moved so I could see my little girl, the little girl who almost lost her daddy numerous times. Eventually they gave in and moved me. I had to be moved into a single room on the ward as I had picked up an airborne disease, similar to MRSA, after the operation in the air over Helmand Province. The disease could be passed through fluid and meant I wouldn't be able to donate blood for at least five years after my recovery.

Eventually I was moved to the ward. I was still slightly spaced out from all the drugs being pumped into my body through tubes inserted into my arms and I was also still hallucinating but nothing like I had been. In my new room, the ceiling felt lower and everything I had seen on the ceiling in critical care, I was seeing in my new room - but closer to my face - the ceiling was moving and came to life every time I looked at it. I was on a spinal bed so had no choice but to look at the ceiling as I was forced to lie down flat due to the seriousness of my spinal injury.

My spinal bed had handrails on it while I was in critical care, but for some reason I was moved off the bed and placed onto one without handrails. That evening while sleeping, I had a dream, the dream was about me, I had been blown up and when I woke up from the dream I was on the floor of my room in a pool of blood. The blast in my dream must have caused my body to react and fall off the bed, face first, hitting the right side of my head. I had fallen on my right cheekbone and cut my eyebrow open with a nasty inch long gash. I lay motionless, slowly choking to death in a pool of my own blood, too weak to cry for help. My lungs were hurting as I breathed in blood through my nose.

I was on the floor for around ten minutes before the nurse found me. She had been called after one of the patients heard a bang from my room. I was then left on the floor, in pain, for a further twenty minutes because they did not have the staff available to lift me up back onto my bed. Because of my injuries I required six members of staff to roll me or shift me - whenever I had to be moved. It was horrible. Half the time I was left naked as the thin sheet covering my skinny, worn out body would fall off, or the nurses removed it as they rolled me about or moved me from bed to bed. Even though the nurses were there to look after me, it still wore me down. The nurses were predominantly female and very young, it was intimidating, I had lost my dignity and I often felt like I wanted to be left alone to die.

CHAPTER THIRTY-TWO
THE IED

I had stories coming at me thick and fast as different Military personnel visited me in hospital. Apparently, while I was patrolling to the Memorial Hill, there was an unmanned drone a thousand meters or so above me. Somebody, somewhere, was watching my every move. As my Driver headed down into the dry stream my team on the ground were fairly close to my Warrior. Although it felt safer to be closer to the Warrior, being too close had its negatives; if the Warrior hit an IED then it would be the end for them. I was told that I had stood on my Commander's seat in the turret, with half of my upper torso exposed to any potential enemy watching on. I did this so I could warn my team as they got too close and to push out to their correct distance. Within seconds of them moving, that was it, an almighty explosion set off directly underneath my position in the turret. The blast blew the under armour - fitted to the Warrior for added protection from the deadly IEDs - upwards, forcing everything sitting above and on top of it upwards too.

Above the under armour is the Warriors hull. The hull was made of solid metal and, theoretically, should be capable of protecting the Warrior against a blast without the added under armour. However such was the sophistication and power of the IEDs to date, the under armour was a welcomed and necessary piece of added protection. On top of the hull, where the IED had struck my Warrior, sat the diesel tank and directly above the diesel tank is the turret. The Warrior runs on diesel fuel. Diesel, as we know, it is less flammable than petrol. The diesel tank always played on mind though.

Throwing a cigarette end into a pool of diesel wouldn't set it alight - like a pool of petrol - but something hotter, like an explosion, would turn everyone inside at the time into nothing more than ash. The diesel tank is made from hardened plastic specially designed for that type of fuel and housed more than seven hundred litres of fuel. You can see the diesel through the tank from the back of the Warrior, you would forget it's there half the time and the number of cigarettes I have had while resting against it is unreal.

As the blast forced the under armour upwards, it then forced the hull up. The hull then pushed the diesel tank up which pushed my turret up and completely out of the Warrior itself. The turret landed a few metres away, hitting the ground hard. The Commander's side hit the ground first and landed upside down.

As the force of the blast pushed everything up, I was shot out of my turret like a bullet from a gun. I had landed some distance away from the Warrior. Unbelievably, luck was on my side that day, if I had not stood up to move the guys forward and remained seated, then catastrophic injuries would have resulted for me. The turret had landed upside down and my Commander's side hit the ground hard, from height and took the full impact. The possible eventualities were endless for me. I could have continued to stand halfway out of my turret as it came crashing down - decapitating my body. Or, if I had still been seated, the force of the blast rippling through the turret's floor directly under where my feet would have been positioned could have caused serious leg injuries, or even worse, an amputation.

The lads told me that I was thrown high into the air as I was blown out of the turret and landed on my upper back and head in the dry stream around ten metres from the turret's position. As the dust settled around the Warrior, my boss and his crew in callsign Three-Zero were left with the sight and the aftermath of the destruction. My Warrior no longer resembled a Warrior, the armour from both sides of the Warrior had been blown far away, the Warrior's road wheels and running gear were also gone, around the right-hand side of the Warrior was a huge, freshly created ditch caused from the blast itself and the Warrior was sat in the middle of it. The ditch now looked like a crater on the moon.

Somehow, my team on the ground had escaped the blast and the flying debris and were absolutely fine. After my team took a deep breath to focus on what had just happened, Blade instantly sprinted over to my position - risking his own life crossing the unchecked ground - to get me. He hit me with a morphine pen as I lay motionless. As Blade was dealing with me, it was all hands-on deck to find the rest of my crew and see to them medically, if they were still alive to require it.

I had left Youngy and Wiggy in the back of my Warrior before the IED hit us, my gunner was in the turret with me at the time of the explosion, my driver was in his seat. My boss had to think fast and put a plan into place and make it happen. He was the best man on the ground - in any situation - and everyone thought highly of him and the Platoon Sergeant and we would bend over backwards for both men. The boss didn't need to tell anyone what to do at the scene because everyone just did what they were trained to do. They went into overdrive, leaving my boss free to call in a rescue mission and the MERT (Military Emergency Response Team), a team made up of medical experts based back at Camp Bastion. The flight to F.O.B Minden was twenty plus minutes long, so every minute it took my boss to write up and send his report, was a minute less for me to live.

There were reports that the drone above had been hovering over me, a thousand metres above my Warrior at the time of the blast and the force of the explosion had pushed the drone off its route. The blast was caught on the drone's camera as the IED set off. I have never been allowed to view the footage. The footage would have been a massive help for my post-traumatic stress disorder and it may well have helped me gain the memories from the IED incident that I cannot remember.

Apparently after Blade rushed over to me and gave me the morphine, he managed to bring me round from being out cold and unconscious and the first thing I did was head for my Warrior shouting for my boys who I knew were still trapped inside the destroyed Warrior.

Surprisingly, nobody had died. The blast was one of the biggest to hit an armoured Warrior in any war zone and the turret being blown clean off the Warrior was unheard of. Thankfully the armour of the Warrior did its job that day and saved everyone inside it. If the armour had buckled and allowed the blast to penetrate the Warrior then that would have been it for everybody. The amount of ammunition inside the Warrior was enough to wipe Afghanistan off the map if it had detonated simultaneously. In the back of my Warrior and around my turret I had a Javelin missile, a number of hand grenades, well over fifty 30mm high explosive rounds and thousands of chain gun rounds. There was enough ammunition inside to send hundreds of terrorists to meet their seventy-two virgins.

My driver was absolutely fine after the blast, he was shaken up, but okay. I was told he was still sitting in his driver's seat in the aftermath of the blast, he was so lucky the blast had struck on my side of the Warrior and not his. The force of the blast would have almost certainly killed him because there is very limited space inside the driver's compartment and that level of force thrusting the under-armour up, would have had devastating consequences for him. In the back of the Warrior my two lads were left with serious foot injuries which required surgery. The reason my boys' feet were damaged during the blast was down to its ripple effect. The armoured flooring took the brunt of the blast and the lads had their feet down on the hull's floor at the moment the blast rippled forcefully along the armoured flooring.

My gunner had also been located, he was found alive, still sitting in his gunner's seat gasping for air and in a huge amount of pain. He had escaped the blast, and the fall, with a foot injury. It was a miracle that nobody died from the blast that day, including my team on the ground. My gunner, like myself, somehow defeated incredible odds and escaped being another pointless death in the Middle-East. Being blown out of my turret reminded me of a game called Pop-up Pirate. You would insert little plastic swords into slots on a beer barrel - with the pirate inside - and when you hit a certain slot, the pirate would shoot up and out of the beer barrel.

With all the lads found and alive the medics stationed with us in F.O.B Minden were now on the ground at my location and giving us medical attention. We were soon evacuated back to F.O.B Minden while we waited for the MERT team to fly in to recover us back to Camp Bastion. Nobody had really evaluated the severity of my injuries, they assumed it wasn't too serious because I was talking. I have one memory of the incident and that was hearing my old Company Commander say to me,

"You can't blame this one on anyone else this time Corporal Lock."

What an absolute tool you might think, but to me that was Military banter at its best.

The MERT team arrived on the ground in a Sea-King helicopter, but I had taken a turn for the worse. I had blood in my earlobes, a sign of severe trauma. I was stretchered onto the helicopter and then we took off and headed for Camp Bastion. As we got up into the air my heart stopped. I lay dying, high above the Afghanistan lands. The doctors onboard needed to act quickly to save my life and they made the decision to operate onboard to stem the internal bleeding that they had recognised as the reason for my heart stopping. They inserted a scalpel and cut a twelve-inch hole up my stomach and through my belly button. I had ruptured my spleen and the blood flowing from the spleen was killing me. As they cut into me - pulling my insides out to stem the ruptured spleen - laying opposite me on another stretcher was Wiggy. He was witnessing me being operated on in the sky. He had his own injuries, but the sight of me dying in front of him and then being sliced open like a samurai sword through paper, had a massive effect on him and still sticks in his mind even to this day.

As the doctors removed my spleen and closed me up with forty staples, my life began to stabilise. The decision was made to keep me sedated, in an induced coma, until the medical experts could evaluate the full extent of my injuries.

I was later told by a source, that I was the first British Soldier to be operated on in the Afghanistan sky. The air and the dust carried an airborne disease similar to MRSA that would put me at risk of serious illness if I contracted it, so it didn't make sense, nor was it a clean operating environment for anyone in need. The risk to life in carrying out such a highly dangerous procedure in the air was massive. It made sense to carry out the required operations in a sterile theatre back at Camp Bastion. I wasn't lucky enough to get a choice, but the choice made was the right one and I am still here to tell my story.

Back at Camp Bastion, while induced in a coma, I was given x-ray after x-ray to ascertain the true extent of my injuries. The doctors decided that I should continue to be intubated for at least a week while my body recovered from the injuries from the second blast in just over a month. It wouldn't make sense to try and wake me up. Rest is best, and no better rest is best while you slept.

With a traumatic brain injury showing up and signs of a bleed on the brain, a seriously damaged vertebrae in my thoracic spine, the spleen removed and a number of broken bones to my shoulder and blade the decision was the right one, besides, I hadn't slept properly in months, so it was much needed.

Whilst I was being looked after, the boys injured alongside me were having treatment themselves. They required surgery at some stage on their feet and legs. The three of them were very young at the time of the blast. Just a few years ago the three of them would have still been in the dinner queue at school while I carried the coffins of two of my friends who had died serving the Country.

Back on the ground in Yatminshia an operation was on-going to recover my Warrior from the blast spot. The Warrior was so badly damaged that it would require dragging the short distance back to F.O.B Minden. The turret also needed to be recovered, as well as the armour blown into the distance. Before the recovery could start the ground would need to be cleared again to make sure it was safe for the recovery vehicles to move in and the personnel on the ground to start collecting the parts blown off the damaged Warrior.

The IED had turned out to be a newly designed device. It was made from plastic which prevented my boys detecting it - they walked over it completely unaware that it was buried in the ground beneath. The device must have been there for some time because there was no ground sign around it, either that or the person who placed it in the ground was a highly trained gardener - but either way the bastards finally got me.

There were numerous reports that one of the snipers from my Regiment had taken out the person who placed the IED down, there is no way of ever knowing if this person who blew me up is actually dead. Nobody knew his real identity because he had never been observed placing the IED into the ground. For all I know, I could have killed him myself long before. He could well have been one of the strikes on the chart hanging in my turret - once part of my Warrior.

Plenty of the terrorists in Iraq and Afghanistan had the audacity and balls big enough to set an IED in the ground. We had plenty of IEDs placed between the two F.O.Bs in my time in Afghanistan. The nerve of the idiots who would set them up - never mind doing it so close to our bases - was unreal and absolutely mental. Surely they were recruited to place these IEDs down because they are insane and suicidal. Did they think they were too clever to don a vest and blow themselves up like the rest of the fuckers? Who knows? Surely if they believed the same ideology as each other then they would want to die and become a Martyr. After all, apparently there's 72 Virgins awaiting their arrival.

I look back at the pictures of the Warrior torn apart by that IED on the 9th June 2009 and think how lucky I was to survive that day. Everything fell into place for me. I don't believe in God, but something or someone was looking out for me that day. I don't believe in luck either, even though I have had my fair share of it, but I do realise something was on my side that day. Everybody has a time and a place to meet their end, that's something I do believe in. One thing I struggle to come to terms with today, when I look back at the pictures, is whether the IED and the injuries to my boys was my fault. I have been told numerous times it wasn't, but I cannot accept it or let it go in life. I can't remember anything about that day, I would like to know if that video from the drone really existed and judge it for myself. See if it will trigger any memories in my fight against my mental health, but it will never happen though, because the Military stopped loving me the day I was injured - just like they do to everyone else regardless of rank. All the help and support also stops. We are nothing more than a chess piece to the Army and the Government, we can be replaced in an instant, yet our bodies that we put on the line can't.

The one thing I do remember about my time serving in Afghanistan is that I was a good Warrior Sergeant and an even better Warrior Commander and as everyone keeps reassuring me, I was not complacent that day. The bomb was undetectable to the human eye and undetectable to the equipment at hand. I did everything right leading up to the blast and if anything I prevented the lads on the ground becoming casualties themselves by pushing them out to their correct distances.

But the brain injury, the PTSD, the depression, the lack of support right from the day I was injured all go against me. It is hard and only those in similar positions understand the real issues with the lack of support - not just from the Government and the Army, but the very charities that have been set up to help people like me. My own Regiment had washed their hands of me and for what reason? For all the good I ever gave, I have been left feeling like a victim and unable to move forward from the past.

CHAPTER THIRTY-THREE
THE BREAK OUT

After falling from the spinal bed during the early hours of the morning, enough was enough. When I was finally lifted off the floor, I had a large wound over my right eye that was eventually fixed together with a couple of butterfly stitches and then I was left alone again. Nobody was concerned about the pain or swelling in my cheekbone and I wasn't checked over by any doctors immediately after the fall. I had a serious spinal injury, yet nobody was concerned that I had just fallen a fair height to the hard floor, potentially making my spinal injury worse. I was left in considerable pain, the pain was thumping away in my thoracic spine - the area where I had damaged my vertebrae. My cheekbone was sore and my eye was stinging, I kept asking the nurses to call my Partner as I was in shock and needed her to keep me calm. The nurses constantly told me that they had rung my partner but she did not answer, but they hadn't. My Partner's phone was by her side all night and the volume was up at its loudest setting, she was staying in accommodation less than a hundred metres away from the hospital's main entrance and could have been at my side within minutes.

The next morning my Partner walked into my room, her eyes lit up to the sight of my face.

"What the hell has happened to you?" she said.

I told her what happened and how I was treated afterwards and she stormed out to the nurse's station and demanded an explanation. She was fed lie after lie about the incident.

Later that day my head started to itch, I couldn't move that well because I was on a high amount of medication and sore. My partner scratched my head for me and as she pulled her fingers out of my hair they were covered in dust. I hadn't been cleaned or washed since the day I was blown up. She went back out to the nurse's station to find out why nobody had bothered to clean me over and to ask if she could wash me. She was told no, she wasn't allowed to touch me,

"A nurse will do it later when one is free," the nurse said.

When the nurse finally arrived, she told my partner to leave the room. Like me, she wasn't having it, she was staying put. The nurses were lovely, but their rules on what they can and can't do just made you want to hate them but it wasn't their fault. I was eventually washed over the best the nurse could do and my hair was still clogged with dust. I would need a hot shower to get the dust out, but unfortunately I was told it was looking highly likely that I would remain on the spinal bed for another ten weeks or so.

Later that day the Military had sent in a lady to see me - shortly after my partner had headed back at to her accommodation, I wasn't in the mood for visitors so early into my recovery, but she came in anyway. The lady gave me the talk on compensation and explained to me that she would fill in my compensation claim forms for me. It was all a bit weird and felt rushed. I hadn't long woken from a coma and I was having my compensation claim forms filled out and sent off. My injuries still hadn't been fully assessed, I wasn't sure if I would ever walk again, it was all to bizarre. When my Partner arrived back at visiting time I had told her about it. Again she asked the nurses why the lady came in to see me against my will when I had told her I wasn't up for visitors. Prince Charles had come to visit the injured lads on the ward and I told them I didn't want to meet the future King in this state and I wasn't up for it and they listened that time. My time in the hospital was becoming a joke, it seemed like the Military were having the last say on how the ward was run. The nurses were mixed, some civilian and some Military.

As the days passed I was becoming more and more impatient, I was being forced "for my own benefit" to lie down flat without a pillow to help my back recover. I suffered with sleep Apnoea as a child and sleeping on my back always started it off, then I had no pillow, I was uncomfortable. I had slept in some difficult positions in my time, but nothing like this. My bowels felt really uncomfortable after being handled during surgery on the helicopter and with all the drugs inside of me I was constantly defecating myself like a new-born baby. Up to eight times a day I would defecate myself meaning that I would need my bed sheets to be changed every time. Every bed sheet change meant I would need rolling and with every roll I would require a number of nurses around me to make this happen. I would need my backside wiped clean of any mess and again this was done by any one of the nurses in the room at the time. I would be partially naked as they rolled me about. My partner would try and cover my private bits best she could, and this one time she witnessed one young female nurse say to another, as they cleaned me,

"oh, look at his cute little bum".

It was humiliating when she told me, but I tried to see the good from it, 'they were here to look after me', I kept repeating in my head to try and calm myself down. I was also extremely sore downstairs, I was covered in bedsores from the constant amount of shit flowing wildly from my backdoor. My Partner was finally allowed to help me out and she began to tend to my sores by cleaning them and applying fresh cream.

Over the days I had become stronger because the humiliation had got the best of me. I wanted out of the hospital and the only way I could escape was to get myself to a stronger state of mind and then flee when I could. But I had a long way to go to get there. I had to eat lying down, I had to try and defecate into a pot lying down after the fuss I made about the humiliation, everything I could do, I had to do lying down. Using the pot as a toilet was horrible, I had to try and lift my back end up as a nurse slid a pot under me. The number of drugs I had in my system meant I was having constant diarrhea rather than a stable poo; the room would stink really badly, and I would always have a visitor walk in on me whilst using the potty - which again embarrassed the life out of me.

Pickle, one of the Mortar Platoon Sergeants, had come to visit me during his Afghanistan leave and walked in as I was on the pot taking another dump. I had been left on the pot for over twenty minutes, which I wanted to believe was down to the nurses being busy and not forgetting me - but my stay on the ward was that strange I didn't know what to think.

A few weeks in I was told that there was a bed available in a Specialist Spinal Hospital in Cardiff and I had the option to be transferred back to Wales and be closer to my family. Being based in Birmingham was a massive pain for everyone. My Partner was torn between being at my bedside and being at home for our four-year-old daughter. It was hard on everybody, it made sense to be transferred to Cardiff just twelve miles away from my home. The transfer could only take place if I could fund a spinal mattress myself between the two hospitals there wasn't a spare spinal mattress even though I was lying on one. I was told if I wanted the transfer then I had to fund it myself. I was again confused because I was laying on a spinal bed. The hospital wasn't willing to part with the mattress. I didn't have the money to buy the bed myself. The bed wasn't overly expensive, but with a mortgage and a family to provide for, we just didn't have the money. We approached my Regiment to ask them to fund my bed, they shut us down instantly. They refused to fund a bed for me, they were one of the richest Regiments in the British Army and they stuck their middle finger up at me. As Corporals, we paid mess bills for the privilege of being a Corporal - so there were plenty of funds available - but I was turned away. As a soldier in general, I was forced to pay Regimental subs monthly. Again I was turned away.

What had I done to my Regiment to be treated like this? I had served nine and a half years with them up until the day of the IED, I had never put a foot wrong in my career, I never once got into trouble, I did what I was told to do and always gave my all.

After being ditched by my own Regiment I turned to a major charity set up to help injured soldiers for the funding. Again I was turned away. The excuse I had from them was they were a new charity and didn't fund individuals, yet one of the boys on my ward was funded flying lessons almost immediately after leaving hospital and his flying lessons were aired on a popular singing contest on the tv that year. During the show the contestants sang a fund-raising song for the charity.

I turned to a number of other charities and again I was turned away with more bullshit and lies. All I wanted to do was get to the hospital in Cardiff and be closer to my daughter. My Company Commander, who had taken over the Company just before I got injured, sent me some good news through his lovely wife who had regularly made the long trip to the hospital to visit me and the other injured lads. He told me his amazing mother had offered to raise the money through knitting blankets and other projects. This was unbelievable news for me, finally someone wanted to help me, yet the charities that were supposed to help, turned their backs. My Regiment finally agreed to hand over a small amount of funds after hearing that the mother of one of their best officers had stepped in to help me.

After all the added stress from the knock backs over this bed, I was more determined to get out of hospital and get home to my daughter. I spoke with my partner and although she wasn't convinced I should leave, she said she would back my decision to break out of hospital as long as the time was right to do so and my injuries were healing.

I was waiting for my weekly MRI and x-ray to come back showing my back had stabilised. The doctor had promised me that when it did, he would get me up and about again if my body allowed. My plan was to go for a cigarette and never return. The brain injury I had made me forget I ever smoked. Even today, ten years on, I still haven't touched a cigarette. I haven't even thought about having one either which is amazing considering how many I was smoking per day before the blast.

Within a week, the scan finally showed my back was stable enough to start my recovery and my escape. The doctor went back on his word though and told me it would be a few more days until I would be in a position to start moving about again. I wanted this catheter taken out of my manhood for a start. Every time I moved about, the tubes from the catheter would pull down hard and make me feel like I was burning inside. I wanted a shower as well, I wanted to go and see Wiggy who was still on the ward recovering. I hadn't been able to see him properly since the day it happened for obvious reasons, but most of all I wanted to get the hell out of this hospital and let my partner care for me back home in comfort, with my daughter.

The day came when I was allowed to finally sit up slightly, we had to take it easy with the movement over the next couple of days just to be certain my back was recovering and still healing. I finally got a towel to rest my head and neck on even though I had a neck brace on. My catheter was also removed, and my quality of life was slowly improving.

I had missed out on the chance to move to the Cardiff hospital because the money would take a little while to be raised and the bed had now been taken by another patient. Plus, I would need a spinal mattress at home anyway, so it made sense to use the funds on a new mattress for my home. I was still pissed off with the lack of support or help that should have been readily available to me. The lads on the ward were getting the support and both me and partner were left bemused as to why I wasn't. The only support we had was my Regiment's Welfare Officer who frequently visited me on the ward, unlike the rest of my Regiment.

In the days to come, I had begun having physio lessons in my room; the objective was for me to gain my balance again and learn to walk, which was a massive issue. Every time I sat up I felt dizzy and sick, every time I put weight onto my legs I just couldn't move them as well I wanted and expected. I was given a Zimmer frame to help get me around and also a wheelchair. The wheelchair would be my way out. As soon as I was allowed to start moving about the ward freely, I had planned the break out. I had a brilliant Welfare Officer who I knew well from my time in 'A' Company back in Paderborn. He had tried his best to make my stay in hospital as good as it could be. Both he and his Second-in-Command gave all their time to look after my partner. They drove her back and forth to Wales whenever she wanted to head home. I knew that between these two men, I could rely on them to help me get out of the hospital. I would be stuck for a lift home if I escaped alone with just the missus. I had to come up with another plan,

I wasn't right in the head stuck in that room after everything that had happened to me. I was slowly coming to terms with the fact my career was over and I now had the added stress of worrying about paying my mortgage and keeping a roof over my little girl's head as well. My life had gone from everything to nothing in a blink of an eye.

I began to get better movement in my legs, I couldn't walk unaided though and I was placed on crutches to aid me whilst moving about. I was told that my recovery would be slow, and I probably wouldn't be running or taking part in sport ever again. Taking part in sport was a major blow to me. Sport was my life. Being told I may never run again wasn't too much of an issue because I hated running anyway and the only time you'll ever see me run again is into a kebab shop or to dodge the rain.

Day after day I tried vigorously to get my legs working properly and strong enough to hold my weight. Doctors kept telling me that I had damaged the top of my spine, not the bottom, so my legs should be ok. I knew my body better than them. I knew I had significant problems, regardless of what an x-ray of my lower half showed the medical experts. I was struggling to move my right arm as well; my rotator cuff would pull and cause me horrendous pain, so walking with crutches was a nightmare, but do-able. I also had a brain injury that the doctor seemed to keep dodging.

I kept pestering the doctor about going home to recover. I would annoy him with the same question every time I saw or heard his voice on the ward - to the point that he finally allowed me to return home to Wales and recover, in my own bed, under the care of my Partner - without the need to break out in the way I was planning. That was it, the break out my way was off, but I was going home and just four and a bit weeks after dying in the Afghanistan sky. I was going home to be with my baby girl for the first time in weeks. I missed that girl so much, having nearly died and then spending weeks lying on a bed doing nothing but think about her.

The time in hospital spent thinking did nothing for my health, all it achieved was to bring back memories of the bad shit that had happened during my career. I constantly re-lived every bad moment in my life. I saw the faces of my friends who had died fighting for this very Country that is now in turmoil over Brexit and my friends who died needlessly through a beasting and a suicide. I saw the innocent, tortured remains of the adults and children butchered by the enemy that littered the lands of Iraq and Afghanistan, I re-lived every round I fired out of my turret and into the bodies of the enemy attacking me and my men, I had visions of being blown up both times, even though I couldn't remember the second blast, but my nightmares would.

When the day came for me to leave the hospital, it was the best feeling I'd had in such a long time. I could now, finally, head home and focus on my recovery without the young nurses calling my rear "a little cute bum" while wiping my mess up. I would no longer have the butcher turn up every morning to painfully insert a needle into my veins to take more blood for testing. I think I gave more blood for tests during my time there than I had in my body. No more painful injections. No more hallucinations.

The Welfare Officer had received the funds for a mattress, thanks to the new Company Commander's amazing mother, who managed to raise the money. I never got the chance to thank her for her kindness and generosity - nor his wife for taking the time out to travel up to Birmingham to visit me. I can't bring myself to thank my own Regiment for finally stumping up a part of the funds either, they made my life hell over the damn mattress in the first place and only gave in when a civilian stepped up to help.

I arrived home to a small number of neighbors waiting outside the house beneath a welcome home sign hung up for my return; each one greeting me as I arrived home. Everyone in the street had known something bad had happened to me because my partner had received the dreaded 'man in the suit' knock at the door, the bearer of bad news. He didn't have much information to tell her when he knocked on the door to inform her about me, because he didn't know the full extent of my injuries or what had happened. He basically explained to her that I was still alive for now and to prepare herself for the worst. She received the news the day she passed her driving test and was waiting for my planned phone call home so she could tell me her good news. But that phone call never happened, and she almost never got to tell me her news.

CHAPTER THIRTY-FOUR
PAIN

As soon as I arrived home from hospital I started receiving unwanted phone calls from the Army warning me that I had to travel to up to Headley Court and start my rehabilitation. First thing that sprung to my mind was fuck off, I hadn't seen my family properly for months and I had almost died. My body was sore and aching from the damage of the IED and these idiots want me back on another ward for God knows how long, and why? So they can cover their backsides. I wasn't going, I told them straight,

"No, I am not ready, I want a month off to recover at home before I go anywhere."

They told me I wasn't in a position to say "No". I would be charged with disobeying a direct order! I wasn't bothered either way because I knew my time was done in the Military, I wasn't stupid. The doctors had already told me that I will probably never work again and the way my own Regiment had treated me since I awoke from my coma pretty much confirmed my time was up.

I made my way to Headley Court just over three weeks after I had been discharged from hospital. It was the day of my daughter's 5th birthday. The Army wanted me in their care and under their supervision and I was being pressurised heavily, so eventually I caved in. Headley Court is a rehabilitation unit for sick and injured soldiers - run by the Military - and with some of the best medical experts in the world caring for its patients. I was placed on a ward almost immediately after arriving and that is where I stayed for two months. I didn't do much, my back was causing me some extreme pain and there were fears that it may be unstable again and might need operating on! As the days and weeks passed, I started to get annoyed and become angry at my care. I wasn't doing anything bar lay down flat on a horrible bed and just think of the horrors I had survived. Occasionally my physio would give me a massage, working on my rotator cuff and shoulder blade, but that was about all I could do. I could have been at home recovering on my own bed, with the only two people in the world who have ever cared for me, but no, the Military want me in Headley Court and in their sights. They can keep an eye on me, whilst accidentally losing my medical paperwork which would screw my compensation claim up.

The compensation hadn't really crossed my mind, I was more concerned about my injuries. My mind just wasn't right after the explosion. I was struggling to remember things I so easily remembered before; like names, numbers, faces, I just couldn't remember. Every time I tried discussing this with someone, I was told there was nothing wrong with me, even though I had evidence that I had a fractured skull and a brain haemorrhage, yet it felt like the Military were trying to cover the injury up so they didn't have to pay out for it. When my compensation confirmation came through the post, the forms filled out by that lady in the hospital - and filled out against my will - it became clear to me that whole thing may be a deliberate act by the Military of misguiding and misinforming both the claimant and the compensation assessors, in order to cut down on the amount of compensation being awarded. I had all these things running through my head because I had nothing else to do but just lay there on my bed and think.

During my stay at Headley Court, Wiggy had arrived on the ward to start his recovery. The other lads had already left prior to my arrival as they were recovering a lot better and quicker than Wiggy was. It was good to see him, I still felt guilty that his career could be over so early on in his young life, even though what had happened wasn't anyone's fault other than the fucker who planted the IED. We spent some time together on the ward and one thing that struck me was what he had seen on that helicopter that day. He was struggling mentally with it; my heart was bleeding inside for him. As the days passed by, we had a visit from the lads who had just finished the Tour in Afghanistan, it was amazing to see the lads who I had worked alongside in Yatminshia and to say thank you to everyone who helped keep me alive that day, especially Blade, Will and my boss. Everyone was buzzing to be back home, they were shocked to see and hear about our injuries because they had hardly any information fed back to them whilst they continued the Tour. Passage of information in my Regiment was terrible and I knew full well what they were like because when my friends were injured in Iraq, all we did was ask how they were getting on with their recovery and each time we were told nobody knew. What made me laugh most about my Regiment was that Headley Court was just an hour up the road, so there were no excuses not to visit and let us know we are not forgotten about.

When the lads visited me for the first time since touching down in the UK, they had time to explain what had actually happened on the day that ruined my life. We had been making light hearted jokes about the whole ordeal and for the first time in a long time, I started to feel like the old me again. Just hearing the boys who mattered most to me talk about what went on over there in Afghanistan, made me feel normal again because we had lived so closely together in a war zone, the talk about life over there was the best medicine. One of the boys had me in tears. An injured Royal Navy sailor recovering on my ward came past in his wheelchair and with a deep squeaky-like voice he said,

"Excuse me please," as he tried to pass through an almost impossible gap.

One of the lads turned around and said,

"What the hell happened to him? Did he fall of his ship and get eaten by a shark?"

Oh how I laughed, something I hadn't done in such a long time.

My platoon were only the second visitors to come and visit me at Headley Court after the occasional visit from my Regiment's Welfare Officer. My Commanding Officer had come up to visit a few days prior to my platoon visiting, but he didn't come to see me or Wiggy, instead he had chosen to visit an old friend and former officer in the Regiment who was also injured in Afghanistan. He gave the officer one of the Regiment's Regimental tracksuits - that weren't cheap to buy - yet I was the one who needed it most as I had no Military sports kit to wear as all my kit was either being worn by some Afghani who had found my clothes after the explosion or had been packed away in boxes and placed into storage back in Tidworth. All I had was a t-shirt supplied by a charity while I was hospital in Birmingham.

The Military guys who patrolled around the ward, to keep us in check, didn't like us wearing our own sports kit during the day and preferred all the recovering soldiers to wear our Military issued sports kit. My Commanding Officer did bring up a Regimental t-shirt for me though and handed it to me while he briefly said hello. The t-shirt was an extra-large in size, I was eight and half stone at the time, the t-shirt looked and felt like a sleeping bag on me. Again, this was another example of how bad my own Regiment were at looking after me and everyone else who was unfortunate enough to get injured. I am, to this day, my Regiment's most seriously injured soldier from the Afghanistan war and yet, since the day of the explosion I feel as though I have been treated like a criminal and banished without any due care.

I can see why ex-servicemen take their own lives after leaving the forces, the support for anyone with injuries that are not visible was appalling and it still is, the whole system should be looked at urgently and that includes the bigger charities.

I had managed to persuade the doctor to wake up and get my brain injury looked at, I was moved downstairs onto the neurological ward with like-minded people. I was finally starting to get the help I had been desperately asking for, but again the experts started playing down my memory and concentration problems as PTSD. I knew I had PTSD anyway, I had known since the day my mate killed himself in Kosovo, that was the day I went into a shell and struggled to climb out of it. I had known what PTSD symptoms I had, as more and more people got diagnosed over the years with it and some of those diagnoses I had. I never wanted to believe it though and I certainly didn't want to visit the doctors about it. My brain symptoms were different to the PTSD symptoms, I couldn't remember anything I was being told, I couldn't concentrate at all, I had a totally new personality that made me miserable and angry. I had become clumsy, my speech would occasionally become slurred and I would stutter when I felt uncomfortable, yet I was told differently.

During my stay at Headley Court I was offered a holiday by a newly formed charity in Jersey. A lovely couple had set up the charity off their own backs, they are the most honest and wonderful human beings I had ever met. They had the full support from the good people of Jersey, who welcomed us with open arms. I flew over to Jersey with my Partner and my young daughter in September and we were put up in a beautiful, five-star hotel with other veterans on the trip. The experience was outstanding, there were loads of activities laid on for us like an island Tour, a zoo trip, we met the red arrows and the charity even laid on a mobility scooter for me to get around. I was on crutches at the time and still struggling to walk, so the scooter was an added boost.

After the amazing trip was over and I had headed back to reality at Headley Court, it was back to the same thing, laying on my bed, thinking the same shit over and over again, followed by the occasional massage and a visit to the brain experts. I was sure I was only placed on the neurological ward because I had kept on and on at them and they wanted to shut me up, so sent me down to the ward.

The pain in my back hadn't eased at all since I left Birmingham hospital. I had been prescribed loads of different types of medications to try and ease the pain, but nothing was working. I was left in agony and it was destroying me. Only a really hot object like a heat pad or a hot bath helped to ease my pain. I went to see a different surgeon about my back pain and he carried out a new investigation with a number of new x-rays and MRI's, it was clear to him that I would require an operation. I would need a cage fitted around my damaged vertebrae to hold it in place and stop the damaged vertebrae from pressing on my damaged nerves. The operation was scheduled after Christmas, so I had to take it extremely easy until then. I told the surgeon that I wouldn't be doing much in activities anyway, other than lay on my bed, but he took the decision for me to continue wearing my neck brace.

Christmas was fast approaching, and I was still in Headley Court doing nothing, my Regiment had barely visited me either. I was left on my own now as well because Wiggy had left. I found it hard to make any friends due to everyone else having their own problems which they were receiving attention and support for. I wasn't getting anything, so I became detached from everyone and closed back into my shell like a tortoise. With Christmas just a few weeks away, we were getting visits from celebrities, but the staff in charge of us were very selective with whom the celebrities sat and spoke with even though most had arrived at Headley Court off their own backs because they cared.

That was it for Christmas, Headley Court would close down for the festive period and I had two weeks off to recuperate back home with the girls. My partner's mum was still living with us and we now had a gorgeous little dog called Lily-mae who was a King Charles Cavalier, she was the runt of the litter and when we went to look for a dog she instantly stood out to my partner's mum who had her heart set on her at first glimpse. Christmas was good, and it was really nice to be at home and around the only people who mattered to me. I was still in pain with my back, it wasn't easing at all and I could not see a future without pain. My head wasn't right either, I wouldn't leave the house when I had to, I had started to hate people as I did not feel comfortable around those I did not know and the feeling left me really on edge, like I was going to be attacked by them. I was jumpy and very anxious and shouty.

My partner had to be resilient to cope with me back then. I wasn't the most pleasant of people during my difficult time. I think back to those days and wish I had been a different person, more like the guy I was before the explosion. My partner wasn't offered any support either, she was now caring for me. I couldn't even put my own socks on my own feet or bath myself and yet she was there for me. I couldn't remember when to take my tablets or which ones to take when I had to, yet she was there. Amongst caring for me, she was bringing up our young daughter too and caring for her mother who had recently lost her husband and had suffered a severe heart attack during my first few weeks at Headley Court. My partner dealt with it all. I had witnessed lads on the ward go through divorces because their wives couldn't cope with the stress, I don't know how she pulled through it all, but she did, and I am the person I am today thanks to her.

After Christmas I headed back to Headley Court where I had only been a few days before I started to kick up a massive fuss about being left to rot on my bed and doing nothing but think. I hated my new life, I wanted help and treatment for my brain, I wanted to sleep more than three hours a night, I wanted the awful thoughts gone from head but all I ever heard from the experts' mouths was,

"Your back is this bad…. or your back is that…"

After I kicked up the fuss I was sent home - where I recovered around the people who wanted to be around me - until the day of my operation. The operation was done in Frimley Park Hospital and it caused the worst pain I had ever felt. After the operation I was on a high number of drugs to help with the pain and again I had started to become mentally abusive towards the staff. The staff were amazing to me, even though I was a cunt to them, they just ignored the abuse coming from my mouth. I can't be too sure if it was the drugs that made me abusive or whether it was my split personality coming out of me every time I had a certain drug in my system, either way I apologised sincerely.

I was discharged from hospital a few days later and I went straight home to recover. This time I was in twice as much pain - I just wanted to die. Every time I tried to move I could feel the layers of my muscle detaching from the areas that had been cut through during the operation, it was horrible. Luckily, after all this time I was free from that horrible, smelly neck brace. I wasn't even wearing the neck brace because I had broken my neck in the first blast - that injury was covered up quickly by the Military - the neck brace was for my damaged vertebrae.

The damaged vertebrae sat in a position close to my neck, so it made perfect sense to keep my neck held still so it didn't cause any more pain or complications to my spine.

After a month of lying in bed while my back recovered, I was finally up and about. I was still using a crutch, but unfortunately still unable to walk properly. The pain was still there as well. The pain just did not want to go away no matter how much medication I was prescribed or the operation I had just undergone. The only thing that was easing the pain was something warm held against it. The operation, in my mind, was a flop; in my surgeon's mind it was a success. My vertebrae were now sitting correctly thanks to the cage and were no longer a danger to my spinal cord and free from touching my nerves. The pain couldn't be explained, so the medical world came up with a new explanation for it - "PTSD" - everything they struggled to fix was blamed on PTSD. They tried telling me that the pain I was enduring was just in my mind and was being caused by the PTSD.

So now, even though I hadn't seen a psychiatrist during my recovery or been given a PTSD diagnosis by one, I apparently had it and that was the reason I was in so much pain. I couldn't concentrate and I could no longer remember a damn thing, maybe the brain did have something to do with the pain. The only way I would get a real diagnosis for my pain was to hope I get booted out of the Army and soon. All these Military medical experts were real arrogant sods, whom I was sure were deliberately ignoring the full extent of my injuries - for financial reasons.

CHAPTER THIRTY-FIVE
JUST ANOTHER NUMBER

With the operation over, I refused to go back to Headley Court and continue my rehabilitation. I was granted permission from my Regimental Chief Medical Officer (Doctor) to continue my rehab under him and his staff at the Tidworth Medical Centre where I was given a room on the ward they have there. Within days of arriving on the ward in Tidworth, I had finally begun to undergo therapy for PTSD and I was soon diagnosed with it. All those months of rehabilitation elsewhere and I did nothing but lay there, staring at the ceiling, doing nothing more than thinking had worn me down. I had nine and a half years' worth of bad memories flowing through my mind continuously and almost all of them made worse by doing nothing more than just lay there, resting and healing.

I had so many good memories during my time in the Regiment and I am still as proud today as I was before I was injured, but almost all of the good memories had been overshadowed by the bad ones. Being left alone to recover and forgotten about by my own Regiment - even though I was still serving - made things worse because it broke me and all for no reason. I began to hate my Regiment, ever since they were renamed the proud standards and discipline they once proudly abided to had started to disappear. I wasn't sure whether this was down to the retention issues within the Army and, looking at the recruitment campaigns today, I guess so. I wasn't the only injured soldier to be passed on and become someone else's problem either. All the lads that had been injured on my Tour, including my boys injured in the same blast as me, had also been shit on. They were back amongst the Regiment and even though they had been down-graded (medical term for working with restrictions and limitations due to injury) they were being forced to carry out the shit jobs in and around the Barracks and frowned upon for being injured.

I was now so glad to be over on the ward because I was closer to my friends again, they were only a few hundred meters away in their own accommodation. The boys would come across to see me when they finished work, also I would be collected by Spanky - who had gone above and beyond for me - and asked the Regiment if he could become the duty driver for me. He would take me across to their cookhouse, so I could eat with the boys. I got to see two of the boys who were injured alongside me, but the third lad, who was my gunner during the second IED, had recently been dismissed from the Army after smoking cannabis. He was given no help for what he had witnessed or went through whilst serving his Country. He was very young at the time, his life had been changed forever, he was forced, like the rest of us, to live through the moments he almost died. Every day leading up to his dismissal was like a life sentence in his head. The Regiment should have stood with him and backed him, they should have asked him why he had smoked the drug, they should have understood what the lad had been through, they should have been there for him and supported him, instead thanks to the Army's drug policy, he was booted out after one mistake. He had smoked it to help him forget his nightmares of war, something the Regiment refused to help him do.

I had known plenty of soldiers who were let off after being caught taking drugs during my time, but it was easy for the Regiment to boot this lad out because he was now nothing to them, just a "Biff" who was frowned down upon like the rest because they had become undeployable through no fault of their own. Most biffs were genuinely injured or had genuine issues, but like every other Regiment they also had some that weren't cut out to soldiers and were to un-trustworthy to hold a weapon on the front line, yet somehow made it through training.

One evening whilst in my room over on the ward, I was visited by a high-ranking officer who looked me in the eyes and told me about a piece of paper sitting on my Commanding Officer's desk with my name and the names of the two lads injured with me on it. The paperwork was part of the Regiment's action plan for redundancies that they were forced into creating, ready for the massive cut in numbers the Government were stupidly about to make. I hadn't even been in front of the medical board yet to determine whether or not I would be discharged. The other two lads had been recovering well and would, at some point down the line, be able to continue doing the job they had almost died doing, yet they also made the list even though they were twice the soldiers the majority of the biffs in the British Army would ever be. Our Commanding Officer had us top of the list and word had it that the he believed we would accept redundancy and leave without a fight, but he was wrong!

I approached the Commanding Officer and tried to demand an answer from him over the list, but I was dragged out of his office as soon as I mentioned it. Next thing I knew, I found myself back in my room on the ward penning a furious letter to the Prime Minister. I was not allowing the Army to end a career I had loved and gave my all for because I had become "just a number". It was down to them to look after me and the other two and help us recover, with the view that one day we may make a full recovery and continue with the jobs we did before. I would never be allowed to deploy again but that wouldn't stop me doing other work.

I have a mortgage, a family to support but no positive future. The extent of my injuries were still unknown and I was in considerable pain almost every minute of every day, I had hardly slept since waking from that coma and all I could see when my eyes did close were the faces of all my lost friends. I hated living because of it, I hardly had any support and what I did have, felt like it was fake. I had felt the staff were forced to help me rather than wanted to help me.

A few weeks into my recovery I was awarded a Joint Commanders Commendation for Distinguished service in Afghanistan. I was told by the same officer who had warned me about the redundancy list, that my precis of citation had been deliberately underwritten by my Regiment because the Military did not want word spreading of me being blown up twice in just over a month and being allowed to continue fighting on the frontline with minor whiplash which eventually turned out to be a broken neck and all the while commanding a Warrior with parts taken off another destroyed Warrior. The number of lads who get bigger awards for less was unbelievable. Mine was pretty much a certificate, something you get in school for doing something well. Don't get me wrong, I was only doing my job, I knew the risks of my job, so any award isn't really something we would hope for or would want, but since I was being screwed over for doing my job, it hurt me.

My Citation wrote:

"Corporal Lock deployed on Op Herrick 10 as a Warrior Commander with Charlie Company.

Due to manning commitments Corporal Lock was quickly elevated to the role of platoon Warrior sergeant, he readily accepted the additional responsibility and was committed to his tasks. He motivated exhausted soldiers to work through the night after a long days patrolling to ensure their Warriors were ready to deploy operations the following day. His soldiers worked the extra hours knowing that he was working alongside them.

Corporal Lock's efforts in the tank park were matched by his exemplary bravery and leadership as a Warrior Commander on the ground. In numerous engagements with the enemy

Corporal Lock exposed his Warrior in order to identify and engage the enemy forces. He inspired his crew with a determination to destroy the enemy. He was the most trusted Warrior Commander when the company were moving to the highest threat routes. His guidance to the barma teams resulted in the discovery of a number of IEDS.

On the 9th of June 2009 Corporal Lock's Warrior was struck by an IED and the vehicle was severely damaged. Corporal Lock was thrown 15 meters and sustained serious spinal and internal injuries. Despite this his main concerns were for the welfare of his crew. Corporal Lock's attitude and conduct mark him out as an exceptional Junior non-commissioned officer."

Within days of my letter reaching the Prime Minister's office I was given a Medical Board and told I was to be Medically Discharged from the Army, I was then sent home to recover alone and handed over to a small recovery unit based in Brecon. The two guys who ran the recovery unit at the time were fantastic to me and partner, they thought for my well-being and for the first time I started to see some light at the end of the tunnel. The Army had funded my home to be adapted for my use. I was now classed as disabled and my home wasn't suitable for me. I only got the changes to my home thanks to the two gents from Brecon who had bent over backwards to help me.

I believe the military funded the house adaptations to keep me quiet about the two IEDs. Shortly before they agreed to release the funds I had appeared in a National Newspaper. The paper had run a campaign on the lack of compensation and support for those affected with Post Traumatic Stress Disorder from the Military and someone who knew me, had sent them an anonymous letter about what I had been through with the two IEDs and the lack of support from both my

Regiment and the Military as a whole. The journalist drove from London to meet me the same day she had contacted me. She was overwhelmed by my story and told me that she would like my support to push the PTSD campaign out there to the people. My story was on the centre pages of the paper.

The newspaper's campaign was successful, but unfortunately nothing changed. Veterans suffering with PTSD are worse off now than ever. They are left struggling and tormented by the horrors of the job, the Government has toyed with our lives, sent us to a war in Iraq that should never have been started in the first place. They are responsible for our aftercare, not the charities. Lives are being lost, needlessly, every week to suicide, veterans are being left homeless and end up fending for themselves while living on the streets because our Councils are not accommodating them, prisons have an alarming number of veterans in them. The Government need to take responsibility and put a real plan into place and stop relying on the charities to take the strain.

So, my time had come to leave the Military. I left having served eleven and a half years and thoroughly enjoyed my job up until the day my life changed. I didn't ask for much, I got on with my responsibilities and did not once mess up - yet that IED had turned me into a criminal within the very place I had worked. I never once thought about claiming for negligence, I could have pushed my Company Commander to send me back to Camp Bastion for a proper check-up. I wasn't to know my neck was broken, the pain wasn't extreme, and it was kept under control by medication.

My entire pay-out was a farce, I had a number of serious injuries and feel screwed over. Deep down I wish I had lost a leg because at least I could still work and employers outside of the Military would give me a chance. I would have received a proper pay-out that reflects my injuries plus the charities would be crawling to help me rather than ignore my cries.

Having injuries that are invisible to the eye are a nightmare, the big charities don't want to know because they can't push us out to make money from us. Normal, everyday people don't care what your injuries look like, they'll still donate because they are good people. The charities seem to think that having a limb missing will make people feel sorrier for veterans meaning they will donate more money. This is the reason so many of us are left with limited support, or none at all. I told one charity that I had been asking for help for over six years, that I was feeling worthless and did not want to live anymore. I was eventually given a space on a feel better about yourself course and I only got on it because of what I said about my life, not because of my injuries and what I had gone through.

For six years they had ignored my cries for help yet certain injuries and you would get the opportunity to travel the world with them. The system is nothing more than a corrupt joke that needs cleansing. Too many individuals are taking the piss with the help. The trouble is, people don't understand what's going on behind closed doors. I know a huge amount of people who have left the Forces and have taken advantage of the charities and the charities allow it to happen with full knowledge. I have been ignored by them even though I have a medical record stating how serious my injuries were. There are people leaving the Military because they have fallen off a motorbike or crashed a car whilst at home on leave and are taking the resources away from people who require them most. If they had helped me when I first asked, then I would be living my life now and not wanting to not wake up.

I finally had my brain diagnosis from an independent specialist, because the Army denied the full extent of the injury. The specialist immediately identified that I had in fact had a Traumatic Brain Injury. I could not do anything about the back injury. I had been to two Tribunals over my back injury and even though I had the medical world on my side, the Army had its fingers in all the pies on their side, so I lost. I was paid out just a four-figure sum for my back injury. I have a cage fitted around three vertebrae and am still in pain.

My life has dramatically changed with both my back and neck now riddled with arthritis. I feel like I have been mugged off for the last ten years of my life. I can no longer do the things I could do with my family. I missed being there to lift my daughter up when she was crying. The medical experts have told me numerous times that my back injury is worse than losing a limb, if I had lost a limb I would have had ten times the pay-out. I guess I am lucky though, because I had not lost a limb, no money is enough for those guys, it doesn't matter if they can continue to work almost normally and receive better care and support from the big charities because they still have to look at themselves every night. I only have scars to look at, so I take my hat off to them because they deserve every single penny.

To this day I struggle to sleep more than four hours a night due to the constant pain throbbing away in my damaged back. I have learned to cope with it and will not let the pain defeat me. I refuse to take any pain relief other than the odd paracetamol because I had become nothing more than a zombie like creature who hated everyone and everything. I constantly felt lethargic and became so depressed I wanted to hang myself. I had that much medication in my system I felt like I was slowly being overdosed. The pain would still be there as well. Since dropping the huge amount of medication that I had to force down my throat with my fingers because I struggled to swallow the pills, I stopped thinking about death. I ditched my crutches soon after ditching the medication, I started to feel better for the first time since I was injured, my beautiful little dog Lily is the reason I started to walk again. My dog would beg me to take her out. She would drag me around the street until eventually I started to lose my crutches one at a time, it looked like a scene from the film Forrest Gump when Forrest started running with his legs in braces, the braces broke off and he just ran and ran.

I am still struggling with my PTSD and I still struggle to understand why I was ditched the way I was after a good career. I have recently looked into the negligence route because the cost of living is higher than my pension. Unfortunately, even though the evidence is there, no legal expert is willing to take the case on. I am only allowed to try and seek advice within the first three years of leaving which I find fascinating considering people can sue for things that happened many years ago in their lives. I spend at least an hour a day pointlessly applying for jobs as employers throw my CV in the bin without realising how good a person I truly am or the skills I have, regardless of the injuries.

I still wake up some mornings wishing I hadn't woken up at all, but the truth is I don't want to die. All I want in life is to be happy, but I feel like someone is out to ruin me. The Military ditched me, the big charities refuse to help me the way they help others who haven't been injured at War. My own doctor doesn't want to know because he has enough problems helping others and it's impossible to gain any sort of employment. I have gone from a positive career to applying for simple jobs that I struggle to get an interview for. My transferable skills and life experience that I have gained from my time in the Army would make me an ideal candidate for most jobs, but people don't want to know. I like helping people and I like seeing the reward from helping people. I often get serving soldiers and veterans contacting me through social media when they are feeling down. Helping others got me the nickname "PADRE" and I often received messages from boys I had not served with or I have never met before, asking me for forgiveness from the lord. I do not believe in God, so the nickname is quite funny.

I have one fantastic charity that has been helping me find employment. They have gone above and beyond to help me find work, but unfortunately, so far without success but that is down to the employers and not the hard work the charity has put in. They have helped me create a fantastic CV, but it gets me nowhere. I am left sitting in my house with my dog starting to hate life all over again and still left wondering what I did to deserve what I have endured since the day the IED changed my life. My poor little dog is now suffering severely with her heart and so far has beaten the odds to last this long, what am I going to do when she's gone?

The fact is I have a six-year recovery gap in my life that I have to explain to employers over and over again and usually over the internet, the thought me of having a big medical record scares them off.

A good friend of mine, who was shot and seriously injured in Afghanistan sometime after I had been injured, left the Armed Forces with limited help and support like me, he was lucky to find himself a good job. He mentioned me to the Company he worked for and after hearing that I too was also injured like my friend and now left struggling to find employment they offered me a job. I trained hard to gain the qualifications that I required to become a Telecommunications Engineer and gained employment with the company as a Fiber Splicer back in 2016, but unfortunately my injured spine wasn't quite ready, so I had to leave less than two months later.

After I left the previous job as a Fiber Splicer, I decided to look for a less physical job on the advice of my surgeon. I finally found another job, but it wouldn't be a less physical job like I was advised to take. I had gained employment at the Airport as a security agent thanks to an ex-serviceman who was interviewing me, it was a job I had always fancied, but I couldn't get along with a couple of the members on my shift because they knew nothing about or understood how PTSD affected people. They had given me hassle from the very first day I started, yet the management turned a blind eye, so after six months of working my hardest, ironing my uniform every day and polishing my boots like the proud soldier I used to be, I made the decision for the sake of my health to leave. The two members from my shift had worn me down to the point where I became even more depressed with life, which made me feel isolated from the other wonderful characters I worked alongside. I often felt alone during the shift and when I had approached my management to raise the issues they just pushed my problems under the carpet every time. My manager even started dodging me whilst on shift, that was it for me I was better than that, so I left.

I have always been a strong-minded person, so I will never let what has happened to me and my body stop me from being the person I used to be or from working to the best of my ability. Looking at me today you would never know what I have been through or what I have had to go through to get myself back on my feet and on the road to normality. People looking at me today would never guess I once died fighting in another Country's war and left to recover alone with minimal help and support.

I hope the Military pick up on the signposts throughout this book on how the symptoms of Post-Traumatic Stress Disorder are being allowed to go undetected within the Armed Forces, because changes need to be made and put in place, so we can put a stop to the needless lives lost to suicide after service. The MOD, Government and certain Charities need to stop picking and choosing who they look after and start recognising that hidden wounds are no different to wounds you can see, we all deserve the same treatment.

For me though, having a fantastic career with everything going for me, to waking up over a week later having to come to terms with reality is what hurt the most. The fact my

Regiment wasn't as supportive as I would have liked them to be, doesn't make me less proud to have served with them. My proudest moments came during my time serving with them and almost all of those I had served with during my career, I would happily do it all over again with.

I was left struggling to find the help I desperately required. I am now strong enough to accept that I have been failed by the system put in place to help me. There are hundreds, if not thousands of Veterans like me being ignored, isolated or even worse, left homeless and living on the streets, their cries like mine go unnoticed. It's time to make a change – it's time to open your eyes to all the suffering, it's time to recognise hidden wounds from all deployments including the Gulf War and Northern Ireland.

I have tried my very best to change my life but it's harder than people think. I see people leaving the Military today and fall straight on their feet with employment and support. I have never fallen on my feet, just my back, my neck and my skull, which is why I am in the position I am today and strong enough to write about it. I never deserved this, I don't blame my Regiment, I blame the Government, the Military of Defence and the bigger charities for capitalising on the injuries visible to the eye. I don't regret my decision to join up either. I just want CHANGE. I want to help prevent anyone else going through what I had to go through with my recovery that has left me scarred and BROKEN BY WAR.

THE END

You are not alone. Please don't suffer in silence.

call:

Samaritans on - 116 123

or

Combat Stress — 0800 138 1619

Hidden Wounds Matter

Chapter Twenty-Five – The First
Callsign 31 after being hit by the first IED. I unknowingly broke my neck.

Chapter Twenty-Eight – The Preparation
Skender confirming the first of three IED finds by Callsign 31 during a single patrol.

Chapter Twenty-Nine – H Hour
Callsign 31 after reaching the furthest end of Yatminshia with no resistance from the enemy.

Chapter Twenty-Nine – H Hour
Afghan Police firing at the Wady whilst locals innocently crossed.

Chapter Thirty-Two – The IED
The second IED to hit Callsign 31 in six weeks. The force of the blast pushed an unmanned drone of its route.

The blast was so powerful it blew the turret clean off the Warrior. I was found with severe injuries some distance away out of the camera shot.

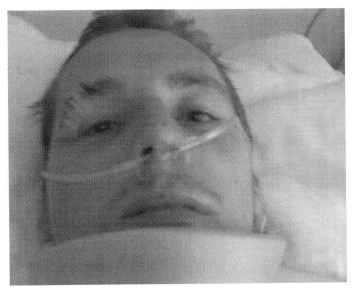

Chapter Thirty-One – Two Times
The following morning after falling from my spinal bed whilst asleep.
The fall left me with a deep wound to the eyebrow and swelling to the
right-hand side of my face.

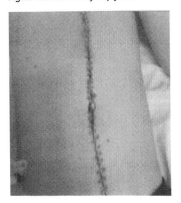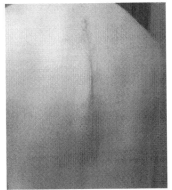

The twelve-inch scar in the picture on the left is from a lifesaving
operation onboard a helicopter whilst en route back to Camp Bastion.
The smaller scar in the picture on the right is from my spinal
operation.

22239328R00184

Printed in Great Britain
by Amazon